TEAM 7-ELEVEN

TEAM 7-ELEVEN

HOW AN UNSUNG BAND OF AMERICAN CYCLISTS TOOK ON THE WORLD AND WON

NEW EDITION

GEOFF DRAKE WITH JIM OCHOWICZ

SPRING CEDARS

Copyright © 2012 by Geoff Drake

All rights reserved

VeloPress edition published in 2012
Spring Cedars edition published in 2023

Cover and book design by Spring Cedars

ISBN 978-1-950484-58-4 (paperback)
ISBN 978-1-950484-59-1 (hardback)
ISBN 978-1-950484-65-2 (ebook)

Published by Spring Cedars
Denver, Colorado
www.springcedars.com

For my wife, Meredith, and my daughter, Andrea, for their love and support.

*—***Geoff Drake**

I want to thank the following people for all that they have done for me over the years. First, my wife, Sheila, who never complained about all my travels and raised a great family that I love. My children, Kate, Elli, and Alex, who didn't always have me around to support them. My parents, Erv and Jeanne, who supported my athletic dreams and taught me the value of hard work and the difference between right and wrong. My first coach, Lyle LeBombard, who taught me how to race. Eric Heiden, for believing in the dream. The Southland Corporation, especially John and Jere Thompson, who believed in this project. Dick Dole, who was always there to support us, and Sean Petty, who always kept us laughing. All the men and women who raced or worked for all the 7-Eleven cycling teams and created so many good memories. Finally, thanks to Jeff Garvey for his friendship and guidance throughout this project.

*—***Jim Ochowicz**

CONTENTS

FOREWORD by Eric Heiden ix
FOREWORD by Eddy Merckx xi
PREFACE xiii
CHAPTER 1 The Lure of Racing 1
CHAPTER 2 Bikes and Blades 7
CHAPTER 3 On Heiden's Coattails 37
CHAPTER 4 What's a Velodrome? 49
CHAPTER 5 Birth of a Team 64
CHAPTER 6 Boys on a Bender 84
CHAPTER 7 Looking for Consistency 104
CHAPTER 8 The Purpose-Built Sprinter 110
CHAPTER 9 A Reluctant Hero 122
CHAPTER 10 Raise the Ranch Dog 133
CHAPTER 11 Olympic Bonanza 147
CHAPTER 12 The Push to Turn Pro 156
CHAPTER 13 A Director with Horse Sense 171
CHAPTER 14 The Kid from North Dakota 180
CHAPTER 15 From First to Worst 194
CHAPTER 16 Not Just Americans Anymore 214
CHAPTER 17 Best in Bordeaux 228
CHAPTER 18 Triumph on the Gavia 241
CHAPTER 19 Ten Days in Yellow 264
CHAPTER 20 Southland Bows Out 278
EPILOGUE 286
SENIOR TEAM ROSTERS 293
NOTES 295
PHOTOGRAPHY CREDITS 303
INDEX 305
ABOUT THE AUTHORS 316

FOREWORD
by Eric Heiden

After I won five speed skating gold medals in the 1980 Winter Olympics, I knew I wanted to stop skating and race bikes full time. I'd always trained on bikes in the summer, and I loved bike racing.

In 1980, my old friend Jim Ochowicz told me he wanted to put together a team. I was getting a lot of publicity for my Olympic medals at the time, and that helped secure a deal. The 7-Eleven cycling team was born.

I had no idea how far we'd go or how much we'd accomplish. Early on we won a lot of races in the United States—mostly criteriums. But Och, as we called him, had bigger aspirations. He wanted to take a U.S.-based pro team to Europe.

And so he did. That first year abroad, 1985, saw a lot of trial and error. We were in way over our heads, and most of the other teams were pretty skeptical of us. If there was an accident, they blamed us first. And they were probably right!

But pretty soon we started winning. First it was stages in the Tour of Italy and then in the Tour de France. All of a sudden the Europeans started thinking, "Hey, these guys are okay."

Now, when I look back at the amazing victories that U.S. riders have had on the world stage, I realize that the 7-Eleven team helped lay the groundwork for that—Americans are now accepted and common in the pro peloton. It's hard for some people to imagine that there was a time when that wasn't true. But we experienced it firsthand, and we helped overcome it, paving the way for the fantastic U.S. successes that continue to this day.

And we had fun doing it. Even now, my 7-Eleven teammates are some of my best friends. The strong bonds continue for all of us.

In some ways, I still can't believe all that we accomplished. For me personally, it was like a second life in athletics. I loved every minute of it. Even after I retired, I stayed connected with the team as a physician. And today, I practice medicine with Max Testa, who was our first team doctor.

This book tells the story of that grand adventure. I hope you enjoy reliving those days as much as I have.

—**Eric Heiden, M.D., Park City, Utah**

FOREWORD
by Eddy Merckx

I started my bike business in 1980, three years after I stopped racing. Soon after I became aware of the 7-Eleven team, thanks to excellent riders like Andy Hampsten. I was also in contact with the manager, Jim Ochowicz. Jim was a good manager, the team had good results, and I liked the riders. I knew America was an important market for my business, and I became interested in sponsorship. So in 1989, when I had the opportunity, I became the bike sponsor for 7-Eleven (and later, the Motorola team).

The 7-Eleven team was the first U.S. pro squad to make a big impression in Europe, and I noticed right away that it had a good atmosphere, like a big family. These guys were good riders, they adapted well to the types and distances of races we have in Europe, and they were accepted in the European pro peloton. Plus, by the time I was involved, the team wasn't made up of just American riders like Hampsten and Davis Phinney—it also included Europeans like Jens Veggerby. It was a complete team.

I had a special relationship with the 7-Eleven team. They were happy to have somebody with my racing and frame-building experience. I took measurements of the riders and fit all the bikes. That was important. Everyone asked me for help, and I tried to assist them all. In particular, I worked with Andy. We made a lot of changes to his bike, and I think he was happy with the results.

We had a lot of memorable experiences together. I remember being at many of the training camps and races. The guys were very professional.

What's more important, in a bigger context, is that the 7-Eleven team also influenced the sport and made it more international. The fact that there was an American team in Europe made cycling more popular worldwide. It was a great thing that Jim brought the team to Europe and was so successful. And there's no question that the team was an inspiration for cycling in the United States. What came afterward was the Motorola team and then the U.S. Postal team. The 7-Eleven team was the foundation for those later teams.

For me the relationship remains a great memory. I was glad to help them be more successful in Europe, and to see the positive influence they had on the sport as a whole. If I had to do it over, I would make the same choice straightaway!

—**Eddy Merckx, Meise, Belgium**

PREFACE

These days, it's common to see U.S. riders compete in Europe and challenge the best riders in the world. It wasn't always so. In a sense, the current generation of American riders stands on the shoulders of what Team 7-Eleven accomplished in the 1980s, as the first U.S.-based pro squad to race successfully in Europe. It was the first American professional team to win stages in a major tour and the first to have worn the coveted yellow jersey of the Tour de France. And in a sport dominated for decades by Europeans, the team had paved the way for a new generation of North American cyclists to find their way into the professional ranks.

This is the story of the 7-Eleven team and its contribution to world cycling. Though the book focuses on the men's amateur and pro teams, 7-Eleven reached into almost every corner of the sport during its tenure, sponsoring a women's team, a track team, and numerous junior development teams. To this day, the women's squad is considered to be one of the most successful in history, with stars like world and national medalists Rebecca Twigg, Connie Paraskevin, and Inga Thompson. The track team, likewise, can claim world and Olympic medalists in its ranks. While these talented athletes are no less deserving of a book, these pages focus on the men's road teams as the genesis of a new generation of American riders who would come to prominence in the 1980s, upending the European hegemony of the sport.

Jim Ochowicz was the person who propelled the whole enterprise forward. He assembled the initial 7-Eleven team, a ragtag collection of amateurs who, in a few short years, completely dominated domestic bike racing. In 1985, aided by an uncanny business sense, sheer tenacity, and more than a little luck, Jim took the whole endeavor to Europe, making significant and long-lasting inroads into what had been, until the arrival of 7-Eleven on the scene, a profoundly insular sport.

Such is the prominence of the team that, while only in existence for 10 years, it is still celebrated by cyclists today. On most recreational rides in America, you can still see the iconic red, white, and green jersey of the 7-Eleven squad, and cycling magazines, blogs, and websites never tire of retrospectives on the team's halcyon days.

More than anything, the time of the 7-Eleven team was one of innocence and possibility, in which the vision of one man, and the talents of his riders, could tilt the axis of an entire sport. This is their story.

CHAPTER 1
The Lure of Racing

In 1980, there were exactly four professional bike racers in America. This was not surprising, given that there were no professional events for them to compete in.

Professional cyclists in Europe came up through a series of amateur teams, eventually earning a coveted spot on a prestigious international squad like Renault-Gitane or TI-Raleigh. But to become a pro in America, you didn't need a team. In fact, you didn't even need a bike. You only needed to fill out a one-page form. Nowhere on the form were you required to state your qualifications, race wins, or years of experience. In a few weeks' time, a hand-typed piece of paper would make its way through the mail from a small office outside Philadelphia. For a fee of $35 and the cost of a stamp, you could become a pro cyclist.

This document would state, in essence, that you were eligible to compete in the Tour de France. That is, if you could find a team willing to have you.

No one would ever claim that cycling in America was a lucrative career. Amateur riders, while more abundant than pros, lived in a state of near poverty; if they earned too much, they would be classified as professionals, making them ineligible for prestigious events like the Olympics. The very best riders—those who placed consistently in, say, the top five—could expect to make at most $250 per race. In the course of a long season, a top rider could expect to make $3,000. These meager winnings would often be accompanied by supplemental prizes, typically samples of the local fare—a jar of honey, apple cider from a nearby farm, a gift certificate to a local shop.

Overhead was considerable. One handmade racing tire, made of silk and latex, cost about $30, and a rider would need 15 to 20 of those tires to get through the year. Then there was clothing ($300), a bike ($1,500), food, travel, lodging, and of course the mountainous quantities of food needed to sustain 20 to 30 hours of training per week. All told, for an investment of 10,000 miles of training and an equal amount of driving, a rider would enjoy the annual earnings of a gas station attendant.

But this was not an equation that a top rider computed or even cared about, for he was doing the thing he loved best. He would train 750 hours a year, ride in every kind of weather, and undergo inestimable pain. He would wash his own clothes, maintain his own bicycle, drive through the night to get to the next race, or suffer the ignominy of sleeping on a friend's floor or in the back of a van. While his body, ravaged by a burn rate of 10,000 calories a day, yearned for wholesome food, he would eat at McDonald's to save a few dollars.

Nor could he expect much in the way of fame or notoriety. While professional riders in Europe were feted as national heroes and celebrated on the front pages of prestigious sports newspapers like France's *L'Équipe* and Italy's *La Gazzetta dello Sport*—papers with hundreds of thousands of daily readers—bike racers of any kind in America were an oddity, members of an esoteric fraternity that existed on the weird fringes of the sporting world. Instead of putting a race in public view, the emphasis was on reducing the potential nuisance to traffic and inconvenience to the community. It was not uncommon for races to take place at 7 a.m. Sunday in the parking lot of an industrial park. The few spectators were most likely friends and relatives of the cyclists. Cycling in America was the quintessential never-heard-of-it sport.

oo

For a young Davis Phinney, pro cycling was something exotic and alluring, a sport he had read about in coveted issues of *Miroir du Cyclisme*, a famous French racing monthly. As a teenager, he stacked the dog-eared magazines like cordwood in his bedroom, poring over them late at night, trying to divine the essence of the handlebar-banging style of his hero, world champion Freddy Maertens. It was nearly all he could think about.

Phinney's attraction to cycling had come in an epiphany. When he was 15, he went to see a bike race with his father in downtown Boulder, Colorado. As he leaned on the race fencing, his experience was visceral, like nothing he had ever witnessed, a symphony of color and noise that prompted a simple, life-changing declaration. "I just got on my 10-speed and said, 'I'm going to be a bike rider,'" Phinney said. He was very nearly alone in his obsession. "I was the only bike racer in a high school of 200 students."

Ron Kiefel, of nearby Wheat Ridge, Colorado, also felt the gravitational pull of cycling, but for entirely different reasons. As a teenager he struggled with the typical frustrations of adolescence and had tried all the usual sports—baseball, basketball, track—with disheartening results. His father owned a small bike shop, and Kiefel started riding for pleasure and escape. Soon he found himself going out for a trip around the block and coming back six hours later. At these moments, the world seemed large and limitless. Cycling was an easy pleasure, an elemental source of enjoyment unlike anything he had known, and it helped him overcome the social awkwardness he had been feeling. It was, in short, a form of salvation. "It kept me out of serious trouble," he said. "All of a sudden I wanted to take care of my body—and *race*."

$$\overline{oo}$$

Phinney and Kiefel were typical of a new generation of athletes competing in the late 1970s, a group of ingenuous and energetic riders on the cusp of something larger than themselves. Bike racing, at that time, was the most improbable path to athletic stardom that could be imagined. Although cycling had been a national passion at the turn of the 20th century, packing Madison Square Garden to the rafters with spectators for six-day track races, it seemed no more popular than lawn bowling by World War II. By the postwar era, cycling had been thoroughly eclipsed as a means of transportation by the automobile and as a sport by America's homegrown big three of baseball, football, and basketball. To be sure, there were a few particularly driven and talented American athletes who left their marks on cycling in the intervening years. Jack Heid, a track racer from New Jersey, won a bronze medal at the world championships in 1949. In the 1960s and early 1970s, American riders like Sheila Young-Ochowicz, Audrey McElmury, John Howard, and Jackie Simes III won medals at the Pan American Games and world championships. While these riders were deserving heroes to their brethren—the people who knew and raced bikes themselves—they were utterly unknown to America at large.

Meanwhile, the sport thrived in Europe. Bike racers were feted as heroes, and tens of thousands of cheering fans lined the roads for three-week-long races, called "grand tours," in France and Italy. For cyclists in America, the Tour de France was unimaginable. Its fantastic dimensions—a 21-day race over thousands of miles of city streets and country roads, through vineyards and villages, in heat and cold, from the sea to the Alps—fomented an irresistible attraction. In the late 1970s, when American riders like Jonathan Boyer and George Mount went off to try their fortunes as European pros, they might as well have been going to fight in a foreign war, far from the view of their native country. In general, when American riders arrived on the scene in Europe, they were considered interlopers and returned home chastised and exhausted.

But the irony and beauty of the bike rider's circumstances were that poverty and anonymity would not deter him. Quite the contrary; it would make him stronger, hungrier, more willing to submit to the pain that is the constant currency of racing. For elite American racers, these many sacrifices put a fine edge on their existence, defining their lives against a backdrop of convention and normalcy.

When young riders like Phinney and Kiefel took up cycling as part of a new generation, they were propelled by a feeling as powerful as anything they had ever experienced, though they hardly understood it: a simple and uniquely American love of riding the bicycle. They immersed themselves in an insular and ritualistic world, helping to resurrect a sport that had languished for decades in the United States. While these riders were aware and respectful of what had come before, it was a sport they would necessarily remake in their own image.

European racing, for decades, was a proletarian discipline, an exit ramp from the hardscrabble existence of being a shopkeeper, miner, or farmer. But this new generation of American riders came from circumstances of comfort and convenience. Their parents were academics, lawyers, engineers. If these young men were to forgo college for racing, as many of them did, it would be an act of volition rather than necessity. They were prepared to work hard, to be sure. But it would be hard work of their choosing, and it would be viewed through a uniquely American prism of enjoyment and even indulgence. They were the progenitors of a new sport, stewards of a pastime that was waiting to be reborn and popularized in a way that had not occurred since the earliest days of the bicycle.

For these athletes, the thought of a career in cycling seemed improbable at best. For the average rider, contemplating the road ahead, there always seemed to be another level, just out of reach. In the United States, cyclists are divided into "categories," based on accumulated placings. A good rider is a Category III or II. Above that is Category I—essentially national caliber—of which there are only a handful in any given state. Beyond that lies a select group of U.S. professionals. And beyond that are those professionals who might be able to stake a claim in Europe. Even today, their numbers are small.

Before 7-Eleven came on the scene, they could be counted on one hand.

o͞o

Phinney, Kiefel, and their contemporaries did not stop to contemplate past failures or the preposterous odds against making any kind of career in bicycle racing. It didn't seem like there was any road that could get them there, but that didn't matter. In bike racing, if one confronts the enormity of what lies ahead—if you look at the endless switchbacks that snake to the top of an 8,000-foot pass—the task seems impossible, too large to even consider. So they did not. They loved the act of riding a bike, drew pleasure from the discipline and the pain. They put their heads down, and they raced.

But inborn talent and youthful bravado were not in themselves sufficient for success on the world stage. Even the most gifted athletes cannot will themselves to victory. While isolation and independence drove the athletes, there wasn't a single one who thought, at some point, that his efforts shouldn't be worth more, that sacrifice and physical prowess should amount to something in this world. Hard work was always a tool they had at their disposal, but it was not sufficient.

Cycling, perhaps even more than other sports like running, did not exist in a pure and unfettered universe. The sport required money, and lots of it. The athletes needed coaching and organization to channel—and, in the case of many of them, to rein in—their exuberance. They needed the best equipment and the wherewithal to travel and compete.

It wasn't so much that they deserved it, as athletes. It was that the *sport* deserved it. Surely, the beauty, pathos, and pain of bicycle racing could appeal to anyone. Someday, they thought, it would get the attention it deserved.

CHAPTER 2
Bikes and Blades

Lake Placid, New York, is a sleepy mountain town known primarily for winter sports and the fact that it receives more than 130 inches of snow every year. Its most prominent features are two Olympic ski jumps, which jut from the landscape like God's own skateboard park. At almost 400 feet, the giant ramps are the tallest things between Albany and Montreal. It is a place where temperatures can hover in the single digits in midwinter, turning the landscape brittle with cold, a crystalline world where you can do an inordinate number of things related to ice, including ice fishing, ice climbing, ice hockey—and of course, ice skating.

One could not imagine a less likely place for the birth of America's most famous cycling team.

In February 1980, Eric Heiden came to Lake Placid to compete in five Olympic skating events, ranging from 500 to 10,000 meters. The last, the 10,000, was considered unlikely for the solid, powerful athlete, whose musculature gave him a clear advantage in the shorter events. If he was to win the 10,000, it would be a little like a 200-meter track runner taking gold in the Olympic marathon —an implausible continuum of athletic ability, for even the best-trained athlete. It was a Hail Mary of colossal proportions. But Heiden, 21 years old and in the best form of his life, thought it was worth a try.

A doctor's son from Madison, Wisconsin, Heiden was as talented as he was improbable. Viewed from one angle, he was the quintessential athlete, with a chiseled physique and massive, 27-inch thighs covered by a dense thicket of veins—piston-like instruments that could propel him around the track at more than 30 mph, for lap after lap. While most elite skaters used 16 strokes on the straights,

Heiden used just 12. He had "a massive motor, and killer instinct," said Ron Hayman, a cycling teammate.

But he was also the inverse of athletic perfection—a shuffling, self-effacing giant who treated the attention lavished on him as a sort of plague. Everyone liked Heiden. Later, it became a rite of passage for members of the 7-Eleven cycling team to have nicknames. Heiden's would be "Gomer," the amiable but simpleminded gas station attendant on *The Andy Griffith Show*. He would frequently say things like "holy moly!"—and mean it.

It was a form of naïveté to think that such a profusion of athletic skill could somehow go unnoticed. But that was Heiden, always trying to wear the invisibility cape over his burgeoning talent. Throughout his life, this ironic mix of traits would become his most endearing feature, propelling him relentlessly to heights of fame that he seemed unable to escape.

But this time, there was nothing that could restrain his talent, or his fame. Heiden won four gold medals in his first four events, setting Olympic records in all of them. In a clear sign of his dominance, he slipped and nearly fell in the 1,500, but recovered enough to win by almost half a second.

All that remained was the 10,000. With characteristic nonchalance, he went to the United States/Russia hockey game the night before—a couple of pals from Madison were on the team, and he wanted to cheer them on. Heiden, in the midst of one of the greatest athletic accomplishments of modern times, relaxed in the stands as the unheralded U.S. team did the impossible, beating Russia 4–3 in the so-called Miracle on Ice.

But Heiden was in the business of miracles, too. He had just seen fellow athletes go beyond the bounds of what had seemed possible, propelled by some mysterious alchemy of athleticism and Olympic spirit. Suddenly, for Heiden, a fifth gold seemed plausible, even likely.

Caught up in the exuberance of the hockey match, Heiden overslept the next day. His coach, Dianne Holum, shook him awake. He quickly choked down a few pieces of toast and headed for the rink. Greatness was in the offing, and the lack of a proper breakfast was not about to stop him now. In the space of a few hours, he won his fifth gold, setting a world record by the yawning margin of six seconds.

It was classic Heiden, his exceptional drive and supernatural ability belied by a self-effacing, almost childlike innocence. He could win five medals and exude all the bluster and pomp of having succeeded at a game of horseshoes. (Piling success on success, Heiden's sister, Beth, won a bronze medal in the 3,000 m, giving the Heiden family exactly half of the medals won by the United States at those Games.)

Suddenly, Heiden was the toast of the sporting world. He was on the cover of *Sports Illustrated* and *Time*. In the coming months he would meet Mick Jagger, drop the opening puck at the Stanley Cup playoffs, and date Kris Kristofferson's daughter. In the space of those nine days, he had become a juggernaut of worldwide fame and publicity.

Heiden's public persona was paradoxical. The more self-effacing he became, the more the press and fans seemed to obsess over him. They found him irresistible, a gentle giant of towering athletic talent who was handsome in a clumsy, lethargic sort of way, with an ambling gait and a tousle of unkempt black hair. To the press and fans, he was unerringly polite and accommodating. Seemingly without trying, he became a media sensation.

It was not his wish to be famous, yet he found he was powerless to evade the acclaim and chaos that surrounded him. In interviews, Heiden would say, "I liked it better when I was a nobody." But being a nobody was no longer a possibility for Heiden, any more than it was possible for a U.S. president to become an average citizen.

What was less well known was that Heiden was already looking to the horizon and to an athletic career far different from skating.

○○

Heiden viewed his success impassively, as if anyone could win five Olympic gold medals in the space of nine days. To him, such things were merely the logical results of prolonged effort and focus. He called this his "Midwestern work ethic." It was a simple algorithm—effort in equals results out—and by his reckoning, it could be applied to nearly anything in life.

Success was early and abundant. Heiden started skating when he was 14, and by 1976, when he was just 17, he had set his first world record, as a junior. He further fulfilled this early promise by winning the world championships in 1977, 1978, and 1979. In his short skating career he set 15 world records and won 7 world championships in a range of distances, making shocking inroads into a European sport. To this day, he is thought by many to be the best skater the world has ever seen.

Madison, Heiden's hometown, was a skating hotbed—the Madison Speed Skating Club, dating back to 1936, is the second-oldest such club in the country, and at that time had sent at least one member to every Olympics since 1972—but in the summer it was also a center of cycling, and Heiden found it hard not to get caught up in the tide of activity that surrounded him. Wayne Stetina, a contemporary of Heiden's who would go on to win numerous national cycling championships, remembers seeing Heiden on skates in the early 1970s and thinking, "I hope he never goes into cycling." But the sport held a magnetic pull for Heiden, as it did for so many of the young skaters who yearned for a sport outside the confines of the small ovals that had been their lives all winter. The sports also had similar physiological demands, making cycling an ideal summer sport.

Heiden started doing weekly training races at a local airfield and found the sport infectious. "I got the bug," he recalled simply. Heiden's father, Jack, bought him a racing bike with sew-up tires for $150. (Jack Heiden, initially indifferent to his son's passion for two wheels, later immersed himself in the sport, competing in national masters racing.) Heiden joined a cycling team associated with Madison's Yellow Jersey bike shop and sponsored by A&W Root Beer, and started riding several days per week.

Heiden's natural aptitude in cycling was obvious to everyone around him, though perhaps least of all to himself. "It was pretty immediately apparent to me that my best talent was in skating," he said. "The rest of world thought I was better [at cycling] than I was. I knew that there were limitations to what I could do." And, though Heiden loved the sport, he was also afraid of it, fearing any injury that might impede his skating. Cycling was an indulgence, a fun but generally superfluous part of his athletic life.

Yet he continued, eventually joining the AMF Wheel Goods team, the strongest amateur team at the time, sponsored by the American Machine and Foundry sports conglomerate. His fondest memory of his early team was not his exploits on the racecourse, but rather that he "really liked the jersey." It was, in many ways, the antecedent of the 7-Eleven squad and included, at one time or another, eventual 7-Eleven team members Tom Schuler, Davis Phinney, and a pugnacious rider by the name of Jim Ochowicz.

Heiden's extreme tolerance for discomfort, a staple of any skater, served him well in cycling. But he found that this intimacy with pain could also be a liability. Because events could last up to five hours, a quick immersion into the deep end of the pain pool would often mean he would be flailing by the end of the race. He would go too hard, too early, chasing down every breakaway, and

Heiden's sheer love of competition and his high tolerance of pain helped him overcome his tactical shortcomings as a bike racer.

have nothing left for the finish. "Even at the end of my career," Heiden lamented, "I was not as smart a rider as I could have been."

He also discovered that the towering muscles that served him so well in skating were a liability in cycling, where excess weight is tantamount to an anchor. Even though he had a scant 4 percent body fat—extremely lean, even by the uncompromising standards of endurance sports—Heiden was a classic mesomorph, 185 pounds of rippling muscle. (The press would later playfully refer to him as a cycling "Schwarzenegger." Indeed, he would struggle with body mass throughout his cycling career.)

Many athletes, particularly in endurance sports, required bluster and cockiness to impel their performances—but not Heiden. His strength came from another place; it was not demonstrative.

At first glance, he looked like nothing special. He had unusually narrow shoulders and a broad nose that made him look more like a boxer than an endurance athlete. At just over six feet tall, he was so profoundly overdeveloped that he walked with an endearing and instantly recognizable limp. He conveyed his essence in his legs, a tangle of veins and rippling muscle, his true power a juxtaposition of calmness and ferocity, like opposite poles of a battery.

Roger Young, a fellow racer, remembers the idea of a second athletic career simmering within Heiden and how it would not let him be. "By the end of 1980," Young remembers, "he was ready to start racing seriously."

"I always knew I wanted to pick up cycling after skating," Heiden said. "It was something I looked forward to."

As Heiden contemplated his professional and athletic future from the vantage point of the Lake Placid Olympics in February 1980, the irresistible attraction of cycling became a piece of a puzzle he was assembling in his mind. It was his nature to be always looking to the far horizon and the next thing of magnitude he could accomplish. A steady and conscientious student, he had always wanted to pursue medicine, following his father's example, and now with the Olympics behind him, he could begin the long and intensive journey toward a medical career. As for skating, the sport had treated him well, but it was time to move on. He would quit skating, after a short, meteoric run. And to fulfill his thirst for competition and balance the hours he would soon be spending on his studies, he would race bicycles. All he needed to get started was some advice from his old skating and cycling friend Jim Ochowicz.

oo

In February 1980, Jim Ochowicz sat watching Heiden circulate the Lake Placid skating oval in long, powerful strides. He could see Heiden's massive thighs pulsing through his one-piece Lycra suit, and he listened as the rhythmic chuff, chuff of Heiden's skates propelled him forward with what appeared to be incredible force.

In the last few months, Ochowicz had been traveling throughout Europe with Heiden, in his role as manager for the U.S. Speedskating Team. On that trip, Heiden had won nearly everything he entered, in every country they visited, a phenomenal display of fitness and dominance. Ochowicz, who had been around speed skating for most of his life, reckoned that the 21-year-old was the most powerful skater he had ever seen. "Eric was way better than everyone else," he remembers. "And everyone else was good." Every time Heiden raced, Ochowicz remembered, he "would win by a sizable margin."

Like Heiden, Ochowicz had devoted his life to sport, sacrificed everything for it. Just a few months before, he had been working construction to fund his own racing career, building a hospital parking lot. He had been competing in both speed skating and cycling since he was 14, and now, at age 28, he was reaching the slow and painful realization that his athletic career was drawing to a close. His racing had not gone particularly well as of late. A few months earlier, while cycling in Germany, he had crashed heavily on a snow-covered road. Then he had rented an austere basement apartment in Ghent, Belgium, where he slept on a mattress on the floor. The apartment had no shower where he could warm himself after long days of training. His goal was to ride the Ghent six-day track race with his brother-in-law, Roger Young. But along the way, he contracted bronchitis riding in the perpetual snow and rain. They completed the race, but Ochowicz returned home in frustration. The events of his life were conspiring to force a change in direction. "I was looking for a way out of racing," he admitted.

Adding to the complexity of his circumstances, he and his wife, Olympic speed skating medalist Sheila Young-Ochowicz, had recently had their first child, Kate, and the burdens of supporting a young family were beginning to bear down on him. In many ways, when he looked to the horizon, he saw a future that was largely uncertain.

But in Lake Placid, he felt strangely liberated. Pragmatic concerns of family and finance seemed to recede in importance. He suddenly found himself in a position of authority and influence. When he first arrived in Lake Placid, he earned extra money by doing the work he knew best, manual labor, helping to build the Olympic ski slope. From those heights, he remembers looking down at the bustle and activity of the burgeoning Olympic town. Now, as manager of the U.S. Speedskating Team, it seemed like the world was watching him and his star skater, Heiden.

o͞o

Like Heiden, Ochowicz came from the bike-and-blade culture of the Midwest. The Ochowicz household, in a working-class suburb of Milwaukee, was one of austerity and pragmatism. His father, Erv Ochowicz, was a tough, cigar-smoking, and occasionally hard-drinking German immigrant who toiled for decades to help build the burgeoning Milwaukee interstate highway system. He expected his six children to apply themselves similarly, aiming for lasting security over fame or indulgence.

Ochowicz remembers a home environment of respectful chaos, in which he shared a room with two siblings until he was 19. The young Jim Ochowicz had a troubling tendency to get into fistfights at school, an early indication of his tenacity and often unyielding drive. His father wielded a great amount of power but was not an unreasonable man. "If he told you to shut up and sit down, you shut up and sat down," said Ochowicz. "He was a tough guy, respected in his profession—he commanded respect." Family drives were measured by the number of cigars Erv Ochowicz would smoke en route, invariably leaving the children with severe headaches.

In this environment, cycling was not thrust upon the younger Ochowicz, but it was there, on the periphery, and he found himself drawn to it. At age 12, he discovered some yellowing photos of his father astride a track bike and decided it was something he might like to try. He started cycling extensively around the Milwaukee suburbs, extending his paper routes in concentric circles around their home. One day his father took him to see some racing at the Brown Deer Park Velodrome. Jim was smitten by the riders' silk jerseys and the feathery, minimalist bikes that had just a single speed and no brakes. It was a world that seemed exotic and alluring, and it was in stark contrast to the lives of earnest mediocrity he saw around him. He decided, with the surety of a child, that he would become a bike racer.

Equipped with this all-consuming notion, Ochowicz viewed everything as an opportunity to race: His paper route became a series of sprints and finish lines. After school, he would pedal furiously around the block, timing himself on each successive lap. He even staged mock races through the local cemetery, often in the dead of winter.

One day a neighbor, Lyle LeBombard, witnessed the 14-year-old Ochowicz locked in one of these maniacal races with himself. (LeBombard's son, Wayne, happened to be a cyclist and Olympic speed skater, with the father acting as coach.) The elder LeBombard approached Ochowicz and asked what he was doing. "I want to be a bike racer," said Ochowicz without hesitation. LeBombard invited Ochowicz to Brown Deer Park for a little coaching. The next day Ochowicz rode the 25 miles across suburban Milwaukee on his brakeless, fixed-gear bike, arriving 10 minutes early for the first personal coaching experience of his life.

The family room of the Erwin Ochowicz home in New Berlin has become a trophy room for their son Jim, 20, who has just been named to the four-man cycle team to compete in the Munich, Germany Olympics. Robert, 13, holds a medal received in Cali, Columbia, last year; Mrs. Ochowicz holds a silver cup won in the Northbrook, Ill., internationals; Ochowicz displays a gold cup from the July 1970 nationals in Detroit, and Bill, 10, holds a trophy presented by the Milwaukee Wheelmen for making the Worlds and Pan Am Teams. (Staff Photo)

From age 12, Ochowicz had an all-consuming passion for racing. Here, his supportive family cradles a few of his trophies.

The elder LeBombard would become a fixture in Ochowicz's life for decades, and his son, Wayne, became Ochowicz's daily training partner. Ochowicz hungered for any advice the older man could offer that would advance his new life's mission. He began to understand that cycling was not all about mashing the pedals; finesse and technique are involved, and sound advice could occasionally trump sheer will and determination.

Brown Deer, a 400-meter track with minimal banking, demanded a very specific cornering method; without that skill, riders would frequently fly off its outer edges and find themselves in the parking lot. Under LeBombard's tutelage, Ochowicz quickly mastered the technique. In 1966, he won the intermediate boys state championship, when he was just 14. The victory qualified him for the national championships at the velodrome in Northbrook, Illinois, where he finished 2nd overall.

He soon fell into a weekly diet of competition common to Midwest bike racers of the era. Small successes impelled him forward, and he began to think that anything was possible. At the end of his first season, he asked his mentor, LeBombard, "What's next?" The answer was the same as for any aspiring bicycle racer of the era: speed skating. Not surprisingly, Ochowicz approached the sport with the same single-mindedness he had applied to cycling, winning the Silver Skates competition at his home rink in West Allis and qualifying for the Olympic trials at age 16.

Suddenly, he found himself in a comfortable place in life. He had energy and a modicum of talent. He had a coach and the support of his parents. Given all these things, it seemed he was living in a dream.

oo

Ochowicz was not known as the most gifted of athletes. But he was, by broad consensus, the most dogged. Later, he would be known as "Sergeant Rock" for his drive and implacable nature. He was not preternaturally gifted, in the way Heiden was, but he tended to make up for it with a "tremendous capacity for work," recalled Roger Young.

If athletic ability exists on a continuum, with perseverance on one end and natural ability at the other, Ochowicz found himself squarely situated on the side of sheer drive. "I trained hard," he said. "And I had the longevity to keep coming back. I would get knocked down, but I would get back up." When he took up speed skating, he approached the sport in the same indefatigable way. "I had endurance," he said. "Anything over a mile, I would just try to wear them down."

He tended to train alone or solely in the company of Wayne. This was not because of any antisocial tendency, but because he existed in an alternative universe of obsession and dedication, where others found it impossible to dwell. One day, seeking companionship, he convinced a neighborhood boy to try speed skating. But before long, it became apparent that the young man did not share Ochowicz's relentless passion for training and incremental improvement. "He didn't take skating as seriously as I did," Ochowicz lamented, "and he faded away."

Ochowicz's devotion to sport was not the direct result of his parents' or any coach's urging. It came from his own mind. "No one ever asked me to train," he said. "Never. I was driven. It was all I thought about, night and day."

When he wasn't training, Ochowicz was scaling girders hundreds of feet above the ground, helping to build Milwaukee's first shopping mall. His father had procured a job—and more importantly, a union wage—for his son. For a teenager living at home, it was a state of extravagance, a financial circumstance created entirely for one purpose: to fund a life of bike racing. Work acquired meaning and value only in relation to sport. He would routinely rise at 4:30, train for an hour, then head to the job site and its hard physical labor until 3:30, then train for another hour at the end of the day. He was in bed by 7:30. He considered the backbreaking labor "power training" and attacked it with the same purpose and aggression he applied to athletics. It was a simple formula. "I worked so I could skate and ride," he said.

Ochowicz began to develop a reputation in both sports. It was also at this time that a couple of speed skating companions, Sally Blanchford and Toy Dorgan, faced with the difficulty of pronouncing his German surname, dubbed him "Och" (like "coach" without the c). And so it would be, for the rest of his life: Och.

∞

In January 1971, Ochowicz made his first foray to Europe, for an international skating competition in Inzell, Germany. It was, in many ways, a trip into the void. He went alone, not under the auspices of a team or coach. But he felt strangely compelled to go.

Throughout his childhood, he had hungered for news from Europe and coveted magazines about European sporting culture. At one point a local cyclist lent him issues of the British magazine *Coureur Sporting Cyclist,* with its grainy photos of the European champions of the day. His favorite book was a dog-eared copy of *World Champions I Have Known,* by the French journalist René de Latour, which chronicled the exploits of such cycling greats as Fausto Coppi, Jacques Anquetil, and others. Ochowicz lived in these pages, and through them he acquired the sense that Europe was the font of all good things in endurance sports. It was a kind of Mecca. He knew he had to go.

It would have been easy for a 19-year-old American, deposited in a strange Bavarian town, to find the alien language and culture unsettling. But Ochowicz, who throughout his life would be unabashedly clumsy with language, was unruffled by the Tower of Babel he found himself in. He remembers, with fond amusement, being unable to discern the sleeping arrangement in the economical hotel where he would stay for 21 days. He recollects a "huge thing on top of the bed, with buttons." Completely flummoxed by his first encounter with a duvet, he simply undid the buttons and slept inside every day. "The maid must have wondered what the heck I was doing," he said.

Soon the Dutch junior team arrived, and they immediately made an impression. As Ochowicz warmed up with them on the speed skating oval, he could see how strong they were. But it wasn't their physical ability that impressed him as much as their demeanor.

A culture of dedication and achievement permeated the team and elevated them above the rest. "Being around that Dutch team—they gave me the impression they were doing something different from everyone else," he remembers.

What he sensed most of all was symbiosis—the Dutch athletes and their coach had a unique chemistry that bred a sense of sacrifice and shared success. What resulted was "a sophistication of capabilities," as Ochowicz called it—the notion that a group of people could perform at a much higher level than an individual. They were, quite simply, skating out of their heads.

It was as if he was observing this team dynamic for the first time. Back in Milwaukee, he had always functioned as an individual, fueled only by his own insatiable drive. "I had never been on a team," he said. "It was all individual. This was the first time I saw people sit down and talk about their sport."

The Dutch coach, in particular, held a fascination for Ochowicz. "They were crazy," said Ochowicz of the Dutch juniors, recalling snowball fights and other high jinks outside the rink. "But when that coach said jump, they jumped." More important, he noticed that the athletes submitted with a facile willingness. "They liked it," Ochowicz remembers. "And without him, they couldn't [succeed]." It was a remarkable demonstration of the benevolent power and influence that one charismatic man could wield over an occasionally unruly and testosterone-infused group of athletes. They were lessons he would not forget.

There was also a cultural dynamic in Inzell that he had never witnessed before. Europeans appreciated a uniquely painful and precise sport like speed skating in a way that seldom occurred in the United States. "I never saw 15,000 people watch speed skating before and understand the sport," said Ochowicz. "I was used to friends and family."

Throughout the rest of his life, Ochowicz's career would cross back and forth between these two worlds: the isolated American sporting culture he knew and grew up with, and the broader European tradition that could appreciate and fertilize his dreams. In time, he and his athletes would help bridge and equalize these disparate worlds.

It had been a remarkable three weeks, a high-water mark in his young life (he also set all his personal records at this meet). Looking back, he would always characterize Inzell as "a time and place of transition." One of Ochowicz's strengths was an innate sense of being in the presence of something larger than himself, a place of growth and maturation. This required powers of recognition, but also openness and a willing nature. "You're figuring out where you fit in, you're moving to different levels," he would say of such

Ochowicz and teammates at the 1971 World Sprint Championships. Left to right: Gary Jonland, Greg Lyman, Ochowicz, Dan Carroll, Bill Lanigan.

moments. "You don't know it at the time, but it's happening. There are certain things that help you later on, that helped you understand yourself and other people."

Before long Ochowicz would be living the life of an expatriate, spending more time in Europe than in America. But throughout his life, he would repeatedly return to Inzell, both the place and its purpose in his life.

o͞o

Despite these strong impressions, when Ochowicz returned to the United States in February 1971, he felt lost. He reflected on everything he had seen in Inzell, all of which stood in stark contrast to his life in Milwaukee. He realized that the dynamic he had seen "was not here. People weren't riding bikes. There weren't articles about speed skating or cycling." He felt adrift, separated from a culture that seemed his natural home. More than anything, he had the sense that the United States had simply not caught up.

"I was trying to figure out what to do," he said of that time. "I didn't know where I was going." Almost reflexively, he started training and working construction, the twin foundations of his daily life. For a while, things fell into a familiar pattern.

But on an April morning, his sister, Jeanne, four years older and living with her husband, woke up with a stomachache. Nothing seemed unusual at the time. But she felt progressively worse throughout the day and was taken to the hospital, where her condition became more grave. That night, with her parents at her bedside, she died. Jeanne Ochowicz was 23 years old.

"It was probably a bowel obstruction, or maybe she choked to death," said Ochowicz. "We don't know. It was a freak thing." There was also speculation that it might have had something to do with an emergency appendectomy she had had when she was 12. The true cause of her death will never be known.

For a while, the world seemed to crumble around him. His father, Erv, an occasionally taciturn man, had always been prone to drinking. Reeling from his daughter's death, he began to drink more. Jim Ochowicz, already feeling rudderless since returning from Inzell, was at a vulnerable moment. The cataclysm of his sister's death and its devastating effect on his parents, cast his life in a sort of pall. "It was a shock, the whole thing," he said. "I thought, 'Should I quit cycling or skating?' "

But at moments like these, the trained athlete welcomes exertion as a familiar truth and a catharsis. It is the one thing, amidst life's many vagaries and injustices, that can be wholly trusted. The athlete puts on his gear, swings a leg over the bike, and does what he knows best in the world. Indeed, for Ochowicz, it seemed to be the only choice he had.

"It woke me up. I decided to get back on the bike, figure it out, and get going again."

oo

It felt good to be riding. And he was riding well, maybe the best he ever had. In the spring of 1971 Ochowicz was selected to go to the Pan American Games in Cali, Colombia, to ride the team pursuit on the velodrome, a 4,000 m event in which four riders draft each other to achieve the best time.

In preparation, he had gone to Chicago to train with a teammate, John Vande Velde. The plan was to do some extensive riding on the road. When Ochowicz arrived, Vande Velde asked him, "Where's your road bike?" Ochowicz, supremely motivated but in a state of blissful ignorance of such subtleties, said, "I don't have one." He had planned to ride his brakeless, single-speed track bike—just as he had always done back in Milwaukee. And why not?

Vande Velde, who had competed extensively in Europe, couldn't brook such a gross training faux pas. Rather than watch

Cyclists in training for the 1972 Olympics in Munich, Germany, starting second from left: Dave Chauner, Mike Hiltner, Ochowicz, Dave Mulica.

Ochowicz suffer in this way, he unearthed his father's old road bike and loaned it to his friend. "You have one now," he said flatly.

Yet the scene was classic Ochowicz. He had the simple notion that if a thing could be done, it would be done, and that convention and societal norms would not be obstacles. It mattered little that you weren't supposed to ride a track bike through miles of Chicago suburbs. Nor, years later, would it matter that U.S. cycling had never won a gold medal in the Olympics or fielded a team in the Tour de France. These were merely technical obstacles, and they could be overcome. None of them, in and of themselves, were sufficient reason to be deterred.

Once in Cali, Ochowicz experienced another infusion of international sporting culture. As he wandered the athletes' village, he "saw people running, riding bikes, and shadowboxing." It reminded him of what he had felt in Inzell, the ineffable chemistry that occurs when athletes compete on a world stage. He called it "a big eye-opener." He could think of nothing he wanted more than to be part of this athletic drama.

The team had prepared well, and they qualified 2nd. Ochowicz felt sure a medal was in the offing. But the night before the final, he contracted dysentery, which he attributed to eating grapes in a country known for inflicting digestive woes on unsuspecting Americans. He spent the next three days in the hospital, drifting in and out of consciousness. In the end he had to sit out the final, while his teammates won a bronze medal. It was at once the fulfillment of a dream—to think that he had helped bring the team so far—and a deep disappointment. Vande Velde, in recognition of Ochowicz's contribution, gave him a medal, in consolation.

oo

The misadventure in Cali only served to heighten and accentuate his drive. Ochowicz could not get enough of international competition. He was infected with the very idea of it. That fall he went to the world track championships in Varese, Italy, again on the team pursuit squad with Vande Velde and company. The team was 9th. The event was also his first exposure to the enigmatic and cloistered world of Eastern bloc athletes. "It was a distinct difference—east versus west," he said. "They couldn't just talk to you. They had people watching them." It was a political and athletic divide that would have huge ramifications for Ochowicz and U.S. cyclists in the coming years.

Ochowicz made the team pursuit squad for the 1972 Olympics in Munich, Germany. Once again, he was smitten by the rarified atmosphere of the athletes' village, where so many elite competitors were gathered in one place. He called it "a whole different level" from the Pan Am Games and the Worlds.

But the team rode disastrously. Vande Velde and another

team member, Dave Chauner, were embroiled in a petty dispute off the track. The team splintered, failing to make it past the first round of competition. Vande Velde called Munich "the worst ride of my life." Ochowicz left in disgust with his speed skating friend, Sheila Young, traveling to his traditional European touch point, Inzell. Vande Velde and his wife eventually showed up, and the group "drowned themselves in beer."

Meanwhile, Ochowicz had no idea what had transpired at the Olympic village in his absence, when Palestinian terrorists took 11 Israeli competitors hostage in what became known as the Munich Massacre. When he returned to the athletes' village he was greeted by machine-gun-toting German police. He didn't realize it then, but the event marked a moment of lost innocence for international sporting events, which would increasingly acquire political overtones and be burdened with tight security and oversight.

In 1973, Ochowicz participated in the world championships in Spain in three events: the 100-km team time trial, the road race, and the team pursuit. His results were unremarkable, but the event left a strong impression. When his races were over, Ochowicz went to see the professional road race. "They looked so fit," he said. "It was another world. They were so cool looking—no helmets or glasses. They were tan and all muscle. Their bikes were like nothing I had ever seen before." In contrast to the meager crowds at the amateur events, tens of thousands of people lined the road for the pro race. At one point, as he sat in the roadside "cabin" that served as a pit stop, a young, bronzed Eddy Merckx pulled in. It was an epiphany on the scale of what he had experienced that day in Inzell. "I was in awe," he said.

Through all these events, Ochowicz was assimilating athletic influences, but also cultural ones. He had a growing sense of what it meant to perform on a world stage, and it became a source of fascination and wonder. As an athlete, he recognized these events for what they were: pinnacles of success and sacrifice. But it was also a public phenomenon, one that could capture the attention of nations. It was a place where one man's personality—a coach, or a team director—could wield influence that would be multiplied and achieve manifold success.

o̅o

Ochowicz had known Sheila Young, of Detroit, Michigan, since he was a teenager. Young had ridden for the famed Wolverine Sports Club, and the two had grown close in the tight fraternity of sport that prevailed throughout the Midwest.

The Young family was an institution in the bike-and-blade community. Both parents had competed, and Sheila's father, Claire Young, was a revered coach for the Wolverines. Sheila's brother, Roger, was a national-level bike rider and Ochowicz's occasional teammate.

Over the years the relationship began to transcend friendship, and on the eve of the 1976 winter Olympics in Innsbruck, Austria, Ochowicz and Young announced their engagement to be married. Just days later, in what must have seemed a particularly auspicious event, Young won unprecedented gold, silver, and bronze speed skating medals, becoming the first woman to win three medals in one winter Games.

Just as quickly, Sheila Young-Ochowicz decided to retire from competition and raise a family with her new husband. (Their first daughter, Kate, was born in 1977.) By this time Lake Placid had been awarded the 1980 Games, and the organizing committee offered Young-Ochowicz a job doing promotional work, capitalizing on her newfound fame. The couple moved to upstate New York, where Ochowicz got a job building the Olympic ski jump. His life soon fell into a familiar routine. "I would ride to work, work eight hours, then train, eat, and go back to bed."

But he soon discovered that his skills were in demand for other reasons. When athletes came to town, "I would help everyone out," he said. "I'd show them where to train and lead rides." It was apparent to everyone around him that he was at ease in such circumstances, and in 1979, he was offered the opportunity to manage the speed skating team during a trip to Europe. "I had to do everything," he said. "Airplane reservations, car rental, manager meetings, and book hotels." What he could not have known was that these logistics were, in fact, a foretaste of his life's work.

oo

About this time, Ochowicz acquired a booklet called *The T.I.-Raleigh Story* by Peter Duker about Peter Post, a winning six-day rider who assembled one of the most successful pro teams of the 1970s. Ochowicz was fascinated by Post's inspirational and occasionally autocratic rule. It harkened back to the remarkable synergy he had seen between the Dutch coach and his young charges in Inzell. He read and reread the book, trying to parse out the unique chemistry of the team and its irascible director. "It gave me the idea I could put a team together and make it work," he said. "He had a model I thought I could do."

By all measures, Ochowicz had done well as manager of the speed skating team. He found the interactions easy, perhaps because he had recently been among them as a racer himself. "The kids liked me," he said. When he examined his life and career, he knew his time as a competitor was winding down. "In my mind, I was done," he admitted. He also knew that sports were the thing he loved most in the world and wondered if he might find some other way to keep his hand in them. "I was thinking I liked working with athletes and could do all the stuff that needed to be done for the team," he said.

All these events—the inevitable end of his athletic career, the obligations to his young family, and the sudden realization that his skills could be applied in a managerial role—were coalescing to take Ochowicz's life in a new direction. Lake Placid had been a wonderful ride, but it had expended its usefulness. "There was no work," Ochowicz concluded in the fall of 1980. "It was a resort town." His house in nearby Ray Brook, which he had painstakingly built, was put on the market. With an air of finality, he rented a truck, packed the family's belongings, and drove back to Milwaukee to start working construction again. A few members of the speed skating team, including Heiden, happened to be in town. A slightly grainy picture shows Heiden and his teammates helping Ochowicz unload the truck, beginning the next phase of his life.

o͞o

In some ways, Eric Heiden and Jim Ochowicz could not have been more different. Where Heiden was lean and muscular, Ochowicz was short and compact. Where Heiden was modest and deferential, Ochowicz was occasionally gruff and pugnacious. But both men emerged from a thicket of athletic activity that thrived throughout much of the Midwest. It was a year-round sporting culture built on the twin foundations of skating and bike riding, and it would provide the underpinning of American cycling for decades. "A lot of the strength of cycling in the U.S. was based out of the Midwest—it all came together and bred success," said Jeff Pierce, who would become Heiden's teammate as well as one of the best pro riders of the 1980s. He would also win a stage of the Tour de France on the Champs-Élysées in Paris.

When Heiden came of age in the 1970s, it was de rigueur for skaters to train on bikes in the summer. In part, this was because there weren't plentiful indoor skating rinks available in the warmer months, but also because the sports were thought to be complementary in their use of musculature and their demands on the body. Skaters rode bikes in summer and skated all winter. "Back

Raised in Detroit, Pierce would become one of America's best pro cyclists in the 1980s, eventually winning a stage of the Tour de France.

then, no one rode bikes in winter," remembers eventual U.S. Pro Cycling Federation champion Tom Schuler. "You stopped in September and weren't back riding until January." The two sports were a perfect dovetail—a year-round fitness solution that kept muscles taut and competitive instincts honed. Perhaps no one exemplified this more than Ochowicz's wife, Sheila, who won world championships in skating and cycling.

To the casual observer, the two disciplines might not seem complementary at all—a bike race can cover 130 miles and last six hours, while the longest speed skating event is 10,000 meters, lasting a little more than 12 minutes. Yet, there is a profound physiological connection between bikes and blades. Both sports emphasize the quadriceps and the bulbous *vastus medialus*—a muscle above and inboard of the knee that can grow to grotesque proportions in the highest-caliber athletes, looking a little like a ripe grapefruit. Heiden was so developed, it seemed as if each leg had two fully formed kneecaps.

In the lab, athletes in both sports registered similarly on the conventional scales of athletic performance. Elite skaters and cyclists had a maximal oxygen uptake, or VO_2 max, of more than 70 ml/kg/minute, which means they could process about twice as much oxygen as a normal person and deliver it to working muscles. They also had a scant 6 to 8 percent body fat, giving their skin a translucent quality, like fine tissue paper. This had the ironic effect of making their immensely powerful legs look almost fragile to the touch, like a china vase.

But if there was one common currency among the athletes, it was *pain*. "Cycling in its purest form is a time trial, and most long-track speed skating is a time trial," said Dale Hughes, a longtime coach for the Wolverine Sports Club, the preeminent Midwest cycling and skating organization. "It's the same mindset—the pain you have to endure."

The pain can be towering and profound. It starts in the lungs, which struggle to keep up with the demand to provide oxygen to the churning muscles. When this aerobic metabolism fails, the body turns to anaerobic metabolism, which produces a few more minutes of effort, but at a painful cost. Lactic acid, a by-product, courses through the legs. It is as if every muscle is being pickled with acid. The urge to vomit rises in the throat. Every fiber screams to be released from this state of purgatory; every rational thought says to stop. The body, in effect, is taking out a loan that cannot be repaid.

For a normal person, this level of physical stress is one of unimaginable agony. But for elite skaters and cyclists, the searing in the lungs and limbs is commonplace—like punching a time card at the office. It's at this moment that the very best athlete will make a choice to act in a way that is the very antithesis of rational. He will find strength where there is none, summon motivation that has long since been drained and expended. He will dig deeper, heightening the sensation, using it as a perverse yardstick of achievement and success. The best athletes, like Heiden, will reach out and embrace the pain, welcoming it home like an old friend.

o͞o

But the commonality of pain was not all that bound the two sports. There was a cultural milieu that surrounded and nurtured the athletes, contributing to their success. They would stay at each other's houses when traveling to events, or park the family motor home in a fellow competitor's driveway for a long weekend of competition. Jeff Bradley, who would become one of the original members of the 7-Eleven team, remembers itinerant summers spent in the family motor home in the company of his younger sister Jacque and older sister Debbie. All three would become national cycling champions. Each week they would follow a procession of other families who would race on the velodromes in Kenosha, Wisconsin, on Tuesdays; Northbrook, Illinois, on Thursdays; and Brown Deer Park, Wisconsin, on Sundays. Weekends were also for road racing—the same assemblage would travel to Chicago, Detroit, Milwaukee, Madison, or any one of a hundred Midwest towns to try their legs against their competitive brethren.

Like Bradley, Jeff Pierce had the quintessential experience common to young bike racers of the era. "We would take my dad's van, pile six guys in it, and within six hours of Detroit where we lived, we had great racing every weekend, spring to fall—Indiana, Michigan, western Pennsylvania, Milwaukee—they were all within reach. That was the culture of the time." Talk of cycling and skating would permeate the conversation at the event, at the dinner table, in the car,

Bradley at the 1982 Tour of Texas, joined his sisters, Jacque and Debbie, as national cycling champions in their youth.

and around the house. Athletics covered everything like a blanket, providing warmth and succor. It was a rich life, filled with sport.

Like the great political families of our age, there were "first families" of speed skating and track cycling, including the names Heiden and Young. During the 1970s and 1980s, a stunning percentage of elite athletes would emerge from this extended family, including world and national champions in both sports. (Their progeny, including Ochowicz's daughter Elli and son Alex, continue the tradition today.)

At times the familial connections seemed to border on incestuous. Athletes would travel to far-flung locations to compete, and the gathering would resemble a reunion. "The Ochowiczes would stay with us in Detroit, and we would stay with the Ochowiczes in Milwaukee," said Roger Young. "It was a tight extended family." Senior members of this elite fraternity would come home, triumphant with medals, inspiring a new generation. "The influence and vision of someone like Ochowicz would permeate everyone, in the infield and in the warm-up house," said Young. And so it went, for decades, a contagion of success and athletic accomplishment.

All these athletes found themselves outside the great tide of youth sports involving a stick and a ball. But once welcomed inside, the Midwest cycling culture strengthened and solidified the young athletes' commitment to cycling—and to each other. It was a mindset that would serve them well when, years later, they would make their first foray into the often-inhospitable terrain of Continental racing. For much of their youth, they had been outsiders in their own country; they would be no less so on the roads of Europe.

o͞o

Much of the prevailing culture sprang from one entity: The Wolverine Sports Club of Detroit, started in 1888. Several members of the 7-Elevens found their start with the club, which promoted speed skating and cycling and was synonymous with an aging and benevolent former racer by the name of Mike Walden. An unassuming machinist with a generous streak for young athletes, Walden believed in what he called "analytical confidence"—breaking down the race into categories and skills and training specifically for them. It was an individualized philosophy that was in sharp contrast to the homogenous approach prevailing in the Eastern bloc at the time, where athletes were assembled like cattle and brutal selections were made in an almost Darwinian fashion. "He never tried to make two riders the same," said Dale Hughes, who would later marry Walden's daughter.

Velodromes, bike-racing tracks composed of paved or wooden ovals, several hundred meters in length, had been a source of national fascination at the turn of the 20th century. While their numbers had dwindled in the intervening years, they still had a firm foothold in the Midwest culture in the 1970s. Given these self-contained venues, it was easy to see how the two sports, skating and cycling, represented complementary cultures. The families would fraternize in the warming house for skaters or the infield for track cyclists. The races, by their very nature, formed a cloistered society in which a man like Walden could have a profound and lasting effect. Walden did not just spawn a love of sport; he spawned a culture, a philosophy, a religion of work and exertion on the roads and tracks of the Midwest.

"The Wolverines, they absolutely loved cycling," Pierce said. "All year long they loved to bring up new talent. They had the knowledge, the passion, and the drive. It was always present in those people."

Though the sports were complementary, many young athletes —including, eventually, Heiden—discovered that cycling had the stronger gravitational pull. For him and for many others, skating may have been more of a cultural attraction than a physical one. When given the opportunity to trade bikes for skates, many quickly made the deal. "I was tired of freezing my ass off," said Bradley, who found the sport mind- and body-numbing. In his grim assessment, "It was 100 meters straight, turn left, and another 100-meter straight." But cycling? "Cycling was just more fun."

CHAPTER 3
On Heiden's Coattails

After Lake Placid, money was falling out of the sky for Heiden, but he would not bend down to pick it up. It was not in his nature. To deal with the torrent of requests and offers that immediately followed Heiden's medal bonanza, a lawyer named Art Kaminsky initially represented him. Though Kaminsky had previously represented NHL hockey players, nothing could have prepared him for the state of delirium that enveloped Heiden after the Olympics.

Kaminsky "had the world's worst job" remembered Michael Aisner, the director of the famed Coors Classic bike race. "He had signed Eric, but Eric never did anything. He never did deals—he turned down more deals than any other athlete." Heiden's focus had nothing to do with meeting the president or being on *The Tonight Show*. "He wanted to be a doctor," said Aisner. And of course, he wanted to race bikes.

It can be difficult for an athlete as highly trained as Heiden to remain stationary for long. The body yearns for activity, and everyday life, without the intense focus of competition, soon begins to resemble a kind of confinement. For Heiden, it was as if this great surfeit of athletic talent and nervous energy simply needed an outlet. "I enjoy knowing what my limits are," he said of his immediate immersion into cycling. "People think of me as driven, but I just look at it as a learning experience." Plus, for someone who had been in the intense glare of the media for months, the bike was, quite simply, liberating. "If I want to get away . . . the bicycle is the best way to do it," he said.

He immediately began crisscrossing the country in pursuit of the next race, riding for the AMF Wheel Goods cycling team, on which he'd been teammates with Ochowicz. He made the rounds of East Coast criteriums in the spring of 1980, including races in Nutley and Somerville, New Jersey, and New York City, among others.

In each case, his results were less notable than the pandemonium that surrounded him. Races that were formerly limited to single columns in the sports sections of the local papers were suddenly being chronicled in the *New York Times* by virtue of Heiden's presence alone. At many events he was shadowed by a crew from ABC's *Wide World of Sports*. The shrieks of teenaged girls, in particular, seemed to follow him deafeningly around the racecourse. In the wake of Lake Placid, Heiden engendered a kind of cult.

He was good, certainly national level, but the press seemed to expect dominance on the scale of what it had seen in Lake Placid. It wasn't to be. The *New York Times*, in fact, was remarkably harsh in its coverage of the Olympic star. It would send a bewildered phalanx of reporters to a bike race, who would watch him circulate in mid-pack. The resulting headlines were in sharp contrast to the adulation that had accompanied his skating exploits: "No Gold for Heiden,"

In the wake of the 1980 Olympics, Heiden refused most sponsorship deals. One exception was television commentary, where he proved insightful and intelligent.

said one. "Heiden Fails Again," said another. Not that any of this mattered to Heiden's adoring public. Nothing could dim Heiden's luster in his fans' eyes.

oo

Heiden had flirted with track cycling throughout his career, and in May he went to the Olympic track trials in San Diego. It was a largely a ceremonial event, since President Jimmy Carter had decreed in January that there would be no U.S. participation in the Moscow Games, in protest of the Soviet invasion of Afghanistan. Some riders elected to stay away entirely. Heiden chose to go, placing a respectable 2nd in the kilometer. The three-lap event seemed to suit Heiden's physiology, both in duration and in its reliance on a high pain threshold, which he had cultivated during years of speed skating events. The superstar atmosphere prevailed here, too, augmented by the presence of basketball star Bill Walton, who had declared an interest in cycling and threw a party to prove it.

That fall, Heiden's interest in track cycling took him to Trexlertown, Pennsylvania, the site of one of the premier velodromes in the country. His friend Ochowicz was there, too—but this time, Och was not intending to compete. He had come in pursuit of the idea that had dogged him since leaving Lake Placid. He was there to build a cycling team.

Races were to take place that afternoon. The languid Pennsylvania humidity pressed down hard on the landscape, threatening showers. Suddenly, thunderstorms blew in with an angry vengeance, postponing the competition. As sheets of rain covered the outdoor venue, both men took refuge in an old barn adjacent to the velodrome, which was used for bike and equipment storage. For Ochowicz, it was the perfect opportunity to present the idea that had been consuming him for the past weeks: Would Heiden be interested in spearheading a pro cycling team?

Rain pelted down across the Pennsylvania farmland, washing it clean, and echoing against the rafters of the cavernous building. The two men were at crossroads in their lives, and the possibilities of that moment seemed to suit them perfectly. Heiden had been looking for a new athletic outlet that could satisfy his competitive urge and complement his goal of becoming a physician. But while legions of high-powered agents and corporations had been trying to get his endorsement for a project—anything—for months, he had steadfastly refused almost every offer. But the proposal from Ochowicz was different. To Heiden, it lacked the mercenary overtones of the other deals. First of all, it was an *athletic* proposal, which by definition made it somehow pure and unadulterated. Moreover, it was being offered not on behalf of a corporation, or an agent, or anyone who, in Heiden's view, was capable of guile or deceit. It was his old friend, Och, a man he knew and trusted. A man who shared his cultural and athletic lineage.

Ochowicz's life, meanwhile, was on a different, but still entirely complementary trajectory. He was envisioning another of the "levels" he was so fond of—the possibility of achieving the next significant milestone in his life. And he saw that Heiden could help him reach it. Given their shared objectives, Ochowicz was not taking advantage of Heiden's star power; he was simply facilitating their new lives. "Everyone needs that," said Ochowicz. "Someone has the dream, and someone has the selling power. Eric had the selling power, and that opened the door to pursue the dream."

Heiden's response was characteristically spontaneous and candid. "He said, 'Yeah, let's do it,'" said Ochowicz. "We were close by then, as a result of those two years [of managing the speed skating team]. We would do stuff together. He was very open-minded."

There was no need for a contract to secure Heiden's participation in Ochowicz's grand plan; it carried the legal standing that came from their shared Midwestern ethic. (In the coming years,

Ochowicz would secure astounding amounts of sponsorship and athletic commitments on handshakes alone.) It was, for all intents and purposes, a done deal. Fueled by his vision and the tacit agreement he had secured in the Trexlertown barn, Ochowicz went forth to procure riders and sponsorship.

∞

Armed with Heiden's imprimatur, Ochowicz found extraordinary success. The state of bike racing in the early 1980s was such that a rider would welcome any overture from a team that seemed remotely viable—but particularly one attached to a man who had just recently been on the covers of *Time* and *Sports Illustrated*. Riders sensed that, with Heiden on board, the yet-unnamed team had possibilities beyond the nickel-and-dime sponsorships from bike shops that they had grown accustomed to. "When you say that Eric Heiden is part of the project, it gives you the ability to get in there and have a chance for a meeting," said Ochowicz. "I told everyone the same story; Eric will race for us, and I will put a pro-am team together. Everyone was like, 'That's cool.' They sensed it could be something big, something different, where they could actually get a paycheck."

At this point Ochowicz conceived the team as pro-am, a combination of professionals (who could accept unlimited salary and winnings) and amateurs (who could accept limited winnings and, by restricting themselves in this way, remain eligible for the Olympic Games). Cycling had, perhaps more than most other sports, been contentiously divided along these lines, with two organizing bodies (the U.S. Cycling Federation for amateurs and the U.S. Professional Racing Organization for the pros) vying for control.

Heiden, by virtue of the few sponsorships he had accepted after the 1980 Winter Games, had already crossed over to the professional side. Therefore, if the team's future was to be predicated on Heiden's participation and star power, it would need to be pro-am. "Eric was technically a pro," said Ochowicz. "At that point, they broke your back for taking money for anything." (Today pros and amateurs are rarely separated in major events, and pros compete alongside amateurs in the Olympic Games.)

As Ochowicz traveled the racing circuit, gathering his informal commitments from riders, his message was one of hope and patience. "I'm telling them to hang in there, we are making progress," he said. "I was trying to keep everyone on board."

It wasn't quite a bluff, but it was close. At the time of these overtures, his hands were empty. He didn't have a dime of sponsorship to back up the offer. "They had no obligation if I didn't find something," said Ochowicz. "There were no terms. Riders just said, 'Go out and do it, and I'm part of it if it happens.'"

In all these discussions, it was not just Heiden's credibility that carried the day—it was also Ochowicz's. He had recently been among them as a racer, and he saw the world as they did. He knew what it was like to be driven to succeed athletically on a national and world stage. But perhaps more importantly, he knew the degree of physical and material sacrifice it took to get there. Their hopes and dreams were his own. To use street parlance, he had athletic cred', and this meant that, for the moment, they were willing to proceed on a hand-shake and a smile.

With irrepressible optimism, Ochowicz went shopping for riders at the Bisbee, Arizona, national road championships in August 1980. It would be his most fruitful fishing expedition and would lay the groundwork for the team over the next 10 years. "I came away from Bisbee feeling good—if we had a sponsor," he said.

His confidence was growing. It seemed that a national team, if not a world-class one, might be in the offing. The more he traveled the country and spoke to riders, the more he was infused by a subtle but sure sense of hope about his new life mission. If anyone could pull off such a thing, he thought, it was him.

And yet, despite Heiden's commitment, and the warm receptions he had received from riders, there was something missing: a title sponsor, and the money that came along with it.

oo

George Taylor, a Dutch sports agent, felt he might be best equipped to deal with the fusillade of offers and attention being lavished on Heiden after the Games. Taylor had grown up around sports, but not as a participant; his father and brother were both sports editors at *De Telegraaf*, Holland's largest daily newspaper. When Taylor was a boy, his father took him to watch the gritty spectacle of spring classic bike races like Paris-Roubaix and Liège-Bastogne-Liège, and it captivated him.

But Taylor's interest lay more in the business side of sports; he came to the United States to earn a business degree in 1969, at age 20. In the late 1970s he formed a sports marketing company primarily focused on soccer; he had been instrumental in bringing the famed Brazilian soccer star Pelé to the United States to play for the New York Cosmos. "Soccer was where I came from," said Taylor. "Cycling was a hobby."

Like any good sports agent, Taylor always had his antennae up for deals. He also happened to know a thing or two about speed skating and was well aware of Heiden's exploits in Lake Placid. "The Norwegians and Dutch are speed skating countries," he said. "Eric was better known in Holland than in the U.S." Indeed, years earlier, when Taylor came to the United States to earn his degree, his father gave him one piece of advice: "Maybe you should do something with Eric," he had said.

So when Heiden hit the mother lode in Lake Placid, Taylor wanted in. "One of the first things I did was to call Heiden in Madison," he said. "I got his father on the phone. He said, 'You should call Art Kaminsky in New York.' We met, and made an agreement that I would represent him personally."

Initially, Taylor was confronted with the same issue that had stymied Kaminsky. Despite the fact that all of corporate America wanted a piece of him, Heiden had to be dragged kicking and screaming into any type of deal. "He didn't make it easy to get sponsorships," said Taylor. "I said, 'You can make a million dollars.' But he never wanted more than four sponsorships. He was not commercial minded. He wanted to be a doctor."

Still, Taylor would not let Heiden's star power go unused. There had to be a way to get him to capitulate. If money and fame held little allure, what could it be?

Whether he was off the front or circulating midpack, Heiden never ceased to fascinate fans and the press.

Taylor's advantage was that he knew the selfless nature of speed skaters. Like cyclists, they were engaged in a sport that required prolific amounts of pain and sacrifice for scant rewards. Taylor had an inkling of the Midwest culture that Heiden grew up with—the almost puritan ethic of work and diligence that surrounded family sporting organizations like the Wolverines. He knew Heiden was driven by something deep and inexplicable, and it was not money Heiden had a sense of altruism toward the sport he loved, but he was also impelled by his Midwest ethic—an overarching desire to play straight, play fair, and embrace honesty. They were traits that tied Heiden to Ochowicz and would constitute the clay from which the entire team would be formed. "He went out of his way to do the right thing," said Taylor. As the team took shape in the coming months, it would be "a Midwest team, with Midwest values."

Thus, if Heiden would not enter into big-money sponsorships on his own behalf, Taylor reasoned, perhaps he would do it on behalf of the sport of cycling, and on behalf of his "buddies"—the close-knit group of athletes he had grown up with and competed against. Indeed, Heiden loved the word *buddies*, and he lived for them, sometimes more than for himself. Ever since he had left skating behind and devoted himself to bike riding, he had begun to see himself as a benefactor of U.S. cycling—a person who, because of his soaring fame, might bring attention and sponsorship to a sport that had been, to date, woefully underfunded and unrecognized.

(It was in fact the second time Heiden had done something big for the sake of his "buddies." Immediately after the 1980 Games, he had also been instrumental in obtaining sponsorship for the speed skating team from the video game company, Atari—despite the fact that he had already declared his intention to retire. The idea of bestowing such a parting gift upon his teammates suited him perfectly.)

Armed with this new tack, Taylor made his appeal. "I said, 'Eric, we need your help. You should help your buddies. If in the cities you can do a few interviews, you can get great publicity.'"

Heiden was well aware of the potential largesse he could give to the sport, materially and motivationally. As he traveled to races across the country in the spring of 1980, he would tirelessly submit to autograph sessions and interviews to promote his new sport. A headline in an issue of *VeloNews* called Heiden "bike racing's best friend" because of the media frenzy he engendered wherever he went. The Coors Classic's Michael Aisner remembers Heiden on *The Tonight Show* starring Johnny Carson, saying "I'm here with all my bike racing buddies." "Johnny would point his finger at the crowd, and they would go '*Yeaaahhh*,'" Aisner recalls. Heiden never seemed happier than when he was, through his own magnanimous nature, propelling the sport forward and into the public eye.

In September, Taylor did manage to arrange a sponsorship for Heiden: a four-year contract with *ABC Sports*, to be a commentator for the network's weekly sports show, *Wide World of Sports*. With Taylor's help, Heiden also left the AMF team and signed with Schwinn for 1981, for an amount that Taylor would only say was "enough to put him through school."

But for Taylor, who was accustomed to multimillion-dollar deals, these agreements supplied just an inkling of Heiden's true commercial potential. He was looking beyond the limited budget that a bicycle company—even one as prominent as Schwinn—could supply. Until then, cycling sponsorship had been mostly "endemic" in nature—that is, funded from within the bicycle industry itself. A so-called nonendemic sponsor—one that did not make bicycles or bicycle products—was rare. Thus, you had teams named for bike makers (Raleigh, Nishiki), bike parts (Shimano, Campagnolo), and bike shops (Wheelgoods, Yellow Jersey). It was a successful model in its limited way, but would be inevitably constrained by the sport itself and the minute amounts of capital it was capable of generating through the sale of bikes and bike parts. And it was incestuous in its appeal, generating the most interest among the already converted—an enthusiastic but tiny enclave of bike racers and racing wannabes. The endemic model would always lack the power and prominence to appeal to a broader audience.

Taylor had the notion that this needed to change, and that cycling was big enough that it could change. In an interview at the time, he hinted at his true intention, which was to pen a deal that was truly worthy of a five-time Olympic gold medalist. Taylor reckoned that Heiden had sufficient draw to be the figurehead for something much bigger, that in fact he might be worthy of an association with one of the world's largest corporations, "like what is common in Europe." He envisioned a team that might be called "Coca-Cola Schwinn, Kellogg's Schwinn, or something like that."

$$\overline{oo}$$

Thus, Taylor and Ochowicz were unknowingly on related missions in 1980, both having to do with Heiden. Taylor was looking for a title sponsor for a team that didn't exist; Ochowicz, meanwhile, was assembling a team that lacked a title sponsor. Both propositions were as empty as they were promising.

In May, both men happened to attend the Tour of Nutley, New Jersey, where they discussed their shared goals. Taylor had heard of Ochowicz through his connections in the speed skating world. In truth, they could not have been more different. Ochowicz had a long history as an athlete; Taylor was a fan and spectator, who came from a family of professional spectators. Ochowicz had a high school education and sports management experience drawn from the cut and thrust of competition. Taylor's approach was more cerebral, born of advanced degrees earned across two continents. Ochowicz was pragmatic; Taylor was academic and philosophical. They knew many of the same things, but they came from different worlds entirely.

Yet they formed a perfect complement. It was the most

natural thing in the world for Ochowicz to chat up a bike company or sell riders on the unique prospects of the team. It was a lexicon he had acquired over 15 years of racing, and it came to him readily. He was less comfortable, at least for the present, navigating the corridors of power in a major corporation. Shrewdly, for now, he was willing to surrender that job to Taylor. "George was really smart, very Euro," said Ochowicz. "You knew he was European in his appearance. He carried himself very well, very professionally. He was the right guy in the right place."

As they watched the racers circulate that day, they discussed their mutual goals. (The object of their attention, Heiden, was in the field and finished well back. Not surprisingly, he garnered the most media attention, meriting a mention in the *New York Times*.) They knew that with Heiden on board, they had a high probability of success in their respective missions. For Taylor, Heiden had the star power to attract a major sponsor. For Ochowicz, Heiden served as a magnet for riders and endemic sponsorship. Given all these things, they established a division of labor, such that by summer the team was being formed on two fronts. "George was looking for a title sponsor—a non-bicycle-industry sponsor," said Ochowicz. "I was mostly working the industry. And I was looking for riders."

A break came in October. In an issue of *Sports Illustrated*, Taylor read that the Southland Corporation, parent company of the 7-Eleven convenience store chain, had agreed to build the Olympic Velodrome in Los Angeles for the 1984 Games, to the tune of $4 million.

Everywhere he looked, in every town, Taylor saw the red, white, and green of a 7-Eleven store, and it made him wonder: If it had that kind of money to build a velodrome, a type of racing almost unknown to the American sporting public, might it also have the money to sponsor Heiden and some of the best cyclists in America? It seemed to him, at that moment, to at least be worth a phone call.

CHAPTER 4
What's a Velodrome?

In the typical 7-Eleven store of the 1980s, there was nothing connected to cycling, or even much a cyclist could consume without committing some grave dietary transgression. Within the famously white walls of a typical franchise, you could find anything from Almond Joy to Alka-Seltzer, ice cream to ibuprofen, all in a space that could be spanned in 20 quick paces. If you were in need of entertainment, you could buy a video, book, or magazine. If you were hungry, you could buy some rudimentary ingredients to cook a meal—or you could take one away, ready to eat. You could find some basic tools to fix a pesky faucet, or an aerosol can of goo to resurrect the flat tire on your car, listing sadly in the parking lot. You could pick up cash at the ATM to entertain a date, or even better, take a flyer on the Mega Lotto to fund any number of indiscretions. If a sugar fix was your aim, 7-Eleven stores served millions of donuts annually, as well as astronomical numbers of candy bars and cookies—a virtual pantheon of junk food. In short, your average 7-Eleven could more than satisfy all the worldly needs of the average American knuckle-dragger. That is to say, people just like you and me.

This emblem of American commerce started in 1927, when an employee of the Southland Ice Company in Dallas started selling milk, eggs, and bread from the ice dock. The combination of convenience and speed immediately resonated with customers, and the chain was soon renamed Tote'm stores. In 1946 the company changed its name again, to 7-Eleven, reaching 100 stores by 1952, 1,000 stores by 1963, and exploding to 7,000 stores by 1981. (Today, the 7-Eleven model has been successfully exported around the world, with stores in 16 countries.) Starting in 1963, its namesake hours of 7 a.m. to 11 p.m. were abandoned in favor of a 24-hour operation.

Many stores could not locate a key to lock the doors if they had to.

But if there was one thing that propelled 7-Eleven stores toward their billions in annual revenue—then and now—it was the collective thirst of a nation. 7-Eleven is all about beverages, serving millions of gallons of fountain drinks annually. 7-Eleven stores may be compact, but they also appeal to the American notion of bigness. One of the most popular items is the "Big Gulp," a 32-ounce drink introduced in 1980. (It proved so successful that it was later enlarged to 64 ounces.) More than a million cups of coffee are served each day. There is also the frozen "Slurpee" drink, which have sold by the billions over the life of the company.

All told, a typical store today will tempt you with more than 2,500 items, presented in a starkly sanitary setting that more closely resembles a hospital ward than your typical market. And there is one thing you can be sure of: Every one of these items will have been selected and presented with the scientific precision that comes from decades of experience, in thousands of stores from Texas to Tokyo. The typical 7-Eleven store may be a matter of casual indifference to the average customer, but make no mistake about it: This is a precisely researched and engineered retail machine, designed to quickly sell you the things you need—and quite a few that you don't. It is a masterful tool for the extraction of money.

oo

In 1980, when George Taylor and Jim Ochowicz were looking to fund their fledgling team, 7-Eleven stores were emblematic of all that America had become and all that the sport of bicycle racing was not: a place of instant gratification and consumption. While 7-Elevens were about indulgence and comfort, cycling was about sacrifice and no small amount of pain. The average 7-Eleven customer, if he owned a bike, had probably not touched it in years and would be no more likely to compete in the Tour de France than forgo *Monday Night Football.*

In all ways, it was as unlikely a partnership as could be imagined. The very fact that such a prominent potential source of atherosclerosis would be associated with one of the world's most demanding endurance sports represented the heights of irony. But Jere Thompson, the second son of the founder, wasn't thinking about any of this when the company began its 10-year association with bicycle racing. He and his brother John, the company chairman, were simply trying to do the right thing.

Jere Thompson was a true company insider. He made the rounds of the ice plants as a young man in Texas and worked in the company's stores in high school and college. In 1961 he was made a vice president, and became president in 1973. Under his leadership, and that of his brother, the chain became a financial juggernaut. By 1979 the company was making a billion dollars every three months, and its uniquely American emphasis on speed and convenience had been successfully exported overseas—the 1,000th international store was opened in 1980.

Thompson had always been community minded, seeking to do the right thing on behalf of the company that had become synonymous with his family. As part of this effort, he served on the board of the Young Presidents' Organization, a Texas-based leadership group for aspiring executives. There, he met a 42-year-old multimillionaire and self-made man by the name of Peter Ueberroth, who, as it happened, had recently been named manager of the 1984 Olympic Games in Los Angeles. The two developed a friendship, and inevitably, the subject of Olympic sponsorship came up. "I got to know him very well," said Jere. "My older brother, John, went to visit him and said we were interested in getting involved." It seemed, to Jere, to be an almost perfect association for his company, flush with overtones of patriotism and goodwill—a perfect outlet for his altruism, and his bank account.

Ueberroth was nothing if not savvy; he had already done an astonishing job enlisting corporate involvement in the Games. It was a time when the specter of the 1976 Olympics in Montreal loomed large: That city had grossly overcommitted to the construction of new facilities and finished woefully in debt. (In contrast, the 1984 Games would eventually make a $200 million profit, unheard of for a modern Olympics, helping Ueberroth become *Time* magazine's "Man of the Year" in 1984.) Among Ueberroth's many coups were McDonald's backing of the swim stadium, and Arco's support of the Los Angeles Memorial Coliseum, site of the opening and closing ceremonies and athletic events.

Part of Ueberroth's genius was in saving money by repurposing facilities that existed in the Los Angeles area. There was, however, one venue that still needed major funding, and that would need to be built from scratch: the 333-meter Olympic velodrome.

o͞o

Few Olympic events can rival track cycling for a low return on investment. It is, perhaps next to equestrian events, one of the most obscure and yet one of the most expensive sports in the Olympic pantheon. Track cycling merits almost no prime-time television coverage, and yet a typical velodrome, with amenities, could cost upward of $3 million at the time. The self-contained events lend themselves to spectating and are thrilling to watch for those in the know. They are, however, nearly incomprehensible to the average spectator. General audiences find it fascinating that the bikes "have no brakes" (a common storyline in the general press), and the events engender a perverse fascination with the frequent crashes. But beyond that, the uninitiated find the events arcane and impenetrable.

In this sense, it was fortunate that the Thompson brothers didn't have any preconceptions. Neither one, in fact, had ever seen a bicycle race. It didn't matter. They were motivated by a fundamental impulse: They simply wanted to do their part for their country and their company.

Ueberroth, known for being forthright, stated his needs to John Thompson in the simplest possible terms: "Why not take on the velodrome?" he asked.

To a large degree, the history of U.S. cycling hinged on the response to this question. But John Thompson, who didn't know a track bike from a teakettle, didn't hesitate a second. He said yes.

○○

Having made this commitment, John Thompson eagerly reported the news to his brother Jere. In what would become an iconic statement in the history of U.S. cycling, Jere Thompson replied in a direct and unassuming Texan fashion. Why, yes, he said. Olympic sponsorship sounded like a fine idea. But he did have one question: *"What's a velodrome?"*

Though he had just committed millions of dollars, John Thompson wasn't entirely sure himself. So the brothers opened a dictionary and looked it up.

In this way the whole sponsorship pivoted on happenstance —the desire of one company to apply its generosity to an Olympic sport—any sport. Were it not for the Thompsons' willingness, merely for the good of the Olympic movement, to undertake a thing they knew nothing about, bike racing's growth might have been stymied for years, if not decades.

"I had never thought about cycling—I never even realized it was part of the Olympic Games," Jere confessed. "That's what Peter [Ueberroth] wanted, and that's what we did."

Although the "What's a velodrome?" story has acquired mythic status in the U.S. cycling community, the Thompson brothers' reaction cannot be regarded as unusual. Lack of awareness of cycling, and particularly track cycling, was pervasive in the early 1980s, and is only marginally better now. The Coors Classic's Michael Aisner astutely points out that it wasn't just the Southland executives who didn't know a fixed gear from a freewheel. "The fact was, no one knew what a velodrome was," said Aisner, in only slight exaggeration.

It would be naïve to say that the company didn't want exposure and brand awareness in return for its multimillion-dollar commitment. The Thompsons clearly hoped to bask in the glow of the Olympics. But compared with the highly refined quid pro quo nature of sponsorship that exists today, the company was opening its checkbook with remarkably few strings attached. Sean Petty, who would later oversee Southland's cycling program, said the decision to fund the velodrome seems remarkable, even now. "You can appreciate the tremendous number of marketing studies that are usually done for something like this," he said. "But this was just fate."

Jere Thompson said there were "no requirements" in those days. "We were just pulling for the U.S. in all sports." This kind of unfettered commitment would become a singular facet of Southland's involvement with cycling, particularly in the early years. Later on, when the company began to experience financial duress, this would change markedly. At the outset, however, it was committed to cycling with virtually no preconditions.

At the time, the company had 7,000 stores. It's unlikely that many of the customers frequenting those stores had an appreciation of track cycling. But they didn't need to. In the eyes of the Thompson brothers, Southland had bought into something that transcended cycling, and running, and every other sport in the Olympic pantheon. They had bought into the Olympic phenomenon.

The deal was formally announced in November 1980. Southland was to pay $4 million to construct the Los Angeles Olympic Velodrome on the campus of California State University,

Southland anted up $4 million to build the Los Angeles Olympic Velodrome in Dominguez Hills and was rewarded with a world-class venue, second to none.

Dominguez Hills, located in Carson. As part of its commitment, 7-Eleven was deemed the official convenience store of the L.A. Olympics. Sponsorship of a team, interestingly enough, was mentioned as an outside possibility.

oo

George Taylor heard about Southland's commitment to the Olympic Velodrome, and like any good agent, he saw opportunity in things that are merely news to others. He was impressed that a company would underwrite a sport it knew nothing about and that its involvement seemed largely motivated by civic pride and altruism. But Taylor knew there were hard financial realities underpinning any such decision, and he couldn't help but wonder, "What do they want to get out of it?"

Taylor already had experience obtaining major corporate

sponsorship for sports that were outside the American mainstream. When he brought Pelé to the United States in the twilight of the soccer star's career, the move was largely credited with a surge in public interest in soccer. (For years, Pelé's bicycle kick was part of the opening montage of ABC's *Wide World of Sports*, exposing millions of people to the game.) In the wake of that success, Taylor had created his own marketing firm, Sports Mondial. It wasn't long before he found himself hungering for another marketing coup, one that could rival what he had done in soccer, and that might involve another unheralded "European" sport.

When he looked at cycling, Taylor saw the same nascent potential that he had recognized in soccer. Growing up, he had witnessed the phenomenal popularity of races like Paris-Roubaix, a one-day "classic" in the northeast of France, whose 161-mile cobblestoned course is lined with spectators from beginning to end each spring. He had also seen the heroics of riders like Eddy Merckx of Belgium and Felice Gimondi of Italy, champions who drew teeming crowds of spectators that Americans might find bewildering. He knew that bike racing had the pathos and power to captivate an audience.

In America, however, cycling was a "third world" sport, unable to garner the money and attention that the stick-and-ball sports enjoyed. To knowledgeable insiders like Taylor and Ochowicz, this snubbing seemed like the height of irony. Here was a sport that demanded the most of an athlete, that engendered the highest levels of self-sacrifice, countless hours of training in isolation, and no small amount of risk to life and limb. Yet, as a competitive sport, it was utterly ignored.

Other sports in this genre included long-distance running, rowing, and cross-country skiing. They had the shared characteristics of extreme physical endurance, self-sacrifice, and, unfortunately, obscurity.

Maybe the pain was beyond the comprehension of most

people. Or maybe not. Taylor thought, "If an athlete like Heiden could be allied with a company like Southland, it might change the entire landscape of bicycle racing in the United States."

Taylor cold-called Southland and was put through to the communications department. He was familiar with the routine—for every dozen companies you contact, maybe two would express interest. And of those, one might call back, if only to say, "The time isn't right," or "It isn't a strategic fit at this time."

But this was different. He was given the opportunity to briefly present his idea to Southland executives Doug Thompson (son of John) and Roger Winter. The three agreed to meet and discuss the matter further at Taylor's Fifth Avenue office in New York City.

Taylor found a receptive audience in the two men. "Twenty minutes became two hours," he said. "I basically told them everything they needed to know—that they should capitalize on their sponsorship by starting the 7-Eleven cycling team." More important, Taylor emphasized that the company needn't sponsor cycling solely out of a sense of philanthropy and community spirit, though those things were certainly important. He explained that they had every right to expect a return on their investment and, moreover, that cycling could exceed all their expectations in this regard.

To make his point, Taylor emphasized a simple fact. "I said cycling, unbeknownst to anyone in the U.S., is one of the few sports where the name of the team is the name of the sponsor." In other words, at every race, in every town, and on the back of every rider, would be the famous red, white, and green logo of the Thompson's convenience store. It was an opportunity to buy into cycling in a way that no company had done previously. He insisted that they would, for all intents and purposes, own the sport of U.S. cycling, from horizon to horizon. It was not far from the truth. With the support of 7-Eleven, Taylor argued, his proposed team would be able to dominate such established cycling events as the Tour of Somerville and the Coors

Classic, and that from coast to coast, wherever there was a race, there would likely be a 7-Eleven store and a 7-Eleven team victory.

Heiden became a great figurehead for 7-Eleven and was instantly recognizable in the red, white, and green. The jersey design proved to be remarkably enduring and changed little over the course of the sponsorship.

The concept, while sound, didn't immediately resonate. Months passed, and Taylor began to wonder if his proposal had fallen flat. Then, in late 1980, he was surprised by a call.

"George, remember me? It's Roger Winter. We have $250,000. Think you could do something with that?" Taylor thought he probably could. "Good!" said Winter. "Call me after the holidays."

Taylor had prepared for this moment, and he knew what he had to do.

"I laid down the phone," he said, "and I called Eric Heiden."

oo

In a way, it was the perfect nexus of events. When Taylor looked around, he saw a fervent patriotism surrounding the forthcoming Los Angeles Olympics. In Southland, he knew he had a well-moneyed, successful convenience store chain wanting to sanitize its image and associate itself with healthful pursuits. And thanks to Ochowicz, some of the nation's best riders stood at the ready, should the team materialize. And Taylor also had Ochowicz himself, who seemed eminently qualified to run the whole thing.

Indeed, it was a combination of factors that could not exist in any other time. Certainly not in the era of Jack Heid or Jackie Simes, decades earlier. But now, in the buildup to the Olympics, bicycle racing was pregnant with possibility in a way that had not been witnessed since the heyday of the board tracks, 80 years earlier.

Yet none of this was sufficient in and of itself. Taylor certainly understood this, and he knew that to succeed, the whole thing would need to be propelled and buoyed by the star power of a certain five-time Olympic gold medalist. No one—from riders, to agents, to sponsors—felt that the team would have even left the gate without Heiden.

"Without Eric, we wouldn't have gotten close," recalled Taylor. "Anyone with the charisma and reputation of Eric was a guarantee for publicity."

"Eric was critical," agreed Tom Schuler, a national champion and future team member. "All of a sudden, George could tell Southland that Eric could be captain on paper. He hadn't really done that much racing, but *everyone* knew Eric Heiden. George was shrewd. He knew it would get Southland's attention."

The company had already provided a charitable largesse to cycling, in the form of the Olympic Velodrome. But this was corporate America, after all—and any further investment needed to show a return, preferably in revenue but at the very least in publicity. And that publicity would come in the form of Eric Heiden.

Heiden had already agreed to the arrangement in principle, in discussions with both Taylor and Ochowicz. When he considered the broad expanse of his life after Lake Placid, the proposal seemed to meet all his requirements. He would be paid to ride his bike and retain the high-level fitness he was accustomed to. He could pursue his medical degree. By being the team figurehead, he would be supporting his Midwest cycling "buddies." And his mere presence would elevate the sport exponentially in the eyes of an adoring public. It seemed as if the whole thing could put him on a trajectory that would take him through the next decade of his extraordinary life.

oo

Taylor had successfully laid the groundwork with Southland, but the sport, and the personalities in it, remained an enigma to the company's executives. So it was only natural that, before committing fully, the company wanted to get a better idea of exactly what it was purchasing with its $250,000. What was this obscure sport about anyway, with its anorexic-looking participants and arcane rituals involving shaved legs and smelly liniments?

By this time Ochowicz was once again living in Milwaukee and working construction, the default vocation of his life for the past

15 years. He was not yet fully confident that the team would supply a new path forward, but he applied himself steadily to the job at hand, as he had always done with all his pursuits. If part of executing his dream involved making his case to a bunch of suits in the big city, so be it.

Taylor helped facilitate a meeting between Ochowicz and Southland executives Roger Winter and Doug Thompson in New York City. Shrewdly, Ochowicz elected to take along one of his committed riders, Tom Schuler, then living in Chicago. Not only was Schuler an accomplished cyclist, he was also a nearly perfect representative for the sport: handsome, college educated, and well spoken. Indeed, the meeting would mark the beginning of a diplomatic and management role for Schuler that would extend well beyond his years as a rider. He would become, in the parlance of U.S. sports, the ideal player-manager. Throughout the life of the team, Ochowicz would strive to sign riders who were both exceptional athletes and good corporate representatives. In this sense Ochowicz's choice of the polished and professional Schuler was nothing short of brilliant.

The pair managed to scavenge suits and ties, as would befit a meeting in Manhattan. This was, more than any other time in Ochowicz's life, one of those "levels" he was so fond of—a characteristic leap into the unknown. He seemed to sense, intuitively, that he would need to master the art of boardroom banter, becoming as conversant in the parlance of corporate America as he had been in the trash talk of the peloton. "It was different from anything I had done before," said Ochowicz of the meeting. "You had a corporate culture—everyone was wearing suits and ties, everyone was serious." Yet, he was no more nervous than he would have been at the starting line of the Tour of Somerville. He found it was a fitting and natural place, a facet of his new life that would become entirely comfortable in the space of the coming weeks, months, and years. It was, to Ochowicz, simply "another space to move into."

Schuler helped Ochowicz land the 7-Eleven sponsorship deal and later assumed the role of rider-manager for the team.

Southland execs had already publicly professed ignorance of the sport they were underwriting to the tune of millions of dollars, as evidenced by the now-famous "What's a velodrome?" anecdote.

Gerard Bisceglia, a sales and promotion manager who would become the head of sports marketing for Southland, remembers that Ochowicz and his athletes were the first bike racers he had ever met in his life. Other Southland execs were no better in this regard. Given this context, Ochowicz deftly grasped his purpose in the initial meeting, which was to convey that "We *did* know what a velodrome was. We had knowledge about cycling that they didn't have."

Southland was apparently satisfied with the performance of the two emissaries, and the deal was consummated in January 1981. It must have gone well for Ochowicz, too. He went back to Milwaukee, where just a few days earlier he had been building a parking lot.

He had been through a lot in the past couple of years, a fast-moving mix of good events and bad. He had basked in the glow of Heiden's success in Lake Placid, and the experience had given him an inkling of a new life for himself, as a manager. He had moved across the country with his young family, renovated a house with his own hands, then just as quickly moved them all back to Milwaukee. Temporarily ignoring his impulse to stop competing, he had tried to make one last stand as an athlete, which had ended disastrously in Belgium, when he became sick and finally surrendered to the inevitable in a dank basement apartment in Ghent.

Yet he was unbowed, and at this moment, all these things seemed to recede from view. He had never felt more sure about his future direction. Now, having conquered any demons that may have awaited him in that New York City boardroom, he seemed to know exactly where his future lay, and it did not involve a pick and shovel.

"I never went back to that job site again," he said.

CHAPTER 5
Birth of a Team

Heiden was perfect for 7-Eleven, a glistening investment that was destined to succeed from the start. But even someone of Heiden's rock-star status could not make a team by himself. A bike racing squad is a complex organism, a confluence of mind and muscle that is sometimes as much alchemy as science.

From the outset, Ochowicz was looking to the far horizon, and he wanted a team that could go the distance. This meant that all the members had to be compatible on and off the racecourse. Ochowicz knew this as well as anyone. At the 1972 Olympics, he had seen how dissension and acrimony could tear a team apart, when openly feuding members of his team pursuit squad dashed any hope of a medal and left Munich in disgust. But Ochowicz had also witnessed the inverse. As far back as 1971, at the speed skating oval in Inzell, he saw how a fully functioning team could elevate its performance above the capabilities of even its best athlete. At these moments, there was something at work that went beyond any mathematical sum of physiology and talent. There was simply no accounting for it. And when he thought back over the myriad experiences of his competitive life, it was clear which scenario he wanted for his fledgling team, and he set about creating it.

Indeed, throughout his career, Ochowicz's greatest skill would not be coaching in the literal sense. He would almost never counsel riders on the specifics of training. His gift, his intuitive talent, was in putting together a team that was compatible. It was the beginning of a uniquely American mode of operation that would persist for the life of the team, and that would send lasting shockwaves through the established cycling hierarchy. He knew that a collegial atmosphere carried some very concrete dividends, providing an essential buffer against the monumental pain and suffering that the sport engendered. In such circumstances, if the team could not rely on each other, no amount of physical talent would compensate.

"Jim had the innate sense that we had to get along socially," said Ron Hayman, one of the original seven riders. "Not just on the bike." It would be easy to dismiss such attitudes as soft or self-indulgent in a sport that valued toughness above all else. But on Ochowicz's part, this was more than just benevolent leadership. In Europe, cycling had been governed for decades by autocratic coaches and team leaders presiding over a Darwinian atmosphere of competition. Though a European foray was still years away, it seemed Asia Ochowicz was already preparing for the difficulties the team would face on the inhospitable roads of France and Italy.

Hayman, with Ochowicz at right, quickly transferred the hard-won experience he had gained in Belgium to his new teammates.

○○

As Ochowicz went forth to sign riders, there was not to be much in the way of salary negotiations. He figured it was simple arithmetic, to be applied uniformly. He just took the amount of the sponsorship ($250,000), subtracted overhead and expenses, and divided the remainder by six, the number of riders he felt he needed for a competitive team. "I just did the math," he said. "There was no bargaining." The figure he arrived at was $12,000 per rider. It was an approach that seems amazing in light of today's litigious and often acrimonious atmosphere of haggling and counteroffers. But economics are a function of their time, and none of the athletes he approached were inclined to dispute the number. Most of them had never seen such a sum before, for any job, much less for riding a bike, a vocation that they hardly perceived as work in the first place.

Powerfully armed with the endorsement of the world's most famous athlete, Ochowicz was, not surprisingly, greeted warmly. He was also accompanied by the great advantage of his personal geography. "I didn't really reach outside my space so much," said Ochowicz of his team-building exercise. "I didn't look for riders from California or the East Coast. I didn't have the need. I had enough people I knew well enough."

But his selections weren't merely a product of familiarity and access. Ochowicz had been traveling around the country for months, leaning on race fencing, watching dozens of events from Southern California to Somerville, scouting the top riders in America. What he saw confirmed what he felt in his heart. Cyclists from the Midwest were among the best in the country.

Ochowicz knew that U.S. racing came from a different bloodline than its European counterpart and required a different horse. In terms of abilities, Ochowicz wanted riders "that could do everything—at least for racing at that time. That meant track and

Most of the team's first races were contested on the American criterium circuit over distances of 50 miles or so. Heiden pictured.

criterium racing and a little road racing. We wanted a team that could win almost any race."

European races, since the earliest days of competition, emphasized distance and terrain. Events were so long that they often started with a "promenade"—a rolling armistice over the course of the first 10 or 20 miles that served to relax muscles and foster conversation. A rider might even be permitted to stop and fraternize with a spouse or relative at the roadside, then regain the peloton, with permission. But once the racing began in earnest, it seemed to more than compensate for the earlier truce, the speeds causing riders to be carved off the back of the group at an alarming rate. Over the course of 100 miles or more, riders would gradually be drained of every ounce of energy and finish limp with exhaustion. Spectators, meanwhile, understood and appreciated the entire pageant, sometimes waiting hours along the roadside for the brief passage of the racers.

In contrast, U.S. racing reflected the frenetic lifestyle of its people. Inner-city criteriums—races of multiple laps around tight courses of a mile or so—hit 30 miles per hour from the opening gun and were punctuated with elbow-banging sprints and frequent crashes. The emphasis, if there was one, was on finishing speed over endurance and hill-climbing ability. For spectators, it was the sporting equivalent of a video game, a kind of rolling catastrophe that anyone could understand and be attracted to.

In time, American teams would need to broaden their repertoire to include longer races and more climbing, following the European model. And the 7-Eleven team, more than any other, would have to learn to accommodate these conflicting demands on the body. But for now, it was all about a fast finish, and about winning races—American style.

o͞o

Perhaps the earliest and easiest choice for the team, besides Heiden, was Ochowicz's brother-in-law, Roger Young. Born in 1953 and already in the twilight of his career, Young would become one of the team's de facto elder statesmen.

Many athletes from the Midwest culture started at a tender age, but Young, who began riding at age 3, was extraordinary even by that standard. Both of his parents raced bikes and skated in an era when such deep athletic conviction, particularly for such obscure sports, was almost unheard of. "My Mom raced in the '30s and '40s," remembers Young, one of four children. "We all did cycling and speed skating. It was always there."

In 1963, the Youngs' world was turned upside down, when their mother was diagnosed with cancer and died. After this tragedy, athletics became more than a family pastime—they were a lifeline. "Sports were always an extended family to us," Young said. "It was a pretty important culture to maintain."

The fact that Young was Ochowicz's brother-in-law made him an attractive choice for reasons of domestic and marital relations. But he was also undeniably talented, particularly on the track and in the flat criterium courses that were then a hallmark of U.S. racing. (He would eventually win multiple national titles on road and track.)

More than anyone else on the team, Young was Ochowicz's contemporary. The two had traveled in the same competitive circles since adolescence and shared the athletic and cultural experiences common to top U.S. riders in the 1970s. They were acutely aware of the embryonic state of the sport in the United States, and when they went to Europe, they generally suffered embarrassing defeats. Young had been part of the ill-fated U.S. foray, with Ochowicz, into the 1972 Olympics (Young had entered the match sprint). "We got our asses kicked really bad," remembers Young of the Munich debacle. They also rode the Ghent six-day together in 1979, after Ochowicz had contracted bronchitis and was looking to exit the sport. Young remembers that race as simply "a disaster."

But these events did not deflate Young or temper his exuberance for bike racing. To the contrary—they seemed to harden him for what lay ahead. Despite "getting his butt kicked every way imaginable," he could think of nothing he would rather do than ride for his friend and relative, Ochowicz. "In 1980, after there was to be no Olympic games, I had a really fun season riding crits, and I decided I wanted this as a career," he said. "I was 29, and my aspirations were to be a six-day track racer in winter and to help out whenever I could. I felt a kindred responsibility, with Och, to help him fulfill his promise to win gold in '84. I saw it as a great opportunity to fulfill what I had in myself."

Young, a talented crit racer, competed with Ochowicz and became his brother-in-law. He was a natural addition to the fledgling 7-Eleven team.

At the same time Ochowicz enlisted Young for the team, he also brought on board a rider from Chicago by the name of Danny Van Haute. A year earlier, Young and Van Haute had both been staying at Ochowicz's house in Lake Placid when Heiden began his remarkable medal streak, and both had been summarily enlisted as bodyguards to shepherd Heiden to the venue and press events. Amidst the madness of that historic week, Ochowicz had mentioned his dream of managing a cycling team, and by the way, would they be interested in being part of it? Now that the dream was a reality, Ochowicz intended to make good on his offer.

Van Haute, like nearly everyone else Ochowicz approached, was wide-eyed at the prospect of riding for a major team. "I said, 'Whatever—let's go!' It was a good deal for me, going from living at home and being supported by my parents and prize money, and all of a sudden having a contract, with expenses. I was on cloud nine."

Van Haute fit the Midwest athletic archetype perfectly. His parents were Belgian immigrants, settling in Chicago in the 1950s. Part of their European heritage was that they "knew cycling," said Van Haute. "They brought me to a bike race, I got a bike, and *boom*." He was racing by the age of 10, in a now-extinct category known as the "midgets." His earliest memories, like those of his contemporaries, were of a life robust with sports. "In the Midwest in the '70s and '80s, there were races every weekend, road or crits," he said. "It was Tuesday night at the track in Kenosha, Thursday night in Northbrook, and Saturday and Sunday anywhere." Van Haute also quickly became allied with the Schwinn bicycle company, which was conveniently located just down the road from his house. "Anytime I needed wheels or tires, they would take me down to 'the cage,' where all the good stuff was, open up the cage, see what I needed, and write it up."

Van Haute progressed quickly, making the Junior Worlds team in 1974. In 1976, he was an alternate for the Montreal Olympics. Like so many riders who would form the foundation of the

7-Eleven team, he was also a Wolverine and dabbled in speed skating and hockey. It was there that he became familiar with a rider by the name of Tom Schuler.

Standing over six feet tall, Van Haute was a formidable presence on the cycling circuit and a perfect fit for the 7-Eleven squad.

oo

Schuler, as much as anyone, would become synonymous with the team, riding in 7-Eleven colors for the duration of the sponsorship and remaining in a managerial role when the squad was eventually reincarnated under another sponsor. Like many of his 7-Eleven teammates, Schuler had an almost genetic predisposition toward cycling. Although he was naturally athletic and dabbled in football, baseball, hockey, and soccer, before long he had eschewed mainstream sports in favor of two wheels. "My gang of neighborhood guys, we were into bikes," he said of his childhood in the Detroit area. "We would take any kind of bike, strip it down, strap on hockey pads, and go mountain biking, bombing down trails in the snow." For an energetic teenager like Schuler, the bike offered an immediate exit ramp from convention and expectations. It was a ticket to freedom. "I would ride to Mackinac Island, with a rack on my Raleigh, and spend a dollar a day. We'd do weekend trips with no money. I really liked the freedom of being on my own."

In traditional sports, motivation could be faint, but structure and peer pressure in something like Little League could compel participation and even excellence. In comparison, cycling was an almost solitary affair. Entering this world required a unique passion fueled by an innate love of the bicycle and the simple act of riding. "When I got into cycling, it was a fluke," said Schuler. "There was no exposure, no path, no funnel. You just knew someone. I had a buddy who liked to ride and we rode everywhere."

Before long he felt the pull of competition. Schuler accompanied a friend to some Mike Walden training sessions and soon after joined the famed Wolverines. It was an immediate fit, athletically and culturally. He remembered a particularly poignant moment with the team in 1971, when he was just 14. He had made the long road trip to the track nationals in Portland, Oregon, and the varied assemblage felt for all the world like a surrogate family. "I camped in a tent next to the velodrome, with the Young family," he said. "It was very much a family thing." With the Wolverines there was an exceptional bond, a feeling of solidarity and uncommon athletic commitment. His indoctrination was at that point complete. "I liked the fact that I was away from traditional sports," he said. "I abandoned all traditional sports and focused on bike riding."

By 1975 he was a member of the U.S. national team, and in 1976 he made the Olympic team as an alternate. He also made the unusual and demanding choice to balance bike racing with college, earning a business degree from the University of Michigan in 1979. It was a decision that would serve him well years later, when he made the transition from athletics to sports management, enabling him to serve the team on the bike and in the front office. It was also in 1979 that Schuler joined Ochowicz and Heiden on the AMF team.

Schuler was one of the original seven riders and the only one to wear the 7-Eleven colors in every year of the team's existence.

Schuler was an obvious choice for Ochowicz as he went on his shopping expedition. He was part of a complex web of athleticism and sporting culture that had been cultivated on the roads and tracks of the Midwest. He accepted immediately.

oo

Throughout the history of the team, Ochowicz would be devoted to the idea of an American roster. But he was also shrewd enough to know when an infusion of international talent could fill a gap or supply experience where the Americans might be lacking.

And so it was with the fifth member of the team, Ron Hayman, the first in a series of Canadian riders who would become tremendous assets through the years. (Five years later, Canadian Alex Stieda would become the first North American to wear the leader's yellow jersey in the Tour de France, under the 7-Eleven banner.) Hayman started riding seriously at age 12, chasing his shadow along the seawall at Stanley Park in Vancouver, British Columbia. Initially a track rider, he made the transition to the road in the mid-1970s, winning the B.C. provincial road championship in 1975. His racing success meant that he made regular forays to the United States, where he sometimes found himself racing against Jim Ochowicz.

Hayman was among the pioneers, a small group of North American riders who defied existing norms and who saw Europe as their rightful proving ground. He understood, early on, that he could either opt for the relatively complacent position of being a successful rider on the short circuits of the United States and Canada, or he could reach for the more aspirational and difficult goal of European cycling. He was wary of the provincial nature of the sport in North America; Europe, as he saw it, was his next logical step. "It was turn pro or get on with my life," he said. So in 1979 he went to Belgium to ride for a pro team, Safir-Ludo.

Unfortunately for Hayman, this compulsion was perhaps too

strong. He had been told that a rider needed to come into the season "lean and mean." Hayman, occasionally prone to excess, took this advice to the extreme, eating like a bird and riding 8 to 10 hours a day. The results were dire and predictable. "I became anemic," he said. "I couldn't get out of my own way."

While in Belgium, his disillusion was compounded by the far more insidious presence of performance-enhancing drugs. "I never felt I had the motor to go with them," he said of the pro peloton. "The only way to make up the difference was to take something." Physically exhausted and mentally disheartened, he came home to reevaluate his career and his life.

Against this backdrop, Ochowicz's proposal could not have come at a better time. Hayman's decision was cemented in the fall of 1980, when he found himself in Lake Placid. "It was very low key," he said of

Hayman, a Canadian, was the first in a series of international riders who would enhance and strengthen the American-based team.

his time at Ochowicz's house in Ray Brook. "We did long rides with Jim, hung out, had beers, and played some golf. We hit it off as a group."

The atmosphere was a 180-degree turn from what he had just recently experienced in Belgium, with the unsavory conduct in the peloton and unrelenting cold and rain. The way Hayman saw it, Ochowicz's fledgling team offered him a way to continue his career in relative comfort. And as one of the older riders, he would be in a position to impart some of his hard-earned and occasionally bitter wisdom.

Ochowicz knew that his endeavor needed a rider with experience and exceptional speed, in equal measure. "I was looking for someone who could be a mentor," he said. Hayman, with his varied and hard-won experience in Europe, seemed just right for the job. Indeed, he was the type of rider Ochowicz would avail himself of throughout the team's history: an elder statesman, a source of wisdom and prudence.

○○

Ochowicz, his passion growing, envisioned a team of six athletes, and he had five: Heiden, Young, Van Haute, Schuler, and Hayman. He knew that a sixth recruit would enable him to apportion riders for different terrains and allow for illness and injury. Six was also the magic number that he felt could be reasonably accommodated in his budget.

To fill the slot, he decided to go to a familiar wellspring, augmenting the team with one more of his athletic and philosophical brethren from the Midwest. As he surveyed the racing scene, two came to mind: Greg Demgen, 20, of La Crosse, Wisconsin, and Jeff Bradley, 19, of Davenport, Iowa.

Demgen had a loose affiliation with the Midwest speed skating crowd, and therefore seemed a natural addition. Like Ochowicz and Heiden, he had Wisconsin roots. Like the others, Demgen had found little success or satisfaction in traditional sports, and in these circumstances cycling appeared as a kind of salvation. "I just got on the bike, and things started to happen," he said. As a member of the Junior National Team, he found early success, winning a stage race in Switzerland in 1977. In 1978 he was part of a four-person team that won a bronze medal in the world junior championships, along with Bradley, former Colorado junior champion Ron Kiefel, and an up-and-coming rider named Greg LeMond.

Demgen began bike racing at the age of 8 and became an 11-time national road, track, and time trial champion.

Bradley, meanwhile, had deep connections to skating—he was on the national team through 1980 under the management of none other than Ochowicz. "He was almost like a second dad," said Bradley. Though he competed at a high level in speed skating, he found the sport had little allure. Cycling, on the other hand, was intriguing. "There was more mystery," said Bradley. "I read European magazines, and dreamed of being involved in European cycling. It was such an exciting proposition." It filled the young racer with a sense of wonder and adventure. "For me it was just a passion. I just loved, as a kid—I just *loved* winning races." Bradley would "win at will" as a junior, according to future team member Davis Phinney, amassing numerous national championships.

By the end of the national championship road race in Bisbee, Arizona, where Bradley and Demgen took 3rd and 4th, respectively, Ochowicz found himself with a surfeit of possibilities. Both riders

Bradley split his time between skating and cycling, but bike racing "was more fun." Pictured (right) sprinting to the line against Brent Emery at La Primavera, 1982, an event that eventually became the Tour of Texas.

seemed perfect for the team, a welcome element of youth and a nod to the future of the sport. But how could he choose just one? The answer was, he couldn't. In January 1981, he contacted both riders with a proposal: Would they be willing to split the $12,000 salary originally intended for the last remaining rider? "They were hesitant to take two young guys—all the others were veterans at that point," said Bradley. "We were kind of a risk." Nonetheless, they accepted. Later, Bradley would reflect on it as "a good deal for 7-Eleven," because "I think we ended up as the winning riders that year."

With the addition of Bradley and Demgen, Ochowicz had succeeded in surrounding himself with riders from his personal geography. With the exception of Hayman, all were from the country's midsection—it was a veritable Corn Belt of cycling talent. "They were all from the Midwest," said Young. "They were the kind of riders Och wanted to get behind." In other words, they were riders like himself.

$$\overline{oo}$$

A bike racing team is a seemingly simple enterprise, a pure and economical nexus of human power and pedals. But when it comes to equipment and operational complexity, it's more akin to readying a military brigade for war.

A professional cycling team, even one as small as the fledgling 7-Eleven squad, has an unending appetite for parts and gear. The riders typically require custom frames, including road and track versions, and backups for the inevitable crashes, all of which have to be ordered well in advance. For 1981, the team piggybacked on Heiden's existing sponsorship with Schwinn, and the Chicago company supplied the team with bikes. "Schwinn was doing Eric anyway, so Schwinn was going to be on board for the team," Ochowicz reasoned. Eventually, there would be separate sponsors for components (derailleurs and brakes), handlebars, seats, tires, chains, spokes, and every other imaginable part, right down to plastic handlebar wrap and chain oil. Each of these deals required salesmanship and no small amount of glad-handing, all of which would fall to Ochowicz.

One of the earliest and most important decisions involved the jersey design. Ochowicz, Heiden, and Taylor had discussed the initial pattern at a meeting with Southland representatives in Dallas, and Ochowicz's mother-in-law had cobbled together the first batch on her sewing machine in Detroit.

They liked what they saw from the outset. The final design was a remarkably effective and iconic piece of Americana, with broad swaths of red, white, and green that were more than a little reminiscent of Christmas. It was a simple, geometric pattern that seems refreshingly austere compared with the frenetic logo billboards that shout across the peloton today. Yet, for all its simplicity, the 7-Eleven jersey was a remarkably effective calling card that was equally recognizable on a storefront, in the chaos of a criterium, or emblazoned across the side of a van traveling down the freeway at 70 mph.

It would also be remarkably enduring. With few changes, the basic design would endure for the life of the team and become one of the most recognized jerseys in the history of cycling. Forty years later, reproductions can still be found online and in bike shops, and it is not unusual today to see one or two on a typical recreational ride. Even more remarkable is the spontaneous way in which the design came about—basically a few people sitting around a table in Dallas—without the armies of marketers and interminable reviews with "stakeholders" that would be part of the process today.

With the design in hand, the clothing company Descente was enlisted to supply the jerseys, shorts, and other apparel. It was a fitting choice, since the company had also made the famous, iridescent gold one-piece skating suit that Heiden had worn in Lake Placid (and that is now enshrined in the Smithsonian Institution).

Lacking a warehouse or other storage space, Ochowicz moved the entire assemblage of equipment into his Wisconsin garage. By this time the Lake Placid house had been sold and his primary residence was in Pewaukee. The house acted as *service course*, the French cycling term for a team's repository of sundry bikes, parts, and clothing, the armaments of a professional racing team.

Thus equipped, the team was in a state of near-readiness. A stretch Dodge van was procured for race and equipment transportation, festooned with spare bicycle wheels on the roof and suitably embellished with the team colors and "7-Eleven/Schwinn Team" emblazoned across the sides in eight-inch-high letters. Ochowicz enlisted Richard Gilstrap, a bike mechanic from Milwaukee, to travel with the team and attend to the bicycles. In the future the squad would be accompanied by a *soigneur* to supply the all-important post-race massages to the riders' aching muscles, but in

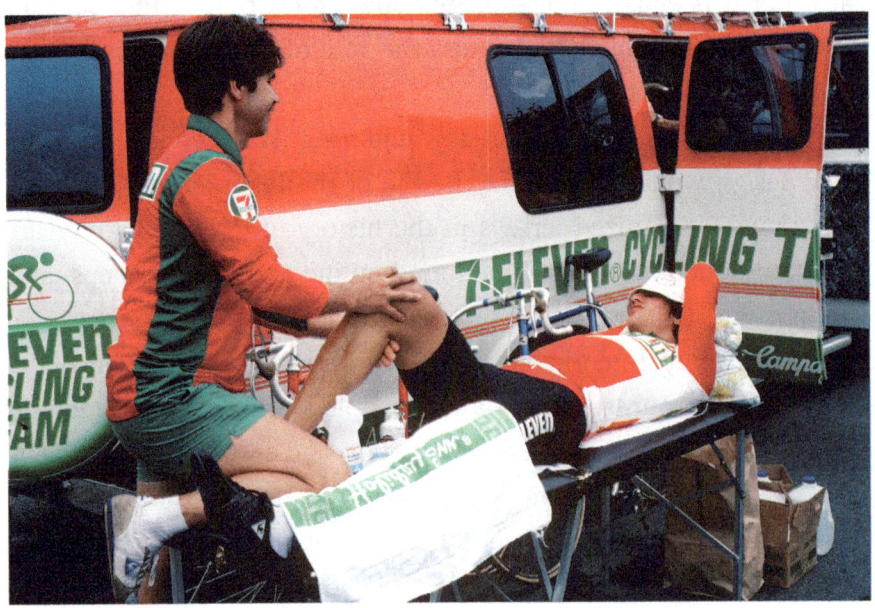

Ochowicz cofounded and managed the team but found himself doing everything from driving the van to designing the jerseys to massaging.

the first year Ochowicz, in addition to his many other duties, agreed to pitch in and do the leg kneading.

All things considered, Ochowicz had done a masterful job of assembling the team—especially given that, by his own admission, he was largely winging it. "It was a combination of what I learned when I was racing, what I learned when I got into management of the skating team, and what I could learn about a pro cycling team," he said. It had been, at least in America, a lost art—if it had ever existed at all. "There was nowhere to go for support," said Ochowicz of his myriad duties.

But if there was no playbook for this particular exercise, it did not show. With these final details in place, the 7-Eleven team, with its ragtag membership, improbable sponsor, and even more improbable ambitions, was born. Corporate America, meet the men with the shaved legs.

CHAPTER 6
Boys on a Bender

Ochowicz had assembled his team, a little rough around the edges perhaps, but at least willing and nothing if not energetic. It was time to collect them in one place and see what he had wrought. He decided that the team's official launch—the first of many spring training camps—would take place in San Diego, where Heiden had enrolled at the University of California to begin his career in medicine. The camp would forever be recognized as halcyon days for the team, a spiritual birthplace that would help establish the work ethic—and the irreverence—that would prevail for the next decade.

o͞o

The atmosphere in San Diego was fraternal, a collection of boys on a bender, the world large and limitless. Bradley remembers consecutive 600-mile weeks, the pavement passing underneath their wheels hour after hour, as if it were nothing at all.

Many of these young men had been riding steadily since age 10. They had raced, as Bradley says, "for the love of it." They had poached floor space in strange towns, parked the family motor home in the driveway of a cousin twice removed, eaten poorly or not at all, all for the purpose of competing in a criterium in some far-flung Midwestern town. For this they would win a pair of sew-up tires, or an apple pie, or maybe a set of steak knives.

Now they were living in a state of munificence and wonder. It was as if they had won the lottery. "It was huge," said Demgen. "We had clothing, a *soigneur* [Ochowicz], a mechanic, and plane tickets would show up in the mail. For most of us, we didn't have a plan beyond picking up *VeloNews* to figure out where to go next weekend."

To these seven young men, San Diego was a training paradise,

First team photo, taken at the San Diego velodrome, 1981. Left to right: Team mechanic Tim Zasasdny, Heiden, Demgen, Hayman, Young, Bradley, Schuler, Van Haute, Ochowicz.

a place where the sun shone relentlessly and infused the landscape with a warmth and luminescence they had never known in Detroit, or Madison, or Milwaukee. They had crossed a kind of threshold, leaving behind the land of the windchill factor and stepping into a place where their talents would not be constrained by the mundane concerns of money or time. They were living in a dreamscape, and in return they had only to do the one thing they loved best: ride their bikes.

For Ochowicz, it was the realization of a dream, but also a time of trepidation. He knew he had a profusion of talent in the riders he had chosen, but also a troublesome abundance of testosterone and wildness. For many of the riders, it was their first time in California, and they found it seductive. "We screwed off as much as we trained," said Demgen. "But we rode five hours a day." Bradley's view was even more to the point. "We were some ass kickers. We wanted to make a big splash. We were possessed. We rode all day, every day. We were determined to be the best team."

○○

No sooner had they arrived than temptation appeared in the form of the U.S. women's volleyball team, who also happened to be conducting a training camp in town. The presence of these Amazons did not go unnoticed by the randy boys, who could not believe their good fortune. "We had a lot of fun with them," said Demgen. "Eric had a condo at UCSD, and we would see them once or twice a week. We had a gas." Assembled together, the two groups of elite athletes made for an ironic mix of athleticism, as bike riders are not known for their stature. "They were all a foot taller than we were," he said.

It was a rollicking time—a delicious mix of physical effort, comic relief, and camaraderie that seemed at times more like a rolling frat party than a training camp. Anything became an excuse to ride harder, farther. They found the effort pleasurable—not like effort at all. Young remembers nearing the end of a 100-mile training ride when talk turned to the subject of who would be first in the showers back at the team hotel. Subtly—imperceptibly at first—the pace began increasing by degrees. By the time they reached the outskirts of town, they were doing 30 mph, attacking each other as if it were the final stage of the Tour de France. "All I can remember thinking," said Young, who was laboring at the back, "was if motivation was this high for a shower, this is going to be a good team!"

In the final miles the group abandoned all propriety, running red lights, riding against traffic and over sidewalks, committing all manner of transgressions—solely for the privilege of being first in the shower. What they didn't know was that they were being trailed by several police cruisers, which pulled up just as they reached the hotel. The cops were livid at the team's blatant disregard for the law —Young even remembers guns being drawn.

At that moment, one of the officers recognized Heiden, the superstar in their midst. Suddenly, tension drifted magically from the scene. Ticket books were put away. The officers said the boys would be released if Heiden would give them an autograph. The deed was done. Heiden, a source of all good things for the team, had performed yet another act of salvation.

Indeed, it was an adventure just being in Heiden's company. Lake Placid was fresh in the public's memory, and he remained a superstar. "It was amazing to go anywhere with him. It was prime time—crazy," said Demgen.

Heiden, in characteristic self-effacing fashion, was indifferent to the madness surrounding him. By 1980, his life had been reduced to the barest necessities, which were to study his premed coursework and to ride his bike with his buddies. He had an amazing ability to be unaffected by the turmoil. Team members recall hosting wild parties at his condo. In the midst of the revelry, there would be Heiden, his books spread about him, studying with unruffled concentration. Heiden found his new circumstance to be an enclave, a place of relative serenity after the madness of the Olympic Games. "The 7-Eleven guys take me for who I am," he said with typical ingenuousness.

It had been a remarkable time. In just a few weeks, the team had gelled, becoming something bigger than the sum of the individuals. But it was more than that. They had established a tenor for the squad, a joyous foundation of optimism and athleticism that would endure for the next decade, propelling them beyond conventional borders of geography and achievement. Ochowicz had created a thing larger than himself.

o͞o

Another event took place in San Diego, something barely noticed at the time but one that would carry monumental implications for the team. Davis Phinney, a young rider from Boulder, Colorado, was in town training. In the previous months he had been living with his girlfriend, cyclist Connie Carpenter, in Berkeley, where she was attending school. Carpenter was cramming for finals, and to improve her concentration, she had summarily banished her boyfriend. The obliging Phinney had elected to go to San Diego to train.

On one ride, laboring alone, he looked up the road to see the 7-Elevens, out for one of their five-hour death marches under the broiling California sun. He remembers a "golden bronze team, shimmering across the landscape," like some kind of apparition. "They definitely had style; there was something right away that was different from other teams. They were flamboyant and wild."

For Phinney, it was an epiphany. He saw the team as his rightful home, a place where his drive and talent could take root and flourish. In less than a year, he would be on it. More important, he would come to embody the team, becoming its perfect personification.

Some original 7-Elevens along with a couple competitors who would later join the team. Left to right: Phinney, Stieda, Hayman, Bradley, Brian Worthy, Kiefel, Terry Anderson, Schuler.

○○

Soon after the raucous baptism of the San Diego camp, it was time for Ochowicz to take the true measure of his new charges—in competition. The fledgling team turned its attention to what would become an annual rite of passage: the two-stage La Primavera road race, later to be known as the Tour of Texas. Spread across several counties but based mostly in Austin, the race would serve, then and for years to come, as a staple of the team's early season preparation.

In time Ochowicz would crisscross the country in airplanes to attend races, but this was a different era, and his position did not carry the privileges afforded to team directors today. No sooner did the San Diego camp end than he began the 20-hour drive from Southern California to Austin in the company of the team's bleary-eyed mechanic.

Though they had yet to turn a pedal in anger, the team arrived with more than a little attitude. "We showed up in Texas in our red, white, and green van, and no one else had ridden a thousand miles," said Demgen, referring to the accepted approach at that time to winter training mileage. "We had ridden five thousand."

Fortunately the team justified its corporate support, and its boyish bravado, with good results. The race itself comprised just two events—a road race and a criterium—held over the course of a spring weekend. Bradley won the 64-mile road race, with Hayman coming in 3rd. Hayman followed up by winning the 40-mile crit the next day, and 7-Eleven riders took numerous top places in each race. "We just cleaned up," said Ochowicz, obviously pleased with his new charges.

They departed Texas with great fitness, but also with the fundamental notion that they were destined for something bigger than themselves. "With Och, we were on a mission that lasted nine months of the year," said Demgen.

La Primavera, Austin, Texas, 1981. At the start line, left to right: Bradley, Young, Schuler, Heiden, Van Haute, Demgen, Hayman.

oo

Van Haute remembers 1981 as an extraordinary year, when the team "had all the confidence that we would win everything we would enter." Schuler, similarly, remembers it as a time when "we would be first, second, and fourth on a regular basis." The 7-Elevens routinely went into events with such bluster and confidence that physical prowess seemed almost secondary; the first blow had been landed before anyone had turned a wheel.

But while success for the team was quick and abundant, it was not without complications. Throughout that inaugural season, the 7-Elevens would be increasingly troubled by the rival Panasonic/Shimano team, which included Bruce Donaghy, winner of the season-long National Prestige Classic series; Hugh Walton, of Canada; and the Stetina brothers, Wayne and Dale, all of them former Olympians. Other persistent antagonists included a compact Canadian powerhouse by the name of Steve Bauer, who rode for

Ochowicz's alma mater, the AMF squad; and Leonard "Harvey" Nitz of the GS Mengoni team.

The Stetina brothers, from Indiana, took particular joy in irritating the 7-Elevens. "They were often spoilers," lamented Schuler. "We measured our success against Wayne." Heightening the insult, the two brothers represented the monetary antithesis of the 7-Elevens. For years, Wayne had been wandering the country nomadically in a motor home in the company of his long-suffering wife, towing an old Volkswagen. He would stay with friends and run an extension cord into their homes to siphon off a little power to cook dinner. "I would go for one or two months at a time," he said. "And I would write the whole thing off on taxes. No one had ever done that before." Stetina's asceticism and denial intensified the pleasure he took in besting Ochowicz's well-moneyed charges. "We beat up on 7-Eleven regularly," he crowed. "For me and Dale, it was a joke—they had all the support and money, but we could beat 'em."

$$\overline{oo}$$

Nowhere were these dramas played out with more intensity than at the Löwenbräu Grand Prix, a $65,000, 10-race criterium series that spanned the country from Boston to Manhattan Beach. It became a focal point for the 7-Elevens. They had sufficient firepower to field two squads in the series, compounding their presence and the severity of their insult.

Though Bauer and Wayne Stetina were 1st and 2nd overall, respectively, the 7-Elevens dominated in their own way, placing riders on the podium in 8 of the 10 races, winning 3 events outright, putting Hayman in 3rd overall, and most important, taking the team competition. They earned 5 out of 10 places in the overall standings. Even Heiden managed to win a race—proving, as he often would in the coming years, that he was more than just a media and sponsorship magnet.

Ochowicz would naturally have preferred clear and complete supremacy in the series. But he was nothing if not a realist, and he was taking note of his antagonists. His team-building exercise at the end of 1980 had taught him the fine art of scouting talent. And so he wondered: Could these challengers become allies? In much the same way that riders from opposing teams can proffer shelter and assistance during a race, perhaps some of these opponents could become supporting members of his team. After all, he knew that Southland was satisfied with the team's performance in its inaugural season, and he was anticipating a budget increase for 1982, freeing him to hire more of the best riders in the country.

He was, in fact, about to embark on a decade-long empire-building exercise that would change the landscape of U.S. and world cycling. Within a few short years, nearly all of his most persistent competitors would be wearing the familiar red, white, and green of a prominent convenience store chain—among them Bauer and Nitz. There was an inevitable momentum to the team. If Ochowicz could not beat his foes, he would make them his own.

oo

Hayman was quickly emerging as the team leader, on and off the racecourse. Prior to 1981, "I don't think any of us had met Hayman," said Demgen. "He had won the Tour of Ireland the year before, and he was definitely the guru our first year."

Part of Hayman's elder statesman role was to impart an air of seriousness to Ochowicz's occasionally unruly charges. "I worked hard," said Hayman. "I put in the hours. We got good volume in those years, and maybe I influenced that. We did 500-mile weeks, and we would finish flat out on the rivet for the last hour and a half. The guys had not done that before. So they had no problem in the actual races."

Hayman was also the animator in competition. "He was good at forcing the race," said Ochowicz. "He knew when and where to make a surge, so you could create the winning move." Ochowicz's strategy in those days was, from the perspective of the other teams, annoyingly simple. He had enough firepower that he could launch repeated salvos until the smaller squads were limp with exhaustion. "We would surge with one rider, create a gap, surge with another, close that gap, then pretty soon we'd have three or four guys in a break of five," he said. Adding insult to injury, Ochowicz frequently still had enough warm bodies to block the chasing main field, ensuring the success of the riders who had made a foray off the front.

But Young recalls that the team became less reliant on specific strategies and rider roles as the season progressed. Early in the Löwenbräu series, the 7-Elevens attempted to impose military precision on the races, sending Hayman off the front or staging elaborate counterattacks to wear down their opponents. Then, according to Young, there was a general epiphany—the team would rely less on carefully orchestrated strategies, and more on "just being generally aggressive as individual riders. That permeated through the rest of the 7-Eleven legacy. . . . Everyone on the team got the impression that they could star and win themselves." Schuler agreed, noting that "the idea was that there *were* no stars."

It was a striking contrast to the hierarchical, European model of racing, where teams would genuflect to domineering leaders. Young called 7-Eleven's approach "unusual for international cycling at the time." It was, in fact, classic 7-Eleven—a reliance on exuberance over all else, success fueled by passion and pure heart.

No bike racing team is ever a democracy, but this one was about as close as you could come. Indeed, it would be a notable trait of Ochowicz's reign over the next decade. There would be team leaders, to be sure—but there was also remarkable depth and equality.

$$\overline{oo}$$

Predictably, the team's stellar race-win success was accompanied by growing resentment on the part of the less-well-funded squads. The team members' characteristic swagger and in-your-face style of racing didn't help. "We were screwing off and winning everything," boasted Demgen. It was the start of what would become enduring us-versus-them warfare on the domestic front. Beginning in 1981, and for years afterward, the 7-Eleven jersey would become tantamount to a bull's-eye. "It was not amicable," said Demgen.

The team members continued to find their luxurious circumstances almost too good to be true. "I hadn't raced in the States a lot, but I never had anything like that before," said Hayman. "It was different from anything I'd experienced. There was a lot of envy. We were getting everything; they were getting nothing. We were so lucky—there was no one else in the States with that support. And it showed."

"It wasn't always a level playing field," added Schuler. "We were serious and full time, and most of the competition wasn't back then."

It was a disparity that did not go unnoticed by their chief rivals. "I was doing a lot of driving, they were flying," said Stetina, with slight exaggeration. "They had mechanics, I was doing my own work. I was having fun, but it's not so good when you should be focusing on training and putting your feet up in the air, not looking after all those details."

But it was more than money that distinguished the squad. There was an undeniable aura surrounding the team, a presence that was coveted by sponsors and race organizers and that the competing teams found maddening. "The van, when you saw that roll into town, you knew something was happening," said Ochowicz. "It was good for the organizers, and good for us."

The 7-Elevens, with their flashy vehicle and even flashier presence, represented a degree of professionalism that was unheard of in the United States at the time. This was not a loose assemblage of sweaty and grease-stained bike riders. It was, more than anything,

7-Eleven's squad enjoyed support in money, travel, and equipment that was the envy of America's itinerant bike racers. Schuler pictured.

a brand. The logo was ubiquitous, on everything from jerseys to shorts and caps, and the bikes were identically equipped. The boys even attended media training to help rein in any off-color metaphors. This was, the rough edges notwithstanding, a professional team, representing a company with almost $5 billion in annual sales and a blanket of retail outlets across the land. It was not just bike racing—it was business.

"Our licenses said we were amateurs," said Schuler, "but we tried to act like a pro team. It was not just money—it was ambition."

oo

It didn't take long for Southland to begin capitalizing on its new marketing vehicle. The company, refreshingly aware of its own ignorance of the sport, hired a public relations firm, Carlson, Rockey & Associates, to do its bidding in the wider world. The agency would do advance work in the cities where the squad was scheduled to race, planting folksy story ideas with the press, most of them about the megastar, Heiden. "They would build up the team with PR, letting everyone know," said Ochowicz. "They would line up interviews, then once we landed, we would do interviews on site. They would always build things up going into town with an article in the newspaper."

Bike racing at the time was as arcane as cricket in the eyes of the American public. Press materials would typically include a primer on race tactics and the perennially misunderstood topics of drafting and pacelines. ("Why do all the racers stick so closely together?" was an almost reflexive question from the general press.) The PR firm even distributed a glossary of bike racing terms, including such insider lexicon as *wheel sucking* and *taking a flyer*.

The glories of Lake Placid were still fresh in public memory, and the media focus was, not surprisingly, directed toward the shuffling giant with the gold medals. But before long, a strange thing began to happen: The team itself began to supplant Heiden in the headlines. Bicycle racing, to the great surprise of the general press, had its own appeal beyond the megastar. And Heiden, who never in his life hungered for media exposure, was more than willing to deflect the public glare onto his buddies and the sport he loved. The polished and educated Schuler, in particular, became one of the primary talking heads as the team roamed the country.

oo

As Ochowicz developed the racing calendar for the squad, he began to focus on places where Southland was trying to augment its business. "Once Southland started to figure it out, that they could leverage their mobile traveling cycling team, we started going to 7-Eleven sites in strong markets such as Florida, Chicago, New York, or Dallas," he said. "Wherever there was a strong market, we would try to do racing damage." It was not unusual for riders to show up at the appointed hour at a 7-Eleven store in, say, a bland Dallas neighborhood, and dutifully sign hats and Slurpee cups for appreciative, if occasionally mystified, patrons. But if even a small percentage of these customers were sufficiently titillated to show up Sunday morning for the race, where the boys would typically dominate, the enterprise would be considered a success. They would then move on to the next town and repeat the exercise, criss-crossing the country for months on end to spread the unlikely gospel of bike racing and Big Gulps to the cycling novices.

Southland also enlisted its franchises to support the team when it came to town. Gerard Bisceglia, sales and promotion manager for the northeast division in 1980, found the high-spirited athletes to be a great diversion, especially compared with his usual humdrum tasks of "ensuring that potholes were filled and windows cleaned" in the 350 stores in his region. Bisceglia recalls store employees showing up at races on their own time, hawking T-shirts and distributing freebies, hyping a sport they knew nothing about, all in the spirit of the mother ship. Retail employees found the sport entertaining, if arcane, and perhaps reminiscent of what they had seen only a year before in the cult classic movie *Breaking Away*. Bisceglia himself found the sport captivating; in a few short years he would head up sports marketing for the entire company, becoming the primary corporate liaison for Ochowicz and the team as they made their initial forays into European cycling.

Within the halls of Southland headquarters in Dallas, the sponsorship was also a compelling curiosity. Bisceglia remembers one employee who was actually a cycling enthusiast and would sometimes ride to work. "It was amazing to find someone on staff who was a bike racer," he said. "He became a folk hero."

But everyone, it seemed, knew Heiden. He would be recruited to attend sales meetings, signing autographs during the breaks and helping rally the troops for another soaring year of profits at the fast-growing company. "Eric was the star" from a corporate perspective, said Southland CEO Jere Thompson. Bisceglia remembers one corporate meeting in Atlantic City, New Jersey, attended by 600 employees, where the keynote speaker was Eric Heiden.

o͞o

Heiden, while essential to the team in every way, bristled at the attention being given him, calling it the "great whoopee." Riders would sometimes be jostled off the podium by fans wanting a piece of the famous skater, even though he might have finished the race midpack. In one interview Heiden flatly declared that the attention given him "stinks," and lamented that his own fame could be casting more deserving riders in the shadows. "I hope what I am doing is helping the sport of cycling," he declared in a remarkable understatement.

His teammates, meanwhile, had no compunction about basking in Heiden's glow, an experience that was a little like being among the entourage of a rock star. Young remembers visiting the Playboy Mansion and meeting Mick Jagger in Heiden's company and also recalls Heiden being whisked away from a race in a limousine so that he could be on time to drop the puck at a Stanley Cup hockey final. "It was a great summer," Young said. "We did things like that all year long." Occasionally, it bored on the surreal. "We'd get back

Heiden submitted to endless interviews and appearances in the interest of advancing the cause of bike racing in America and his cycling buddies.

from a training ride, and someone would call—his attorney or something—and he'd say, 'Do you want to go to the Johnny Carson show? It was just a fun time."

Indeed, comic relief was ever present. As in any good fraternity, all the boys had nicknames, most of them bestowed by Demgen in his role as team joker. Heiden, as noted earlier, was "Gomer," named for Gomer Pyle, the languid and occasionally dim-witted mechanic from the *Andy Griffith Show*. Schuler was

"Ploughboy," due to the fact that he had sold oats in high school. Van Haute was "Verbist" (or "Verbeast"), named for the famed Belgian motorpacer Carlton Verbist. Hayman was "Skin," owing to a certain part of his anatomy. Demgen himself, with his round face and tendency toward avoirdupois, would be forever known as "Doughboy." Ochowicz, owing to his implacable nature, was—of course—"Sergeant Rock."

oo

Ochowicz exuded power in the way of all good coaches and managers. Diplomatic and accommodating with the press and sponsors, he was a gruff insider to his boys, alternately profane and chummy, as would befit the good-old-boy culture that inevitably prevailed during the long summer months on the road.

There was such a surfeit of restless power on the team that it frequently seemed that Ochowicz's chief challenge was one of containment rather than inspiration. "Och knew that we had a lot of energy and enthusiasm," said Hayman. "He knew if we couldn't break out, we would have been destructive socially."

He was a friend to his charges, for he had recently been among them as a racer himself. Far from his days of racing fitness, but still harboring competitive fires, Ochowicz was fond of riding with the team in a heroic but ultimately doomed fashion. (For years, the mechanics kept a bike in the support van for him.) Ochowicz would depart with the team on grueling six-hour rides, and would soon be racing, head down, as if to beat men 10 years his junior. "He would get out there and stretch his legs," said Bradley. "We loved having him on the rides. He was a gas. He would just laugh it up."

The most nuanced aspect of Ochowicz's new role was knowing when to be a friend and confidant, and when to establish the psychological distance that signifies control and authority. The few compliments he bestowed were measured rather than effusive, and he would keep his boys in check with faint praise. They remained eager to please and sacrifice for him, like hungry greyhounds. He was the law unto himself. He was Sergeant Rock.

"We were a piece of work then, trying to get away with whatever we could, and he had to lay down the law," said Bradley. When this more hard-edged aspect of Ochowicz emerged, it could have profound effects. "One time, when we were living in Texas, we had all been out on the town," said Bradley. "I came straggling in one morning. We had duplexes in this neighborhood, and three or four of us, we were talking, letting it all fly. I look in the corner, and there is Och, sitting there. He busted us, caught us in the truth of the moment. He was an expert in that. He knew everything. He was the master."

Ochowicz astutely recognized that his role was changing, and he needed to adapt to the new realities that accompany being in a position of authority and responsibility. "It was hard to pull away from being a rider," he said. "I had to try to not be their friend anymore. It was a struggle. I had to decide how much distance was needed. If people aren't doing their jobs, that's where you start to separate the friendships from the business." Ochowicz's artistry was that he never let this necessity spill over into harsh authoritarianism. "I was always friends with riders to a certain degree, and I still am. But when there had to be hard calls, I had to learn how to make them and back them up. I could bark a little when I had to," he said of these periodic chastisements.

o͞o

Ochowicz relished the opportunity to "move into a new space." Managing the team was yet another of the characteristic leaps that formed the prime impulses in his life. The focus was moving from the inward and necessarily selfish perspective of an athlete to a more encompassing view that, if not broadened to the world at large, had at least grown to encompass his newly acquired athletic family. It was a degree of complexity that was new for him. If, in the past, his concerns had been about his own body and the next race, those responsibilities now had been multiplied to what seemed like an ever-expanding constituency of riders, sponsors, organizers, and press. It was a lot to keep track of.

"I was making the transition from athlete to manager, and learning about the difference between the two," he said. "I was pushing myself into another space in cycling. As a rider, I never had to get involved in operations and the industry. Riders are more concerned about training and diet and their own families, and when they leave for a race and when they come home. I had to transition to where I was thinking about a whole group of people and sponsor stuff and working with organizers and the industry. You need to know where the hotel is and when the race starts. And we need 50 more tires, and who will give us those for free?"

Though he rarely advised on matters of training, Ochowicz was entirely confident in the realm of race strategy, and his disciplinary salvos included what he called "race barking." He developed a system that could rival that of any third-base coach in the major leagues. "The riders knew where I stood on the racecourse," he said. "I always wore a hat, like a baseball hat. If there was a break, and I had my hat on, they could keep working. If my hat was off and I gave them a split, it meant the break had to stop working, and the field should chase.

"The racing piece is about respect. They need to trust you in that role, whether to let the break go, or not go. They have to trust your judgment. You have to control all that."

These broader responsibilities also raised questions of demeanor and conduct. He was, like never before, onstage, and he had a role to play. He had acquired a suit, and found he was using it more often in his many meetings with Southland executives, organizers, and potential sponsors. In his competitive career, he had expressed his opinion freely and been forced to engage in small indulgences for the sake of his racing and his own life. Now he was part of a complex web of interaction that was essential to the success of the team.

○○

Despite his progress in this new managerial role, Ochowicz, along with George Taylor, decided to procure some help to impart an air of seriousness to their charges. They enlisted Herman Krott, coach of the Dutch Amstel/Heineken team, to spend two weeks with the boys toward the end of the inaugural season. Ochowicz, still in the process of defining his relationship to his riders, found Krott's guidance essential. "He would watch me coach, and at night we would go for walks and he would critique me," he said. "He would tell me about relationships with riders and that you had to separate yourself and still be friends. You had to make a distinction between yourself and them."

But Krott may have gotten more than he bargained for with the Americans. "Och was looking for someone to give us direction," said Demgen of the time spent with Krott, whom the boys largely ignored. When the European coach recommended more fresh vegetables, the recalcitrant 7-Elevens would have none of it. They put the concept in practice by eating microwave popcorn. "Bradley and Demgen were brutal with this guy," said Young. "They gave him a hard time. They were rebelling against any scientific training."

Ironically, *VeloNews* ran an article on Krott that hailed him as the root cause of the team's recent and spectacular success. The headline, however, may have been more telling than the article itself.

It said, simply, "Dutch Coach Finds Americans Need Discipline."

CHAPTER 7
Looking for Consistency

Although the team achieved remarkable and consistent success in its first year, it was not a free ride. One glaring exception to the team's relative dominance was the 1981 Coors Classic stage race. Ochowicz recalls the team as being "hot and cold. We were either really good or really bad. And we were really bad at the Coors in '81." Indeed, the race would always be a place of mixed fortunes for the team, a playing field on which it would achieve some of its greatest results, and its most stinging defeats. "It was the only event we had difficulty with," Bradley said flatly.

The Coors, set against the spectacular backdrop of the Colorado Rockies, was the closest thing that America had to the epic, mountainous stage races that defined the sport in Europe. The race was founded in 1975 as the Red Zinger Bicycle Classic, a promotional vehicle for the famous brand of spicy tea. In 1979, the event was purchased for $1 by its promoter, Michael Aisner. The race would become synonymous with Aisner, a dynamo of a man who talked in a staccato narrative that was as exhausting as it was entertaining. He enlisted the Coors Brewing Company, based in Golden, Colorado, as title sponsor. During the next eight years, Aisner and the 7-Eleven team would become inextricably bound together in what is still considered the most successful and dramatic stage race in American history.

In 1981 the 7-Elevens set out to dominate the race in a way that would befit their emerging reputation as America's premier team. Ochowicz rented a spacious house in the resort town of Breckenridge prior to the race so the boys could do epic training rides, acclimate to the 9,000-foot altitude, and recover with massage and therapy in the evenings. They hunkered down as if the Olympic

The American racing scene was vastly enhanced by the efforts of Michael Aisner (pictured right, with French racing great Jacques Anquetil), the indefatigable promoter of the Coors Classic who designed stages to reward– and frustrate–the team.

Games had already arrived. "We trained our asses off," said Hayman. "We did every big climb over 9,000 feet." Young and Van Haute, who were considered track riders and were not slated to do the Coors, rode their single-speed bikes until they expired, then dragged themselves into the team van.

But it was all too much. What started as admirable focus and dedication soon became consumptive excess. The boys' very motivation contained the seeds of its own demise. When race day finally arrived, "We couldn't get out of our own way," said Hayman. "Three weeks later I had the best form of my life—but not during the race." For his part, Ochowicz had learned a valuable lesson. "We were there too long, and we trained too hard," he said. "The guys were tired."

∞

The event itself comprised 11 stages, a mix of time trials, criteriums, and long road races that conveyed its increasingly international flavor. Race director Aisner had a remarkable sense of promotion and, for a nonathlete, an even more remarkable sense of what made for high drama in a bicycle race. One year after the U.S. boycott of the Moscow Olympics, he arranged an entry for the powerful and well-prepared Russian team. "When I first announced that the Russians were coming, I got letters from racers, who were friends, who said the Russians will come and take all the prize money away. They said, 'Why would you do this? It will ruin the race.' My silent answer was, 'Then get off your asses and beat them!' One racer who responded positively, and said 'Bring 'em on,' was Greg LeMond. He said, 'I will show them what wheel to get on.'"

Indeed, LeMond, fresh from his first season racing as a pro in Europe with the French powerhouse Renault/Gitane team, won two stages and the overall race by almost five minutes. It was an almost single-handed display of dominance, with Soviet riders shadowing him in 2nd, 3rd, and 4th. Demgen was the top-placed 7-Eleven rider, in a dismal 16th place. The race was particularly frustrating for Hayman, who a year earlier had won two stages as part of a composite team with race winner Jock Boyer, one of the first U.S. riders to make it as a European pro. (Interestingly, Heiden's sister, Beth, had won the women's event that year.)

The race was the first of many encounters with what would be an enduring challenge for the team: the split focus on American-style racing, with its abbreviated distances and frenetic criteriums, and the epic, vertiginous demands of a European-style stage race. The Coors itself would experience this transition over the years. "The race was moving away from criteriums and more toward the mountains," said Ochowicz. "We didn't have the right riders for that race, in terms of the whole race. We had a few that could do it, then we had others that just didn't belong."

It was a division of labor that would never be resolved in any simple or lasting way, as the landscape of American racing shifted as fast as the composition of the team. Ochowicz would juggle the two variables over the next 10 years, never with complete success. In a few short years, when resources permitted, he would attack the problem by creating two, nearly exclusive teams to meet the challenge. But in this initial foray, the team had foundered.

o͞o

The last big race of the year was the Great Mohawk Cycling Classic on October 24, and the 7-Eleven team intended to finish its inaugural season with a flourish. In addition to its symbolic appeal, the race had another draw: money. Sponsored by a carpet company, it offered an unprecedented $70,000 prize list.

The weeks leading up to the race had not gone particularly well for the boys, however. These were still young men, prone to the excesses of youth, and they had started celebrating their season too early, with a week of debauchery before a race in Charlottesville, Virginia. "We drank like crazy the week before," said Hayman. "And we got trashed." At one point in Charlottesville, Schuler was off the front in a breakaway and promptly ran out of gas. With his head presumably pounding, he faded to 11th. The team's missteps that day were particularly costly; by virtue of their poor placings in Charlottesville, they surrendered the season-long National Prestige Classic points competition to archnemesis Bruce Donaghy and the Panasonic/Shimano team. Suffice it to say, Sergeant Rock was not pleased.

But this embarrassment, along with some gentle upbraiding by Ochowicz, only served to heighten the team's motivation for the Mohawk race the next weekend. "As we were working our way up the coast, we were in dry counties for a few days, and we got in some good training," said Hayman of the intervening week. "We wanted to redeem ourselves in the Mohawk race. We came in very focused."

With their toxins purged and their motivation piqued, the team achieved one of its most dominating and lucrative victories. Hayman lapped the field and picked up $15,000, the largest purse of his career. Heiden was 2nd, Bradley 4th, and Young 7th, for total 7-Eleven spoils of $25,000. "We pretty much took the whole purse," beamed Bradley. And after the shame of the previous weekend, perhaps most satisfying was that they limited their season-long rivals, Panasonic/Shimano, to a meager $1,500.

It had been another rollicking 7-Eleven performance, with embarrassing lows and spectacular highs crammed into a few weeks of testosterone-infused excess. Whatever—it worked.

From almost any perspective, it had been a good year. "Southland was satisfied," said Ochowicz. "It set the stage for going forward. There was enough success to justify the sponsorship and increase the operating budget and reach into larger space with the team." Adding to Ochowicz's good feelings about the season, his wife, Sheila, made a spectacular comeback from childbirth to win the world sprint championship for the third time that fall (she had also won in 1973 and 1976).

Southland's support for cycling continued to expand, even beyond the team. In the fall, construction commenced on the Olympic Velodrome, and the company announced a series of track races for the following year, cosponsored by *Bicycling* magazine, that would take place at seven tracks in North America. Bill Scott, manager of the company's Olympic Planning Committee, called it "yet another step in Southland's major commitment to cycling in the United States."

o͞o

While the team was alternately goofing off and winning

everything in sight, unbeknownst to them, Ochowicz was fermenting his grand plan. He was looking toward the Olympics, certainly, but also toward a farther horizon. "He wanted to take this thing to heights I didn't even realize when I was on the team," said Demgen. In a sense, the enterprise had become a vicarious racing experience for Ochowicz, a means for him to achieve everything he had failed to do as a rider, for reasons of ability or circumstance.

The team was now a manifestation of himself, a vehicle of hope and aspiration through which he could achieve remarkable things. "I didn't think, as an athlete, he had as much fun as we did," said Demgen. "He saw an opportunity to take things where he couldn't go himself."

Did winning come too easily? Sometimes it appeared so when the team seemed to dominate races at will. Hayman pictured.

CHAPTER 8
The Purpose-Built Sprinter

In 1981, Davis Phinney was living the life of the itinerant bike racer, competing against the powerful 7-Eleven squad as the "token male" on the Puch women's team of his then-girlfriend, Connie Carpenter (the two were married in 1983). To Phinney, the 7-Elevens lived in a state of decadence and splendor, a condition that sent him into simultaneous fits of disgust and jealousy. The truth was he longed for it.

The 7-Elevens would fly to far-flung cities, stay in hotels, and arrive at races in the red, white, and green 7-Eleven van like rock stars. They would have their legs rubbed while a mechanic fettled their bikes. Feed bags would be meticulously prepared and handed out at midrace. Clothing, bike parts, and no small amount of fame all seemed to flow like water.

In contrast, Phinney and Carpenter found themselves traversing the country in a wheezing Volkswagen Rabbit, which she had inherited from 1978 Red Zinger Classic winner George Mount. If that weren't bad enough, Phinney suffered the indignity of having to serve as the mechanic for the women's team. "I was so fried from going to races with the ladies and making sure their bikes were always clean," he said. "My bike was a disaster." But in Phinney's view, being an athlete was a matter of piling sacrifice upon sacrifice, and the indignity of wrenching the women's bikes was something he was prepared to endure to achieve his ultimate goal, which was to be a professional bike racer.

At the same time, he knew it was not the optimum situation for an aspiring athlete. As Phinney and Carpenter crisscrossed the country, he had ample time to think back to the previous spring, when he had seen the 7-Elevens training in San Diego, a wondrous apparition of athleticism and spirit. Over the last few months, the demands of being a privateer against the powerful team had left an indelible impression, and the contrast of their prosperity and his austerity burned inside him with a dull glow, fueling a passion for change. The team had seemed like something he might want to be a part of back then, and it seemed even more so now.

◌◌

As a child, Phinney had an extraordinary drive that was apparent to everyone around him. Once, at Boulder High School, a teacher told him he would never make it as a professional cyclist. In Phinney's mind, the fact that anyone would even make such a statement was ample reason to challenge it. He found the very prospect alluring. Years later, when he was a successful European pro, he would recount the story of the teacher at Boulder High again and again. He was proud of his defiant and obsessed nature.

Phinney saw a linear path toward his aspirations. It was a simple formula: He would squint his eyes, envision the task at hand, apply prodigious amounts of work, and the thing would be done. In some ways, he found the work to be the easiest part. Later he would become famous for 500-mile weeks. Indeed, compared to the vagaries and unpredictability of a race, doing withering amounts of training seemed a straightforward and entirely pragmatic exercise, like cooking from a recipe book. It was a causal relationship, steady and sure.

Phinney's particular obsession began one afternoon in 1975, amid a Technicolor blur of team jerseys and the whir of double-butted spokes. He had gone to watch the North Boulder Park stage of the Red Zinger Classic (a race he would win overall 13 years later, in its subsequent incarnation as the Coors Classic). "I saw the color and speed, everything about it," he said. Just being there flipped a switch in his teenaged mind, prompting a simple, life-changing declaration: He would be a bike racer.

Throughout his life, Phinney would measure himself on a tangent—by a defiance of norms. It wasn't just the speed and flash he found alluring; cycling was appealing for the very reason that no one else was doing it. "It seemed so exotic and cool," he said. "I was trying to figure it out. It was so underground." If the great mass of students at Boulder High made a right turn, Phinney would go left. It was his nature. "I was very much on my own in those days," he said, the words conveying a sense of satisfaction rather than isolation or despondency.

Even at 15, it was clear that Phinney was not one for half measures. Cycling quickly became the only thing in view. Within a year, he was competing in Category I and II races in Colorado—the top amateur class. "By '76, I was a bike racer," he said flatly.

What followed was a physical and cultural immersion in the sport. Like many young riders of his era, Phinney looked to a distant shore for inspiration: Europe. Viewed from the American heartland, Continental racing existed in an alternative universe—a clandestine

After seeing his first race at the age of 15, Phinney had one goal in life: He was going to be a bike racer.

and painful pursuit shrouded in mysteries like shaved legs and expensive silk tires sewn together with cotton thread. Tradition infused everything, occasionally spilling over into superstition and ritual. Riders denied themselves food in order to stay eager and whippet thin; they abstained from sex to heighten their drive; they routinely donned nothing but a towel, covered themselves in liniment, and had their legs vigorously rubbed by a heavily muscled, sweating *soigneur*. European cycling comprised a cult-like array of arcane rituals that found easy prey in an impressionable American like Phinney. Peeling back this curtain was an integral part of the sport's appeal.

o͞o

In 1976, Phinney met a fit but occasionally troubled young man by the name of Tony Comfort. Comfort knew the secret handshake of this new world and helped Phinney gain entry. If Phinney was obsessed, Comfort was maniacal—he worshipped all things European, to the degree that he adopted an Italian nom de guerre in deference to the cycling culture he loved: Antonio Conforti. His obsession was pure and transformational, apparent to all around him; in time, Conforti would be credited as the inspiration for Dave, the protagonist in the cult classic film *Breaking Away*.

Phinney remembers first seeing Conforti at a local time trial. "I said, 'Who is that pro?' I watched him sign in and thought he signed in as a '[category] I.' But it was an 'I,' for 'intermediate.' He won the time trial over everyone." At the time Conforti was riding 400 miles a week, according to Phinney—a huge number for the growing musculature and bones of a teenager. But it was a level of effort that resonated with Phinney and conformed to his more-is-better worldview. He had found a spiritual soul mate; they shared the same ailment. When Conforti came to Boulder High a year later, the two began training together.

Significant athletic accomplishment often takes seed as a

fantasy, a thing kindled through the dreams of youth. Conforti and Phinney shared a common vision, and it propelled them violently forward, infusing their lives with the two-wheel sport and its associated milieu. Conforti remembers that he and Phinney "would walk home from high school, go to my house, and look at European magazines." The pair even adopted personas. Conforti was Felice Gimondi, the legendary climber and winner of all three major tours (France, Italy, and Spain). Phinney, meanwhile, was Freddy Maertens, the irrepressible fast man in a sprint and eventual winner of two world road championships. "We would talk about who we were and who we wanted to be," said Conforti. They lived in a world of joyous naïveté, in which the distance between these two things did not seem at all insurmountable.

The pair hungered for information from Europe. Their window into the sport was the French cycling magazine *Miroir du Cyclisme*. "There was so little information at the time," said Phinney. "It was like finding gold treasure to find a *Miroir*." Though the pair couldn't read French, the subtext conveyed in the gritty, race-action photos was clear enough. There were the great pros of the era—Merckx, Gimondi, Bernard Thévenet (winner of the 1975 Tour de France)—their mud-covered faces contorted with pain. There was the aftermath of a crash, a rider's body crumpled and bleeding at the roadside. There were the great sprinters of the age—Maertens and Sean Kelly—banging handlebars violently at the end of a six-hour race. In *Miroir*, Phinney saw the pathos and pain of racing. It was a terrifying beauty, and he wanted more of it.

For the two adolescents, cycling was more than a sport; it was a kind of religion, a form of worship and idolatry. It even had an altar. "I had a room, and I had all these *Miroirs* with Merckx and Gimondi," said Conforti. "We would go there and hang out. It was a shrine, with autographed photos and trophies. It was my whole life."

The pair traveled to events, living the ascetic and carefree life of itinerant bike racers. "We liked what we did so much," said Conforti. "We didn't think much about it. Life was cycling. You traveled, had fun, met people. Your life was outside high school. We just loved what we were doing."

○○

Phinney was the prototypical daydreamer, a habit that, for some, is destructive or leads to apathy. But in his case, his fantasizing was a force propelling him forward—a springboard for what was possible. In his mind, even the most mundane activity would assume epic overtones. He remembers "riding home from school, wearing jeans and a backpack, in the dark and the rain. I pictured myself as [Francesco] Moser, winning a race in Europe. That became a common thing for me."

Cycling was a strong current that coursed through his life, and there wasn't a single activity that wasn't connected to it. "Later, when I was 19, I got a job at Celestial Seasonings packing bulk tea," said Phinney. "It was the most boring job you could imagine, putting tea on palettes. I had one picture of Freddy Maertens, who won 56 races in 1976. I had a photo of him from Paris-Nice, and I would set it in front of me—I was trying to *be* Freddy Maertens. I could always visualize it. I had that photo for years and years."

Phinney, still in his teens, was visualizing a world in which he could achieve spectacular glories—and then he set about making that world real. "I became really good at envisioning what I wanted to do," he said. "It helped me greatly as a bike racer." Mostly, these imaginings centered around one, consuming goal: "I wanted to win more than anyone," he said.

His friend Conforti saw these qualities immediately in Phinney and knew intuitively that he was destined to play on a larger stage. "He was a natural, gifted athlete," Conforti said. "He had a good personality. People liked him. He had all the cards in his favor—he was a good-looking guy, he was in the right place at the right time."

Above all else, Phinney was supremely motivated. There was never a vast distance between the visions he was concocting in his head and the reality of his life on the ground. "He had a general excitement about him," said Conforti. "He would get pumped up and confident that he would do it."

But there was a downside to such unwavering commitment, and both young men, in time, would suffer the consequences. The same drive that enabled them to excel could also hurt them and alienate them from friends and family. Conforti said he was "100 percent when I needed to be 70 percent. I was too serious and would get discouraged." He remembers one season when he failed to make the Junior World Championship team; a promising young rider by the name of Andy Hampsten was chosen instead. Conforti was "devastated, heartbroken." The effects resonated for years. Phinney, similarly, would learn the cost of obsession. He put unrelenting pressure on himself and his teammates, barking commands in races and occasionally acting like a petty dictator. It was a complete contrast to his friendly demeanor off the bike. "I was such a bull about winning," he said. "I could have been more forgiving." In future years, this unyielding drive would result in friction with some teammates and even cause the departure of a few. Many would soon learn that, with Phinney on the team, there often simply wasn't enough room for others at the top.

o͞o

It wasn't long before Phinney's insatiable drive started to produce results, and he won the Rocky Mountain Championships as a junior. What had seemed like an outlandish career decision that day at the North Boulder Park criterium—to devote his life to bike racing—had begun to seem plausible. He remembers it generally as a time of fulfillment and self-realization. Phinney was beginning to see

Phinney was a gifted athlete with a muscular build—a perfect physique for the blindingly fast sprinter he would become. Pictured leading, 1982.

that different riders had different skill sets, and that his compact, muscular build lent itself to one attribute above all others. "I realized I had a good sprint," he said.

It was a meal ticket he would cash in with spectacular regularity for the better part of two decades, his name becoming nearly synonymous with the discipline. Every national class bike racer of the era carries a mental image of Phinney, bent over the handlebar in the last 200 meters, his face in a maniacal contortion, his over-large biceps bulging as he yanks on the handlebar, the bike creaking and groaning underneath him in protest.

Indeed, Phinney was purpose-built for sprinting, with explosive leg power augmented by his substantial upper body musculature. Photos of Phinney on the bike convey a bodybuilder-like presence that completely belied his real stature. Despite efforts to starve himself and atrophy his considerable mass, he always seemed to look as if he had just left the weight room, his shirt sleeves pulled taut against his biceps. Though he was only five foot nine, he always "tried to exude a big presence on the bike." (It can be surprising, after seeing photographs of purpose-built sprinters in a race, to meet them in street clothes, where they often convey a Walter Mitty–like presence.) Indeed, Phinney in a sprint was a fearsome thing. Future team manager Mike Neel put it succinctly: "You don't mess around with a Davis Phinney."

It was a physique that would serve him spectacularly in the comparatively short, flat races that predominated in the United States at the time. But later, as he expanded his repertoire to longer and hillier events, his physical bulk would become a liability, just as it had for Heiden.

Soon Phinney discovered another, unfortunate by-product of his chosen discipline: crashing. "I wouldn't back down, which meant that I crashed more than a lot of guys," he said. "One went with the other. I became fearless." Before long, the sight of Phinney wrapped in gauze and hobbling from yet another encounter with the pavement became a common thing. The irony was that, rather than being discouraged, he seemed to relish and derive strength from these incidents; road rash became a badge of courage. In his mind, he was a warrior.

o̅o̅

By the time Phinney turned 18, cycling had moved across his sky like an eclipse, casting everything else in shadow. It seemed there was only one way forward in his life, and it did not involve the perceived tedium of college and professional life.

Though he came from a middle-class family, Phinney soon realized that bike racing was taking him in another direction entirely, away from the cultural momentum he saw all around him. "When I turned 18, in my third year of racing, I decided I absolutely did not want to go to college," he said. The declaration was initially dismaying to Phinney's father, Damon, who was a successful engineer and envisioned his son continuing his schooling, which would of course lead to a life of conventional success and prosperity. "My Dad's whole thing was to get an education," he said. "That's how you got a respectable job and a family."

Phinney wanted respect, to be sure, but it was of a different sort. While other students at Boulder High plotted their assaults on college and careers, Phinney sat in class squinting his eyes, trying to augur his future in bike racing, choreographing sprints at the end of Paris-Roubaix and the Tour of Flanders, bumping elbows with the great racers of the day. "I was a daydreamer," he said with a hint of resignation. "I did everything but pay attention in class."

The elder Phinney eventually had to accept that his son would never find comfort in a life of convention. "My parents were nonplussed," said Phinney after declaring his life mission. In 1977, father and son drove to Seattle, for the national championships, and to Vancouver, British Columbia, where he was 3rd in a criterium. "That was the first time that my dad realized that 'this guy could be good,'" he said. It wouldn't be long before his father would become one of his greatest boosters, crisscrossing the country in support of his son's obsession.

○○

Phinney had more than simple physical gifts. He had a public persona, a countenance that was immediately appealing and frequently disarming. One minute he would be relentlessly demanding in a race, barking commands and using his elbows to define his space in the peloton. Then, moments later, he would be happily fraternizing with other racers or romancing the media. He was a sponsor's dream, successful and filled with bravado on the racecourse, amiable and appealing off of it. Michael Aisner, director of the Coors Classic, called it "the good and bad Davis, the angel and the devil." Such qualities made for high drama, particularly for a populace that needed an emotional hook to get involved with a sport that was still on the margins of popularity and understanding. As Phinney accumulated wins and increasing fame, said Aisner, "he embodied everything this sport needed to help sell itself."

Indeed, the press found him irresistible. It helped that he was, by broad consensus, magnetically handsome. (Later, a poll in the Denver Post would proclaim him one of the state's "10 Sexiest Male Athletes.") He was also eminently quotable. He would endure interview after interview, answering the same questions over and over, waiting patiently for the next one, delivering his measured responses with professionalism and charm, saying things like, "I'm out there to win the race for myself, but I'm also out there to get the

Phinney delivered crisp sound bites that made him irresistible to press and fans—augmented, of course, by his good looks.

crowd fired up and give them a show. It's flash and it's style and it's speed and it's color—that's what makes the race."

More than anything else, Phinney had the right combination of confidence and humility. Tom Chew, who was an early teammate of Phinney's on the McDonald's team, framed it this way: "Arrogance from someone who is not great is intolerable. Arrogance from a champion is tolerable. But being a good person and talented is the best of the three." In this sense Phinney was in the same class as his future teammate, Heiden—the quintessential self-effacing champion.

oo

In 1981, Phinney had signed on to be part of a fledgling team backed by Yoplait yogurt, but the sponsor withdrew and the squad dissolved in acrimony before the season had even commenced. Suddenly, he was a privateer, competing against the best teams in the nation. "I went all over the country racing against them on my own," he said. "Basically, I didn't have a team."

He couldn't help but compare himself to the 7-Eleven team, a powerhouse of talent and corporate support. It seemed to him that "they had everything—all the goodies. I was totally jealous."

So when Ochowicz approached him for the 1982 season, he was ready. At the time, he viewed the offer as "almost what would be considered a decent salary: $11,000. It was great—support at a whole different level." He accepted immediately.

It didn't take long for Phinney to assume the quasi-management role he would have throughout his career with the team, advising Ochowicz on everything from setting the race calendar to choosing equipment to team selection. And as he surveyed the national scene, it seemed to Phinney that one rider stood alone from the rest. So he approached Ochowicz and spoke plainly. If there was money in the budget, he said, Ochowicz should also hire Phinney's old friend and rival, a tall, sleepy-eyed rider by the name of Ron Kiefel.

CHAPTER 9
A Reluctant Hero

If most successful athletes are impelled by cockiness and bluster, Ron Kiefel was the antithesis, a shuffling giant whose power and speed unfolded like a chrysalis once the starting gun went off. He had an endearing mix of eccentricities, a diffident youth from an immigrant family who knew how to play an accordion and ride a unicycle. It was perhaps inevitable that in the 7-Eleven fraternity, Kiefel's nickname would be "Wookiee," the tall, benevolent, and decidedly hairy creature from *Star Wars*.

Unlike Phinney, who was almost fanatically compelled to succeed at racing from age 15, Kiefel felt only a mild gravitational pull. It was a nonchalance that followed naturally from his unassuming personality. He embraced things gradually, assessing their true value and place in his life.

A self-described "scrawny kid," Kiefel experienced the typical athletic frustrations of adolescence. He tried track and field, wrestling, baseball, and a host of other sports. Nothing resonated. "If there were 100 runners, I was 50th," he recalled. "I remember being so dejected." Almost pathologically shy, Kiefel found that success and popularity were eluding him, and as he plodded into the middle of his teenaged years, he began to feel increasingly isolated. And then, when he was 15, cycling appeared as a kind of salvation, providing a path toward acceptance and away from the social awkwardness he had been feeling.

Kiefel did not come from a culture of comfort and convenience, and his reactions to things were measured and sure. His father, Eugene, was born in the Ukraine and grew up in Odessa, on the Black Sea. Persecuted in his own country, he was forced to flee with his extended family via Poland and Czechoslovakia. Very much a self-made man, Eugene Kiefel worked at a series of small jobs, but soon became keen to open a small business in the new country. "It was between a Dairy Queen, a rental business, or a bike shop," said Ron. "He chose the bike shop." Thus Kiefel found himself quite literally surrounded by bikes from the age of 13. He could hardly avoid them. (The postage-stamp-size shop Eugene opened, Wheat Ridge Cyclery, later became a sprawling 30,000-square-foot success story, run by his son, Ron Kiefel.)

It would have been only natural for Kiefel to reject cycling, in the way that young men rebuff the passions and livelihoods of their fathers. Instead, he found it alluring. He started working in the shop after school and on weekends, sometimes riding a unicycle to get there. But more important, he began to explore the area around Wheat Ridge, a vertiginous landscape hard by the Rocky Mountains, crisscrossed with roads that were perfect for cycling. "As soon as I got on the bike," he said, "I had this sense of adventure. It spoke to me in volumes."

Davis Phinney may have been only 20 miles away in Boulder, but psychologically, the two teenagers were in different landscapes entirely. The bike was not a weapon with which Kiefel could conquer the world, or that might provide a testimonial to his power and drive. It was a vehicle of discovery and wonder, and he assimilated its joys naturally and easily. While Phinney was pursuing his own passion for cycling with characteristic fury, Kiefel was exploring Colorado's Front Range with childlike innocence. "I would go out for an hour and get back six hours later," he said. "I just liked to ride and explore." The bike became a vehicle of transformation, physically and emotionally. "I was always shy—I still am," he said. "As I started to get more confident, I could talk to people. All those things came together when I was 14 and 15, and it kept me out of serious trouble. All of a sudden I wanted to take care of my body—and race."

A mechanic in his father's employ, Bob Junge, encouraged

Kiefel to try his hand at competition, and in 1976, he entered his first event at the sprawling Denver Tech Center. There, he had the foundational experience common to newbies in the sport: He touched wheels with another cyclist and crashed. For most riders, this would have brought the day to a disappointing close. But Kiefel had other plans. He dusted himself off, rejoined the field, and won the race—"by a significant margin," recalled Junge.

Long and lean, with a sleepy, droopy-eyed countenance that belied his incredible speed and power, Kiefel quickly began accumulating results. Though intensely competitive, he was not prone to zeal and infatuation. His father, Eugene, remembers having to forcefully extract race reports from his son. "How did it go?" he'd ask after a day at the races.

"Oh, pretty well," Ron would answer.

"Really? How well?"

"Oh, I won," the younger man would demur.

o͞o

Every successful cyclist learns that genetics have bestowed one gift above all the rest. For some, it's the ability to conquer endless climbs. For others, like Phinney, it's an explosive sprint. Still others may find their natural home in the individual time trial, an event that supplies an almost clinical measure of one's ability to tolerate pain. Kiefel, though a good all-around rider, soon learned that his greatest asset was an explosive turn of speed on an uphill finish. Coming into the final sprint, he would appear as if out of nowhere, flying along the road edge, his expression pained and maniacal, his long legs moving like levers in some vast machine. It was as if he had a switch on the dashboard that could ignite hidden afterburners. "If it was uphill, it was over," said Wayne Stetina, a frequent competitor and multiple-time national champion. "He was unbeatable." Phinney went even further, likening it to magic, a dose

With his long, lean build, Kiefel was deceptively fast. He could generate devastating power on uphill finishes, as though he possessed a hidden afterburner.

of elixir that Kiefel would summon at the most critical moments. "He could open up this bottle at the end of a race," said Phinney. "It was a wonderful skill."

For much of their teenaged years, Kiefel and Phinney contested the same piece of real estate. At times it seemed like the 103,000 square miles of Colorado were not big enough for the two of them. Their intense competitiveness was apparent from their very first encounter, at the 1976 Colorado junior state road championships. Both riders remember the event clearly, as the race would provide a foretaste of their respective roles in what would become one of the most productive duos in the history of American bike racing.

Even as a teenager, Phinney was displaying the autocratic nature and relentless drive that would become his trademarks. As the pair closed in on the finish as part of a small breakaway, Phinney began exhorting his companions to do more work—including Kiefel.

"He was yelling at us to pull," said Kiefel. In answer to Phinney's theatrics, and with the finish fast approaching, Kiefel put in one of his fearsome accelerations. "By that time, I was gone," he said. "That was my first race with Davis. He was 2nd." Phinney was dumbfounded at what he had just witnessed. "It dwindled to a couple of us on the very last lap," he said. "We got to a hill, and he took a flier. He was unbelievable on a finish hill. We made a turn, and I couldn't even make a dent in the guy."

The placings would frequently be reversed in the years to come, but the dramatic roles had been established. There was Phinney, issuing admonitions and commandments. And there was Kiefel, every bit as capable, producing results in his own understated way. Or, as he was fond of saying, "I always let my legs do the talking."

Things in the junior ranks quickly crystallized to just the two of them. "Pretty much from that point on, at every race in Colorado, it would end up being the two of us, pushing each other to the wall, doing anything we could to beat each other," said Phinney. Kiefel recalls it more succinctly, saying that the pair simply "tried to rip each other's legs off." But both young men also realized that the intense competition carried dividends, raising their collective game. "In a couple of years, we became pretty dominant in Colorado," said Phinney. And when they finally became teammates a few years later, it was if they had already gone 10 rounds and reached a draw.

o͞o

Kiefel remembers seeing the 7-Eleven team for the first time at the Tour of Texas, a glittering display of bluster and bravado. At the time, 1981, he was riding for the ill-fated Yoplait team. "There were Bradley, Demgen, and Van Haute, pulling up in the van, full of piss and vinegar," he said, recalling the 7-Eleven's team arrival on the scene. He also remembers them training shirtless, cultivating their tans, exuding an extravagant mix of vanity and psychological gamesmanship. Such displays were at the heart of the team's persona from the very beginning. They had talent, to be sure. But they also had an uncanny ability to knock other teams off balance before the racing had even started. Kiefel characterized them simply as "highball guys. They carried a huge attitude." Heiden, the superstar, seemed to generate his own weather system of press and popularity. "It was a bit intimidating," said Kiefel.

But while others may have fallen prey to the team's theatrics, Kiefel, ever steady and unflappable, was underwhelmed by the show he was observing. "I said, 'That's cool, but it's not me. I'm here to race.' It didn't stop me from racing hard against them."

Few racers have been as unflappable as Kiefel.

Kiefel may have been unruffled by the 7-Elevens, but they were noticing *him*. Roger Young in particular remembers one race in which Kiefel embarked on a solo foray. Such a direct affront to the 7-Elevens could not go unanswered, and they made it their business to reel in the upstart. But Kiefel ignited his afterburners, and despite the team's collective efforts, they were surprised to see him recede into the distance. Young remembers that "it took one of the most remarkable chases of the year" to bring Kiefel back. "I almost felt bad. But afterward we all said, 'If there is any space on the team next year, we ought to pick up that guy.'"

Kiefel, in his usual fashion, was letting his legs do the talking. And he was being heard. In 1982, the offer came from Ochowicz: Would he like to join the team?

$\overline{oo}$

For Phinney and Kiefel, being together brought a palpable relief. They had been battling each other so intensely, for so long, that finally being teammates seemed like a form of armistice. Colorado had been their Gettysburg, a place of bitter battles and ultimate resolution. "There was a point in our careers where either he won or I won—we attacked each other really hard," said Kiefel. "In a race Davis would pull, I would pull, then he would pull harder. . . . I think when we finally became teammates, we had such respect for each other, we didn't have to prove anything."

Duos in sports can be a rare and beautiful thing. One thinks of Joe Montana and Jerry Rice in football, or Michael Jordan and Scottie Pippen in basketball. In the most obvious sense, these are physical collaborations: the passer and the catcher, the guard and the forward. But there is more: the commanding presence and the faithful lieutenant, the charismatic flourish of talent and the steadying hand. In the best of these historic duos, the more imposing presence knows that he relies utterly on the assistance of the other.

When it works, there is a tidy math of talent and synergy, and an inescapable reality that the sum is greater than the parts. Phinney and Kiefel were all these things.

Almost immediately, they began to accumulate wins, often in a predictable pattern: With a few kilometers remaining, Kiefel would begin his advance to the front, with Phinney conserving energy on his wheel. With a kilometer to go, Kiefel would begin one of his blistering accelerations, establishing a pace that was so high that other riders simply could not come around. But as in all such leadouts, Kiefel's effort contained the seeds of its own demise—the pace was simply too much for him to sustain to the finish. It was at this precise moment, with Kiefel beginning to flag, that Phinney would make his move. Until that moment he'd ride in a pocket of relative calm amidst the chaos; then, he would unleash his fury. Rising out of the saddle, his trademark biceps bulging, his elbows flailing to the sides to fend off potential interlopers, Phinney would rev his legs to a frightening velocity, sprinting for all he was worth to the line. And more often than not, he'd hit that line first.

It's long been accepted lore that a racing cyclist can accelerate, flat out, for a maximum of 200 meters. Beyond this, speed will begin to trail off, unsustainable, owing to fatigue and metabolic processes in the muscles themselves. There is simply no more fuel for this type of anaerobic, energy-intensive effort. Consequently, nearly all finishes are marked with a cone or banner, to indicate the real beginning of the sprint, the 200-meter mark. Phinney's entire racing universe—the locus of his professional life—existed inside this mark. It was the realm in which he chose to live and excel, his office for 15 years. And as regularly as clockwork, it was Kiefel who transported him there.

"He knew me perfectly," said Phinney. "If he launched me, 90 percent of the time I would win. It was a wonderful blend of talent, friendship, and respect."

For Kiefel, out of the dozens of wins that followed this script,

Kiefel (right) was more than Phinney's (left) lead-out man. A remarkably versatile rider, he won national championships in the road race, time trial, and team time trial in 1983.

one in particular exemplified the dynamic that existed between the two riders. It occurred at the Coors Classic stage race, an event that would come to define their careers. There was a breakaway of four ahead of them, with a 40-second gap. "I just looked at Davis, and he looked at me," said Kiefel. "I just nodded, *okay*. I just went to the front as hard as I could. That was my specialty—I could accelerate for a few kilometers. We managed to catch the breakaway, and just blow by. Davis was on my wheel. That, for me, was the most incredible day. We

The Coors Classic was the biggest race on 7-Eleven's schedule. Pictured, Kiefel celebrating a stage win in Boulder, Colorado.

just took matters into our own hands and won. The announcer was shocked. He said, 'Where the hell did they come from?' "

Kiefel, more than capable of winning himself, was often runner-up in these situations. "There were times when we did our jobs so well we were 1st and 2nd," he said. "For me, that was like winning."

oo

As they achieved more success, and the pair began to earn the attention of the media, it was Phinney who found himself in the limelight. He had a model's good looks, was ever-ready with a sound bite, and had a way of endearing himself to the press and fans. Kiefel, meanwhile, tended to assume the supporting role, on the roads as well as in the public eye. "Davis was the media star," Kiefel lamented. "I was the media knucklehead." It was all part of the equilibrium that defined their relationship. "I taught him patience, he taught me how to have more charisma," said Kiefel. "He taught me how to put myself in a position where I was uncomfortable."

For Michael Aisner, director of the Coors Classic, the pair made a compelling tale of stardom and sacrifice that he could sell, over and over, to the general media. "Here is this blowhard beating his chest like the incredible hulk," he said of Phinney. "But what got him there was this quieter, European-oriented kid who played the accordion. That was the beauty of it: this one-two combo. It filled reels of tape."

In this sense, their respective positions at the finish seemed to reflect their personalities as well as their physical attributes. There was Phinney, ever-demanding and frequently domineering; and there was Kiefel, characteristically self-effacing. For Phinney, any loss was a crushing injustice, a condemnation of him personally and professionally, and it tormented him. "He was just so damned tenacious," said Kiefel of his teammate. "He hated to lose. He would be so upset. I would be like, 'Oh well, at least we tried. . . .'"

But Kiefel also understood that Phinney elevated and illuminated his own abilities, just as he did Phinney's. "I would lead him out, because I knew he would win. If he led me out, there was a 50 percent chance I would win."

If he found this inequity to be an injustice, Kiefel did not frequently show it. Successes were communal, a shared dividend that carried the pair to the pinnacle of U.S. cycling with remarkable regularity in the 1980s and early 1990s.

CHAPTER 10
Raise the Ranch Dog

In the early 1980s Southland saw itself as the great benefactor of the unheralded sport of cycling, and it went on a shopping spree to prove it. In an 18-month period, the company funded a men's team, a women's team, added a men's track team, devoted $3 million to the construction of a new Olympic velodrome, paid $1 million to be the official convenience store of the Olympic Games, and became a title sponsor of a national track racing series, the 7-Eleven/Bicycling Magazine Grand Prix.

It was a dizzying binge that left other sponsors gasping in its wake. One such casualty was Schwinn, which initially furnished the team with bikes and equipment. "We were amazed at the money Southland was able to spend on the sport and the team," said a Schwinn spokesperson. "We couldn't go 50/50 anymore."

For a company of Southland's soaring profitability, the goal became nothing less than to catapult the sport to new heights, putting its familiar colors on everything from team vans to event banners. And it had the wherewithal to do it. In 1981 the company had gross sales of $5 billion (equivalent to about $15 billion today), and was showing every sign of continuing on the same trajectory indefinitely. "They were opening stores like crazy," said Ochowicz.

Ochowicz found himself in the heady position of spending the company's money. He had been watching and learning in the team's inaugural year, mentally marking his chief antagonists. So in the fall of 1981, amply armed with Southland's checkbook, he began what would become a reliable tactic of pillaging competing teams for their best riders. He had every intention of bolstering and augmenting the superteam he had created.

For the road, in addition to Phinney and Kiefel, he added a

promising Canadian by the name of Alex Stieda. Blond and compact, Stieda had a persona much like Phinney's—smiling and accommodating off the bike, aggressive and occasionally domineering on it. "Alex was a guy that was on the front," said Ochowicz. "If guys were taking laps, Alex was in there as much as Davis." But it was also a circumstance that set the two riders up for an inevitable clash of egos that would play itself out in the coming seasons.

The always smiling Canadian Stieda was easygoing off the bike but an intense and driven competitor in the saddle.

The next order of business was to strengthen the team's presence on the track. Of the six cycling events included in the Olympics, four took place on the velodrome—a venue funded by Southland and bearing the company's name. Thus, any medals garnered there would be doubly satisfying for the convenience store. With this in mind, Ochowicz traveled to the University of Michigan to visit Mark Gorski, a powerful sprinter. It would be one of his most fruitful shopping expeditions. The two men had ridden together on the AMF team, a familiar wellspring for Ochowicz that had also produced team members Phinney, Kiefel, Heiden, and Schuler.

Just months earlier, Gorski had suffered a devastating crash at a meet in Japan, where he was knocked unconscious and broke his collarbone. Although he had recently won an Olympic trials event and seemed primed for the Games, he suddenly found himself contemplating an exit from the sport. "I was in a bad way, physically and emotionally," Gorski said. In the circumstances, Ochowicz's offer to ride for the team came as kind of a salvation. "Och, and his offer to join, was a large part of my reason to try to come back," said Gorski. It was a strategic addition that, in two years' time, would pay huge dividends for Ochowicz, and for Southland.

The initial impetus for a 7-Eleven women's team came not from Ochowicz, but from the original architect of the Southland deal, George Taylor. For 1982, the women's team comprised a promising group of teenagers, including Rebecca Twigg, Sarah Docter, and Jacque Bradley (sister to men's team member Jeff Bradley). Ochowicz, whose consuming passion had always been a men's professional team, was nonplussed. "I think Jim wasn't happy when I suggested they add a women's team," said Taylor. "From his perspective, that meant some of the budget now would go to a women's team." Indeed, Ochowicz would have almost no involvement with the women's squad until after the Olympic Games. Until then it would be a separate and autonomous operation, with its own coaching staff and equipment sponsors.

The 7-Eleven women's team launched in 1982 and included Rebecca Twigg (left) and Jacque Bradley (right). Twigg would go on to become a multi-time national champion, world champion, and Olympic medalist.

For 1982, Ochowicz also brought back the seemingly indefatigable mechanic Richard Gilstrap. Prior to Gilstrap's arrival, Ochowicz had run the team's shop—its *service course*, in cycling language—out of his house in Pewaukee. His garage had become a chaotic mother lode of bikes, parts, and clothing, all of which he was managing in addition to his hundreds of other duties. In these circumstances Gilstrap, plucked from a bicycle shop in Milwaukee, was a godsend. He was capable of prodigious amounts of work, everything from cleaning the bikes after every race to the endless tedium of gluing tires to wheel rims, to mind-numbing drives across country in the team van. "He was the pioneer pro mechanic," said Ochowicz. "And he did it with a lot fewer tools at his disposal than most. We never lost a race because of a mechanical." Indeed, every 7-Eleven rider of the era carries the enduring image of the hardworking Gilstrap, head down in the parking lot of some nameless hotel, cleaning and servicing bikes until the small hours of the morning. Despite the withering workload, he would remain with the squad through the better part of a decade.

Gilstrap, posing with his first service truck in Europe, was the team's stalwart mechanic for nearly a decade.

In the spring of 1982, the bigger and better-funded team again turned its attention to the Tour of Texas. In typical 7-Eleven fashion, there would be ample misbehavior counterbalanced by voluminous amounts of training. In the early days, racing generally took place on the weekends, leaving plenty of time for training in the Texas Hill Country—as well as abundant midweek high jinks.

The Tour of Texas—part race, part training camp, part coming-out party—was a smorgasbord of physical indulgences. After all, who could expect young men to restrain themselves in a town like Austin, where the beer and music flowed so freely?

Issues of restraint and propriety arose almost immediately. It became obvious to Ochowicz that the boys could not be entirely trusted with the impeccably clean 7-Eleven van, particularly after hours. This presented a dilemma. With the van off limits, how could the boys indulge in their after-hour visits to the bars and musical haunts of Austin and environs? Together, they hatched a plan. They would pool their money and buy the "cheapest car that ran in Austin, Texas," according to Demgen, which turned out to be a blue Plymouth Satellite of indeterminate vintage, purchased for the princely sum of $500. The hapless Bradley was elected owner, which meant he had to register the wreck at the Department of Motor Vehicles in his name.

The "Ranch Dog," as it was to forever be known, became the means for these athletes-cum-delinquents to perform all manner of quasi-legal escapades and misdemeanors across the Lone Star State. If there was ever an object that became emblematic of those early, carefree days for the team, it was the Ranch Dog.

The first order of business was to personalize the Ranch Dog by painting huge, red bull's-eyes on the hood and doors. Thus emblazoned, the car would make its evening rounds to the bars and clubs of Austin. "It was an undercover mode of transport," remembered Gorski. "The analogy comes to mind of *The Blues*

Brothers," he added, recalling the famous film in which John Belushi and Dan Akroyd, as the timeless characters Jake and Elwood, wreak havoc in an aging American land yacht.

The car suffered gravely at the hands of the boys. It was rammed into walls, parked by Braille, and generally taken for granted. It soon became riddled with dents. "We came out of a race and took out our frustrations on the car," remembers Gorski. "Everyone drove it— everyone shared in the abuse."

Heiden, the good and decent aspiring physician, also revealed a wilder side of himself. Seeking a little ventilation in the heat of the Texas Hill Country, he at one point did an about-face in the rear seat and used both of his piston-like legs to summarily punch the rear window out, whereupon it slid across the trunk, breaking into shards on the pavement. Instant air conditioning!

Texas was a joyride, a rollicking, near hallucinatory experience for a bunch of guys who not long ago had been driving to races with their parents and sleeping on the floors of whoever would have them. It was not quite a state of grace they were living in, but it was perhaps as close as a bunch of bike riders could get to such a place.

But before leaving Texas, there was the small matter of the Ranch Dog. It was obvious that the car couldn't accompany them during the remainder of the season: Traversing the country in a paint-daubed jalopy did not exactly constitute an approved marketing activity from Southland's perspective. So what was to be done? The 7-Elevens put their heads together and determined a final and fitting resting place for the vehicle that had suffered so greatly at their hands, and that had served them so well. There could be no other conclusion: an act of euthanasia was in the offing. After days of relentless abuse, the Ranch Dog was driven into a riverbed and summarily abandoned, smoking and hissing. It may yet be there today.

Forsaken but not forgotten, the car became emblematic of the spirit of enthusiasm and recklessness that would propel them through the coming years. Twenty years later, at a 7-Eleven team reunion, a T-shirt was made to commemorate the forlorn vehicle. In bold letters, beneath an image of the old Plymouth, the shirt proclaimed, "Raise the Ranch Dog."

oo

Despite the wildness, the surfeit of energy, and the predilection toward trouble and youthful delinquency, there was also an underlying sense of purpose and seriousness to the team. With Phinney and Kiefel on board, the atmosphere began to shift in small ways, from the rowdy, fraternity-like days of the San Diego camp to something more determined and focused. "With the leadership quality of Davis and myself, we took the team from a bunch of good riders to some-thing dedicated to winning," said Kiefel. "Davis and I were very serious; we were able to bring a little more discipline."

Kiefel brought a little more discipline to the team.

Phinney saw the squad's mission as his own. His persona and that of the team were indivisible, and anything less than a victory constituted a personal failure. The boys weren't there just to be a presence or to conveniently fly the flag of their well-moneyed sponsor in prominent races. They were there to win—every time. "When I joined 7-Eleven, I thought this is a very exclusive club, and only extra special riders would get in. I felt like we needed to create an absolute gold standard in the domestic arena," Phinney said. To his teammates, he was messianic; to his competitors, there were hints of megalomania. "A lot of people might look back critically at how dominant I was in those days, in all ways," he said. "But I always delivered. I could have let someone else win, but I didn't even think about it. That's what we were there for, to win."

It all worked with maddening precision. Competing teams found the domestic scene exhausting and occasionally demeaning. In one 1982 criterium in Las Vegas, the squad resembled a pack of angry and unyielding bees, launching repeated attacks and counterattacks that left competitors limp with exhaustion. "You'd catch one, and the other one behind you would take off," said one flustered competitor, who could only watch as the 7-Elevens garnered 6 of the top 10 places.

$\overline{oo}$

In addition to being a designated race leader, Phinney started to act as Ochowicz's trusted advisor, influencing everything from the choice of riders to clothing suppliers. Ochowicz was patient with his interventions, and the relationship blossomed. "Och would take my calls," Phinney said. "I would talk for hours. There's this whole myriad of stuff that goes on in a bike race, and that was my nature to define every angle. He listened to me. I would make notes and tell him that we need to talk to this sponsor, et cetera."

The pair shared a singular bond, with a foundation of

pragmatism and an intuitive sense of what it took to succeed in sports. "Och and I have a common thing, in that both of us went to high school and that was it," said Phinney. "All of our formative education came through experience, sports, and bike racing."

Ochowicz was also a foil to Phinney's hyperactive nature. Phinney was always theorizing, hatching plans, developing scenarios. "The great thing about Jim, he was relatively unflappable," said Phinney. "He was 'The Rock'—solid as a rock. He always gave the appearance of being calm and in control, even when he had no idea what he was doing."

Kiefel, too, became a sounding board for Phinney's expansive view of athletics and the universe at large. Phinney would launch into one of what he called his "soliloquies—and Ron would take it all in. Our personalities were complementary. I thought about every nuance of the training. He was more quiet and soft-spoken."

It was a remarkably effective chemistry that served to catapult the team to domestic dominance in the early 1980s. Indeed, on any given weekend, somewhere in the United States, it was likely that one of the 7-Elevens was winning a race on the road or the track.

oo

Given Phinney's domineering presence, it was inevitable that turf battles began to erupt on the team. "I was probably overly selfish," said Phinney, for whom the formula couldn't be simpler: Get him to the finish line, and he'd sprint to the win. But as obvious and repeatable as the strategy may have been to him, it was bound to take a toll on his teammates. In particular, Hayman—the unquestioned team leader in the team's inaugural year—began to bristle at Phinney's apparent coup. "I was getting frustrated," said Hayman. "Davis was so dominating." As a result of this simmering rivalry, Hayman left for a team founded by Fred Mengoni, a New York real estate magnate and long-time cycling benefactor.

Stieda, the superfast Canadian, also quickly found himself being overshadowed by Phinney. "Alex was a similar person to me," said Phinney. "A lot of times we would get in a break, and it would be, 'I want to win. No, I want to win.' We were competitive, because we were similar."

As Ochowicz's de facto assistant, Phinney also began to shape the composition of the squad. "I influenced the direction of the team and the riders on the team," he said. "I was very strong-minded—if people on the team weren't helping out to the best of their ability, they went away, and I had a say in that."

All the riders from the team's inaugural year had stayed for the second year, but 1983 marked the beginning of an annual and occasionally sad series of team changes that would continue for the next decade. The initial exodus included not just Hayman, but also stalwarts Van Haute and Demgen. "Davis was calling the shots as much as Och," remembers Demgen with a hint of dejection, "and I wasn't chosen for '83." Ochowicz's brother-in-law, Roger Young, now 29, found himself "getting his butt kicked every way imaginable," and ended his racing career. (He would remain connected to the squad as track coach.)

○○

Many of the 7-Elevens came from backgrounds of comfort and convenience and struggled with the tug of higher education and careers. In choosing to race full time—even for a team as prominent and well-funded as 7-Eleven—they had opted for a life of sacrifice and questionable glory over security and convention.

Even at the highest levels, only a few could count on a salary or sufficient fame to propel them through the rest of their lives. Devoting themselves full time to cycling was a risk: If they took this detour now, in their early 20s, would they ever go back to college? Or in 10 or 20 years, would they be living the peripatetic lifestyle of a team manager or the patchwork existence of a bicycle shop owner (as Kiefel and Bradley eventually did)?

For some, either sure of their abilities or naïve to any other outcome, it was a simple decision. Phinney, even at age 16, "absolutely knew" that he wasn't going to college. For him, bicycle racing was a once-in-a-lifetime opportunity, and he would gladly forsake security for the chance to travel the world and—just maybe—earn the fleeting recognition that comes from athletic success. After all, who could resist the temptation to step on the podium in some foreign nation, redolent in the stars and stripes of your native land? The memory would be stored like a cache of gold, the sense of sacrifice fresh and poignant even 30 years later.

Then there were those who, with mixed success, tried to straddle the divide. Schuler, Kiefel, and others were among the team members who would try to patch together a life of college and racing. Not surprisingly, the one gleaming exception was Heiden, who never once wavered from his medical goal. His drive was enviable. "I should have gone to school like Gomer," Stieda would lament later. But he would only half mean it. For Stieda, and others like him, the prospect of success on the roads of Europe was, in the mind if not the wallet, worth far more than any college degree.

But the team was growing, too. As Ochowicz looked toward the horizon, the Los Angeles Olympics loomed large. It was, after all, Southland's original motivation for underwriting the team, and Och needed to manipulate the composition of the squad to ensure its success. For years, he had been courting an unassuming cyclist by the name of Leonard "Harvey" Nitz, an accomplished track rider who was also very capable of winning road races. In 1983, Nitz finally accepted his offer.

With Nitz aboard, it seemed that things were falling into place for the Games. Ochowicz had Nitz and Gorski on the track. For the road events, he had the reliable Phinney/Kiefel combination as well as another recent addition, Andy Weaver. For the inaugural women's Olympic road race, Southland had hired the promising Rebecca Twigg.

Nitz, a track specialist who took silver in the 4,000 m team pursuit at the 1984 Olympics, was equally at home in road races.

Meanwhile, the company was feverishly overseeing the construction of the Olympic velodrome that carried its name at Cal State Dominguez Hills, in Carson, California. Gorski was so consumed by his gold medal mission that he took up residence nearby, in Orange County, to observe every facet of the track's construction. It seemed the attention of a nation was directed at Los Angeles. Now, more than ever, it was time for Ochowicz to justify the fanfare that had surrounded the team since its inception.

While no one at Southland had known what a velodrome was in the fall of 1980, they certainly did now. "The Olympics," Ochowicz said, "was everything."

CHAPTER 11
Olympic Bonanza

On May 7, 1984, the Soviet Union announced it was boycotting the Los Angeles Games, an action taken at least partially in revenge for the indignity of President Carter's boycott of the Moscow Games four years earlier. Responding in solidarity, 13 other East bloc nations quickly followed suit, including cycling powerhouses East Germany and Czechoslovakia.

On the day the boycott was announced, Mark Gorski and the other leading U.S. track sprinters were competing in the Soviet Union, against the very riders they would have faced in L.A. Though fraternization across the Iron Curtain was frowned upon, the athletes shared a common frustration with what they perceived as an intrusion into the pure and sacred world of sport. "I kind of commiserated with them," said Gorski. "We were fierce competitors, but we respected each other. I knew what they were going through, given what I went through in '80. I was there back in the day."

Modern Olympics have become inseparable from the politics of nations. And with the same surety, each passing Olympiad brings a predictable response from the athletes and coaches who have dedicated their entire beings to sport. There is a collective sigh, after which they go about the somber and sacrificial business of training and preparation. Sport is the thing they know best in the world, and there is no choice but to go forward. "They just wish," said one U.S. cycling coach with resignation, "that the Olympics would be left alone by the politicians."

o͞o

With the boycott came the specter of the "asterisk"—the idea that any medals earned in L.A. would be tainted by the absence of some of the world's best cyclists. Indeed, at the time, 5 out of 8 world track champions hailed from communist nations. In Olympic events at the worlds, 14 out of 24 medalists were from the other side of the Iron Curtain.

Meanwhile Gorski—Ochowicz's star track rider—had been riding well, perhaps the best he ever had. In late July, he won the Olympic trials at the new 7-Eleven Olympic Training Center in Colorado Springs, soundly beating his chief American rival, Nelson Vails.

It was a different story in international competition, however. In the 1983 world championships, Gorski had placed 5th, behind four East bloc riders. In international meets in early 1984, he was unable to take a single ride from the reigning world champion, Lutz Hesslich of East Germany. (The match sprint is decided on the best of three rides.) Another East German, Michael Huebner, beat Gorski in two of the three meets. Unquestionably, in the absence of these riders, the playing field would be seriously tilted in favor of the Americans.

It seemed the spoils would increase even further when, on May 28, the International Olympic Committee decided to allow more athletes per nation in each event, to compensate for the absence of the Easterners. In the men's road race, for instance, the United States could field four riders instead of three. Each country would also be allowed one additional sprinter and an extra individual pursuit rider.

The U.S. national team, under its new coach, Eddie Borysewicz, was arguably better prepared than it ever had been. Many riders had been sequestered at the new, high-altitude training facility in Colorado Springs for months. Now, in the absence of the East bloc nations, and with the additional riders, it seemed like a medal bonanza was in the offing.

o͞o

For Southland, the boycott was at once an affront and an

opportunity. The Thompson brothers had gotten involved in cycling out of patriotic zeal. This was, after all, the height of the Cold War, and medals at the Games had become symbolic of political as well as athletic superiority. But now, as a result of the boycott, it seemed that these global implications had been reduced and cheapened.

On the other hand, if the company applied a pure marketing calculus to recent events, it seemed certain that the boycott would only increase its exposure—and the booty that American athletes stood to gain at the company's freshly completed velodrome.

If the boycott rankled the American public, the feeling did not linger for long. On the contrary, there was such punch-drunk enthusiasm for the Games that it completely obscured the gaping holes in the international field. The East bloc cyclists were already complete unknowns, and in the patriotic delirium of the Games, their absence would go largely unnoticed.

Ochowicz, too, had little time for remorse. "You still have to beat somebody," was his simple summation. Whatever philosophical and moral implications surrounded the coming Olympiad, they quickly receded from view, and the focus was on one thing only: winning, regardless of who showed up to race.

o͞o

For Ochowicz, the Olympics fomented a simmering war with the heralded national team director, Eddie Borysewicz, or "Eddie B." As national coach, Borysewicz had dominion over rider selection and training in the months leading up to the Games. But since many of the nation's top riders wore the colors of a familiar convenience store, they found themselves in positions of dual allegiance.

Ironically, in the absence of the Cold War athletes, the Americans had an East bloc coach in their midst. Borysewicz, from Poland, was more than a knowledgeable coach—he was a personification of the communist training ethic. His position as U.S.

national coaching director, in a country generally thought to exist in a cycling back water, was augmented by an aura of mystery and arcane knowledge. He recommended, for instance, that riders eat recently slaughtered venison and abstain from "girl chasing." His advice was delivered in an almost impenetrable accent that enhanced and enlarged his image. In general, he viewed the state of American cycling as laughable. He called U.S. riders "fat guys with mustaches." Almost without trying, he found himself a demigod among the hairy-legged heathens of U.S. bicycle racing.

Ochowicz, accustomed to being a figure of absolute authority to his riders, chafed against any power-sharing arrangement with Borysewicz. Skirmishes arose regarding everything from the choice of clothing to team selection and preparation. "Eddie and I did not get along," he said simply. "We had strong personalities." While Borysewicz wanted his best riders sequestered at the Olympic training center, Ochowicz wanted them out racing on behalf of his sponsor. "The guys didn't need to sit in Colorado Springs," said Ochowicz defiantly. "Good riders don't train, they race. Eddie and I didn't agree on all these things." Gorski, himself an object in this tug-of-war, called it "an us-and-them mentality. It was the national team, and the big, bad guys in the green and red."

For Ochowicz, it was all about one thing: trying to "put as many guys on the Olympic team in every discipline as we could." In the end, he was wildly successful. Out of 23 Olympic team berths, 9 belonged to 7-Eleven. This included Gorski (men's sprint), Twigg (women's road race), Phinney and Kiefel (road race and team time trial), Nitz (individual and team pursuit), and Rory O'Reilly (kilometer).

With the selections made, it was time to put any controversy that may have existed behind them and gel as a team. No American had won an Olympic medal since 1912, and if there was ever a time for the United States to prove that it had moved into the modern age of cycling,

Rebecca Twigg, shown here in the Tour of Texas, was a medal hopeful for the inaugural women's road race in the 1984 Games—and she delivered.

it was now. Whatever hurt had been suffered on either side quickly passed, and the athletes focused on the Games in a near state of frenzy.

oo

The first day of the Games, July 29, foretold the coming landslide. Phinney's wife, Connie Carpenter, won the gold medal in the inaugural women's Olympic road race. Twigg, the 7-Eleven rider, was inches behind, taking the silver. "This is it guys," said Carpenter to the men's team, holding up her medal. "Go for it."

And they did. In the space of eight days, the U.S. team won 9 medals (including 4 golds), out of a possible 15. The U.S. won medals in 6 events—and 7-Eleven riders figured in 5 of them. Besides Twigg, 7-Eleven medal winners included Nitz, Gorski, Kiefel, Phinney, and Andy Weaver.

Since the Games opened with cycling, the sport received unprecedented coverage in the major media outlets, including *ABC Sports, Sports Illustrated, Time,* and *Newsweek*. If there was any talk of the "asterisk," it did not seem to fester in anyone. For a nation that had not won an Olympic cycling medal in more than 70 years, the Games could only be regarded as a resounding success.

The match sprint final became a duel of two dominant American riders when Gorski went up against his friend and rival, the charismatic Nelson Vails. The two had been trading victories for more than a year, Vails winning the 1983 Pan American Games, Gorski besting Vails at the national championships. For both men, even before the Games began, it seemed increasingly likely that it would be an all-American final. "It ended up pretty much being between me and Nelson," said Gorski. "We could see that developing from a mile away." In the months leading up to the Games, the rivalry only intensified. They trained in different cities, with different coaches.

In the Olympic final, Gorski took a risk, using a bigger gear than he had all season. "If you make a mistake in gear choice, in a sprint, it can be fatal," said Gorski. "But I said, 'Screw it—it's the Olympics.'" Fortunately for Gorski, in the biggest race of his life, the gamble worked. "I accelerated like never before." He won in two straight rides out of a possible three.

In that moment, any talk of an asterisk was irrelevant. "I feel in my heart I could have beaten [then-world champion Lutz] Hesslich or anyone then and there," he said. Indeed, his fastest 200 m time— 10.49 seconds—was just 0.04 off the Olympic record.

Gorski had put in a career ride, and he relished his win, as he had every right to do. Afterward, he took a lap of the velodrome with his infant son in his arms, attended a press conference, then rode his bike back to his hotel through the suburban streets of Los

After a discouraging stretch of injuries, Gorski found support with 7-Eleven and won the gold medal in track's premier event, the match sprint of the 1984 Olympics.

Angeles. His life was about to assume an unprecedented period of chaos and notoriety, but this was a cherished moment of anonymity. As he passed by the nondescript tract homes in the late afternoon, he had a feeling of absolute satisfaction and accomplishment. "I would see someone on the street—it was just a Friday afternoon in their life, but it was life-changing for me," he said. "I was riding home from the biggest day of my life, and they had no idea. It was a feeling of contentment and satisfaction. You don't often have days like that."

For Ochowicz, too, it was a moment when all seemed right with the world. He had delivered on a promise: A 7-Eleven rider, competing on a venue paid for by the company and bearing its name, had won a gold medal. The Thompson brothers' investment had paid off spectacularly. "The Gorski win was huge for Southland, and for us," said Ochowicz. "That was the ultimate objective."

oo

Almost as memorable as the Games themselves was the aftermath. In a remarkable show of extravagance, Southland rented the cruise ship from the television series *The Love Boat*. Docked at Long Beach harbor, it became a place to fete key executives and VIPs. Bob Hope gave a private show on board. Ochowicz, flush from his recent success, stayed for two days with his wife, Sheila, and their growing family.

The company also agreed to underwrite an "Olympic Medalist Tour": a five-day extravaganza involving chartered jets for medal winners from all the sports. For the athletes, the whole thing bordered on the surreal—a dreamlike sequence that started with a huge medal haul and finished with a transcontinental party. Gorski remembers a "ticker tape parade on Broadway in New York City, a party at Studio 54 all night, a trip to the White House, and a private trip through Disneyworld in Florida."

"During the ticker tape parade, [fellow medal winner] Andy

Weaver and I were sitting in a convertible, looking at each other. It was snowing paper in the sky, with just hundreds of thousands of people hanging out the windows. We're just going, 'This isn't real. I can't believe it.'"

Ochowicz, too, was living a dream. The team was about to enter its fifth year. As he thought about all that had occurred, it seemed he had come a long way from Milwaukee. But it also begged the question: What's next?

It wasn't hard to summon an answer. In fact, it had been there all along—ever since he had read *The T.I.-Raleigh Story*. He had been carrying a notion, barely acknowledged, even to himself. He would create a U.S.-based professional team, and they would ply the storied roads of Europe, alongside the best cyclists in the world. And just maybe, if all went to plan, they would compete in the world's most famous bike race: the Tour de France.

CHAPTER 12
The Push to Turn Pro

Just a year earlier, the Olympics had been an overarching goal, casting all else in shadow. Now, in retrospect, the Games seemed a mere diversion on the way to something much greater. The first few years for the team had been a fine ride, but when Ochowicz thought about it, he realized that something bigger was calling. In fact, he said flatly, "I had no interest in staying in the U.S. with an amateur team."

The very idea of an American team pitting itself against the world's best pros represented a kind of heresy. In the late 1970s, when solitary Americans ventured overseas to test their legs as European pros, they found themselves rebuffed as interlopers and returned chastised and exhausted. Only Greg LeMond had penetrated that cloistered world in any lasting way, and he had done so as part of a European team.

In America, it seemed like the 7-Elevens had achieved a position of easy dominance. So why go to Europe, relegating themselves to positions of anonymity and no small amount of suffering?

Ochowicz seemingly did not stop one minute to consider what had come before. He would not be bound by geography or convention. Since age 14, he had been consumed by one, supreme goal: to strive for the pinnacle of the sport, regardless of the continent.

Ochowicz did have an ally in his madness—someone nearly his equal in measures of ambition and hubris: Davis Phinney. "I don't know if I can take total credit, but Jim and I sat down after the Games and said, 'What do we want to do?'" said Phinney. "Out of that discussion, we decided to turn pro." It was the beginning of a unique alchemy between the two men. For the next decade, they would be twin catalysts, each urging the other toward ever more ambitious goals.

Not everyone subscribed to the new mission with equal enthusiasm, however. Ochowicz's soaring ambition exceeded even that of most of his riders. Kiefel had been faithfully attending the Colorado School of Mines, and it seemed his life as a bike racer might soon reach its natural end. "Being a pro was never my push," said Kiefel. "I had to decide if I wanted to finish my degree. I had a career path." Under pressure from Ochowicz and Phinney, he eventually relented. Heiden, in the throes of medical school, agreed to remain on the team as a figurehead and make occasional forays to Europe. Nitz, the perennial amateur, had his eyes fixed on the next Olympics and elected not to go. (At the time, turning professional would preclude participation in the Games.)

George Taylor, the original architect of the Southland deal, was another prominent dissenting voice. He and Och had been on divergent paths for some time. Taylor had started the women's team against Ochowicz's wishes. He had convinced Southland to build a second velodrome in Colorado Springs, home of the United States Olympic Committee, and had successfully lobbied the company to sponsor the 1986 world cycling championships as well, also in Colorado Springs. In broad terms, Taylor's vision was domestic and egalitarian. He envisioned an enduring amateur presence, based on success in the Games, involving men and women—something that would generate wide appeal in the United States and support Southland's primary market.

For his part, Ochowicz was less interested in the intricacies of media impressions and marketing than he was in pure athletic success on an international scale. So at the end of 1984, ignoring Taylor's entreaties and armed only with his own soaring ambitions, Ochowicz flew to Southland headquarters in Dallas to make his case for a European professional cycling team.

The company's original sponsorship had arisen from patriotic fervor. But what Och was proposing—a pro team in Europe!—bordered on the irrational. For one thing, it would be expensive. For another, any publicity the team might gain would be primarily overseas, far from the home market. In pure financial terms, it was hard to see how the company could possibly benefit from a bunch of recently minted pros toiling anonymously over the high passes of France and Italy. If the original backing of the team had been impetuous, this would be a Hail Mary of colossal proportions.

But Ochowicz inspired confidence in his riders and his sponsor. He had run an impeccable operation for four years. His athletes, though occasionally unruly, had been tutored and polished into a precise media machine, winning almost at will and smiling unfailingly in the public glare.

The company was also predisposed toward such experiments like never before, and for one reason: Its coffers were full. More than full—they were overflowing. Fueled by America's insatiable appetite for convenience and speed, sales were by now exceeding a billion dollars every three months. And, to be fair, the company's overseas presence was also growing. It had opened its 1,000th international store in 1980, and by 1985 that number had more than doubled to over 2,500, making the ostensibly risky venture of a European pro team at least a little more palatable.

Ochowicz's blue-collar background didn't hurt him one bit in Southland's corporate boardroom. He'd become comfortable with the company's decision makers, and he figured he was as much a part of their sports sponsorship plans as anyone. In his view, there was no reason to be timid. Never one to mince words, he told the assembled Southland executives simply, "These guys need to go to Europe now."

What he didn't say was that he really wasn't interested in any other outcome. Managing a pro team was his dream, and he intended to move forward, no matter what. "There may have been resistance," he said, "but it didn't matter."

In the end, though, there was no lengthy wrangling over strategy or details. The Southland company executives acceded to his request—once again, without the nuisance of a contract—and Ochowicz flew home to Wisconsin, full of hope. And just a hint of trepidation.

oo

With Southland's handshake blessing, Ochowicz began a mad scramble to secure much-needed equipment, cars, clothing, and race entries—the armaments of a European pro campaign. It was like marshalling forces for a ground war. The first event—the early season Étoile de Bessèges, a five-day stage race in southern France—was only a few months away.

Never inhibited by a lack of language skills, Ochowicz flew to Milan with Richard Dejonckheere, an experienced European team manager and brother of longtime pro cyclist Noël Dejonckheere. Together, the pair skillfully procured cosponsorships for everything from handlebars to musette bags. What Ochowicz discovered was a prevailing curiosity—if not a ringing endorsement—of the notion of an American team pitting itself against the world's best professionals. "We were different," he said. "They didn't even know who we were, but they liked the idea. The doors were open."

With the squad's new mission at hand, Ochowicz gathered his riders together for a training camp outside of San Diego, where America's most famous pro, Greg LeMond, was also logging his early season miles. Full of hope and promise for their new undertaking, the team seemed unusually inspired. "That was a special group of people," said Ochowicz. "They were not opposed to training hard. When it came time to go to France, they were ready."

But was Ochowicz? His jaw set, he was about to embark on the greatest adventure of his life, an all-consuming passion that would eclipse everything else for the coming decade. His family, his life in Wisconsin, and everything else that was familiar and simple seemed to recede to pinpoints in his rearview mirror as he made his way to southern France to prepare for the team's first race as full-fledged pros.

The very earth seemed to shift under his feet. "When I packed that bag," he said, "I knew it was never going to end."

∞

In late February, the team gained entry to a small Italian race, the Trofeo Laigueglia, on the Mediterranean. Since its inception in 1964, the race had served as a traditional season opener in Italy. It was deemed a semiclassic—not on par with such heralded one-day races as Milan–San Remo or Paris-Roubaix, but important nonetheless. Past winners included none other than Eddy Merckx and Freddy Maertens.

Early results for the team's spring 1985 campaign had been mixed. They had entered two small French stage races. There were glimmers of hope when Phinney took 4th in the final stage of the Étoile de Bessèges. Shortly thereafter, in the five-day Tour of the Mediterranean in southern France, Kiefel crashed in the opening time trial but then placed a highly respectable 2nd in a mountain stage. In other ways, however, it had been a rude baptism for the freshly minted pro team. The weather—despite expectations for the sunny south of France—had been horrific, and the pace was unlike anything they had experienced in the United States. "We had to get used to a new style of racing," said Kiefel. "At first they would go along at 30 kph and I said, 'This is easy.' Then they'd hit the climb and go faster. For the last hour, I'd never gone that fast. Then I began to understand what it meant to be a pro." It was painfully apparent that this was not the Tour of Somerville, New Jersey.

But Laigueglia, just two days after the conclusion of the Tour of the Mediterranean, offered a new opportunity. The 160-km race—about 100 miles, start to finish—comprised two large loops. What the team didn't know was that there was also a small finishing circuit. Kiefel said this obliviousness was characteristic of the squad's early days in Europe, a state of blissful ignorance that shielded them from the true, overwhelming scale of the thing they were undertaking. "We didn't know all the details," said Kiefel, acknowledging that in many ways it was better that way. "It was typical of the American team."

Adapting to the speed and distance of European racing was a challenge for the team. Kiefel pictured, 1985.

As the end of the race approached, Kiefel found himself the only remaining American in the front group. He was plotting his approach to the finale, when "all of a sudden everyone took a sharp left" onto the finishing loop that had previously escaped their reconnaissance. "I had no clue what was going on," said a bewildered Kiefel. To his credit, he decided to go with the flow. "I felt good," he said. "It was the right kind of climbing for me."

Kiefel then found himself in the company of Vittorio Algeri, the Italian national road champion. Algeri pulled hard at the front. Kiefel took his turn, then Algeri pulled yet again. "Then I said to myself, 'I'm not pulling again,'" said Kiefel. "'You're the Italian champion, and I don't have anything to lose.'"

In the circumstances, Kiefel was aided by anonymity. The Americans were essentially unknown to the European peloton, and the peloton was an unknown quantity to them. It was a state of mutual ignorance that, in the early days of the team, would often work to their advantage. "I basically didn't know who all these guys were, except [Giuseppe] Saronni," said Kiefel, referring to a prominent Italian pro who had previously won the worlds and the Giro. "They were just bike riders. And they had no idea who I was."

Algeri started to accelerate with 500 meters to go, which Kiefel took as an invitation. "I was always a fast sprinter out of breakaways," he said, "and this was perfect."

The next moments unfolded in a dreamlike sequence. Kiefel's teammate, Jeff Bradley, had a perfect vantage point at the back of the main group. "All I remember was there was a two-kilometer climb to the finish," said Bradley. "I was dying. As Kiefel was going off the front, I was coming off the back. I thought, holy crap—we were ecstatic!"

Kiefel, exhibiting his trademark uphill sprint, beat the Italian convincingly, winning his—and the team's—first professional race.

o͡o

It was classic Kiefel, the reluctant hero—a star despite himself. For the entire team, at that moment, the world seemed to shift on its axis. "That was when things started to change," said Bradley. It may have only been a semiclassic, but it didn't matter. Kiefel had won a professional race, from the front, in the true style of champions, with the likes of Saronni and Algeri trailing in his wake. More important, the boys had conducted themselves like professionals. For riders who not long ago had been crisscrossing America in a 7-Eleven van, frenetically waging war on the humdrum criterium circuit, the win seemed almost hallucinatory, a tantalizing glimpse of future possibilities. "After that we thought, 'Hey, we can do this,'" said Kiefel. Laigueglia, in the pantheon of 7-Eleven wins, would always be regarded as one of the team's major milestones.

That night the 7-Elevens had plenty to celebrate. Wine was not always allowed at dinner, but this time the table was awash with it. As glasses were being raised, a figure approached the table. It was the Italian hero Francesco Moser, a former world road champion and, in the previous year, winner of the Giro d'Italia and the demigod of two-wheel sport in a nation obsessed with all things two-wheel.

As the dark and handsome Moser approached the table, the 7-Elevens looked up expectantly, as if a verdict was about to be rendered—an assessment of the day and their place in it. Just then, a broad smile came across Moser's face. "*Complimenti*," he said.

$$\overline{oo}$$

For Ochowicz, brimming with confidence, the spring campaign had provided a glimpse of what was possible. "Once we won Laigueglia, lights went on in our little camp—and within pro cycling," he said. It was time, he thought, "to see what we could do in a serious stage race—to see how we really stood as professionals." And so the idea was hatched: why not a major European stage race? Why not the Giro d'Italia?

Initially, there were plenty of reasons why not. For one, Och didn't have enough riders to field a competitive squad. Second, and perhaps more important, "I didn't have the money," said Ochowicz. "The Giro was not budgeted for." And third, the team had not been invited to the race. These last two problems would be solved by an ebullient businessman and cycling fan by the name of Erminio Dell'Oglio, the head of a company that made, of all things, industrial washing machines. Dell'Oglio agreed to cosponsor the team and provided critical connections within what Kiefel called the Italian cycling "mafia."

The Giro, a "Grand Tour" that precedes the Tour de France on the yearly cycling calendar, had long been considered the world's second-most prestigious bike race, second only to the Tour. But whatever the Giro laced in glitter and media glare, it more than

Dell'Oglio, who owned the Hoonved washing machine company, provided essential backing and insider connections.

made up for in the passion of its riders and its people. For three weeks each spring, the entire boot of Italy seemed to hold the event in a warm embrace. Families lined the roads, staking out picnic spots for hours in advance, eating prosciutto and drinking chianti. Every detail and subplot was agonizingly discussed in cafés and endlessly chronicled in the pink pages of the sports daily, *La Gazzetta dello Sport*. Riders were feted as national heroes. In the cities and in the countryside, the nation seemed to lapse into a state of suspended animation each May. So fervent were the Italian fans that they had earned their own place in the country's lexicon of sport: They were the *tifosi*, and with their banners, blaring horns, bells, shouts, and occasional illegal pushes administered to faltering racers on the Giro's formidable mountain climbs, they were as much a part of the race as the competitors themselves. The Giro was a crazy, wonderful carnival in which the 7-Elevens, fueled by their own passion and excitement, would find a natural home for years to come.

Ochowicz certainly understood that the Giro would be a proving ground—a consummation of all he had worked for in financing and assembling the team. But he also saw that changes were needed. Leading up to the Olympics, his emphasis had been on building a team suited for the frenetic inner-city criteriums and circuit races that dominated American-style bike racing. That team structure had served 7-Eleven spectacularly through an intoxicating period of domination and success.

But now they were entering new territory, of geography and of the mind—a place where the old formulas simply would not work. Aside from the team's annual trek to the Coors Classic in Colorado, there had been a conspicuous lack of distance and long, switchback climbs. Now they were facing a 4,000-km test, punctuated with consecutive 200-km days and climbs spiraling up 3,000 meters. And it was not just about climbing; the Phinney/Kiefel combination, so chillingly effective in America, would merely be one of dozens of such

For the newly minted pros, the 1985 Giro d'Italia was a leap into the void. Left to right: Kiefel, Phinney, Dell'Oglio, Boyer, Ochowicz, Heiden.

duos, all of whom had been equally lethal in their own countries. In every sense, they were about to enter bike racing's big league.

What Ochowicz needed was more depth and horsepower to survive the rigors—and inevitable illnesses—of a three-week race. Even more, he needed a rider seemingly not of this country—someone more at home in the vertiginous landscapes of Europe's highest mountains than in the industrial parks and urban circuits of America.

Ochowicz had this notion firmly in mind when the team made its annual spring trip to the Tour of Texas, won handily by Phinney. At that moment, to Ochowicz, the team's domineering win seemed almost gratuitous. It wasn't a bore, exactly—every win was important, and Phinney's victory was another jewel in the 7-Eleven crown. But Ochowicz couldn't help himself. Every time he looked at the results sheet, a diminutive climber named Andy Hampsten, then riding for the Levi's-Raleigh team, popped out at him. Hampsten, in Och's estimation, was a rider in search of a suitable geography. And Ochowicz was pretty sure he had a suitable geography in mind.

○○

If the mesomorph Phinney was perfectly suited to the cut and thrust of U.S. criterium racing, Hampsten was the inverse, a featherweight package that seemed to be composed solely of legs and lungs. National coach Eddie Borysewicz called Hampsten, at just over 130 pounds, "skinnier than his bike."

He was, however, a package almost perfectly engineered to go uphill. For years, Hampsten had been laboring against the likes of fast men like Phinney and the Canadian Steve Bauer on the American criterium circuit. "Racing in the early '80s," said Hampsten, "was all about chasing Phinney and Bauer." But in any race with climbs longer than a kilometer, Hampsten would come to the fore, often with spectacular effect. In the Coors Classic, he had placed in the top 10 the previous three years, including a 2nd place in 1984. "I would do my best in the Coors," he said, "which was the only major stage race with mountains."

Hampsten grew up in Grand Forks, North Dakota, surely one of the flattest parts of the country, if not the world. So from the outset, it seemed he had no canvas on which to express his true abilities. But cycling held a mysterious attraction, and at 13, he started attending group rides organized by a local bike shop. "These were dead flat rides," he said. "I mean dead flat."

In 1977, when Hampsten was 15, his family went to England for the summer. He began training with a local club in Cambridge and doing time trials. "After England," he said, "I really got the bug." He spent the next summer racing and working in a bike shop in Madison, Wisconsin. "I would get out at 2:30 or 3, and go ride," he said. "I started racing every weekend." It was there, in Madison, that he was exposed to the bike-and-blade culture of the country's vast middle section. "The Midwest was one of the best places to be racing," he remembered. "Heiden was there, and all the speed

Though he hailed from the board-flat North Dakota prairie, Hampsten was a gifted climber, able to initiate breaks and then ride away from the pack.

skaters." More than anything, he found it infectious—an intoxicating mix of athleticism and inspiration. "It was the perfect time to be a teenager and race bikes," he said.

It was also a time when the slightly built Hampsten got his first inkling of his true calling in sport. "Often the guys my age—the juniors—were faster and more clever than I was," he said. "But I was a stronger climber." Indeed, it soon became apparent that he was a kind of athletic expatriate—a rider in search of his preferred terrain. "There were so few races in the mountains," he lamented of the racing at the time.

In 1981, he moved to the budding cycling mecca of Boulder, Colorado, where he could train on the long switchback climbs that suited his physiology. It was also a time when he began to envision an alternative future for himself. Not content with his growing success in America's bigger events, he began to consider other options. "I knew after a year or two of being amateur that I wanted to race international stage races, with the intention of turning pro," he said. "I went to criteriums, and it was great to do well, but it was just a stepping stone. By 19, I already had the idea that I wanted to do mountainous races in Europe."

But how? A European cycling career, at that time, seemed altogether improbable for a solitary American—even one as suited to the task as Hampsten. In the meantime, at the urging of his parents, he had been sporadically attending college, with an eye toward another future altogether. Hampsten came from a distinctly cerebral household. Both of his parents were English professors, and they found his headlong venture into cycling to be occasionally disconcerting. "My parents were hoping I would go back to school," he said. Suddenly, his world seemed to be closing in, and he began to wonder whether his cycling career might simply be reaching its natural conclusion. "My objective that year," he said, "was to make it on a pro team or stop racing."

Meanwhile, he had seen the resounding success of the 7-Elevens on the domestic front. "7-Eleven won all the races," he said, "at least the crits." The squad had undeniable appeal—it was polished, well moneyed, and seemed to be thriving under Ochowicz's steady and determined hand.

Hampsten had been approached to ride for the team in 1980, and again in 1984. But each time, the option held little appeal. "They didn't know whether they were going to go to Europe or just do the criterium circuit in the U.S.," he said. Besides, Hampsten was faithful to his current Levi's-Raleigh team and its director, Michael Fatka.

By 1985, though, things were different. Ochowicz's offer, coming as it did at such an athletic and personal crossroads, had irresistible appeal. Ochowicz was proffering a one-month contract to ride professionally in Europe, at the pinnacle of sport. Conveniently, Hampsten could still ride for Levi's-Raleigh in the United States. It was exactly what Hampsten had been waiting for: a chance to test himself against the best in the world, in the vertiginous landscape he had dreamed of since he was a teenager. It was nothing less than the culmination of a dream.

CHAPTER 13
A Director with Horse Sense

Ochowicz was growing more confident in the athletic composition of his team. In Hampsten, he had his climber; in Phinney, he had the consummate sprinter; and in Kiefel, he had a fast and faithful lieutenant. These were the known quantities, and they could be counted on to produce results.

But he needed something else—a contribution that was not so much physical as emotional and philosophical. For all his European experience, dating back to his youthful skating adventure in Inzell, Ochowicz was in many ways still an innocent abroad. He had no personal experience in the pro peloton and remained chronically challenged by foreign languages.

What he needed was an insider—someone who could gain the confidence of his riders, help them navigate the insular society of pro racing, and speak the gritty dialect of the peloton. He knew his team was a nuclear power plant of testosterone and ambition. Now he needed someone who could corral this energy and apply subtle restraints and direction.

And he needed someone who had paid the requisite debts of pain and perseverance.

o͞o

Ochowicz had known Mike Neel from their days racing together for the Turin bike club out of Chicago. They were frequent partners for Madison racing on the track, and both men were part of the 1976 Olympic cycling team in Montreal. Now retired from racing, Neel had been drifting from one coaching job to the next, selling bike parts on the side.

In many ways, Neel was a world apart from his old racing

Neel (left) and Ochowicz (right) were track racing partners and teammates in the 1976 Olympics. Neel was a natural choice for European team director.

colleague. He was from California, which was inevitably perceived by the Midwest cabal as soft and undisciplined, a place of experimentation and indulgence. While Ochowicz had been pounding out laps on skating ovals and velodromes in Wisconsin, Neel, a self-proclaimed 1960s hippie, was fighting his way through the fog of Berkeley, California, antiwar protests. And if northern California was seen as suspect terrain, Berkeley seemed to be spilling over into anarchy, a bastion of liberalism that could not be more different from the disciplined milieu of the Midwest that had spawned Ochowicz, Heiden, and many of the 7-Elevens.

And if Ochowicz's path forward was linear and purposeful, Neel's was as meandering as a switchback climb. He was one of a handful of riders who made brave journeys to Europe in the early 1970s to try their hands in the professional sport. Culturally, if not athletically, he fit in immediately, proving himself adept at language, moving easily between French and Italian, and eventually securing a place on the Italian Magniflex team. In 1976, he earned perhaps the greatest result of his career, a 10th place in the world professional road championship, held that year on a 288-km course in Ostuni, Italy. "I was the only American, so I didn't have to work for anyone," he said. Instead, he rode his own race, followed wheels when he had to, and, on the sixth lap, briefly took the lead. In a remarkable photo, he can be seen crossing the line just a few bike lengths behind the legendary Eddy Merckx (the event was won by Freddy Maertens).

Neel continued riding through 1980 and even considered himself a candidate for the early incarnation of the 7-Eleven team. But his life was not uncomplicated. He wrestled with a drug problem. Before long his cycling career, his business dealings, and his marriage were in tatters.

He recovered enough to procure a job coaching the 7-Eleven junior team in 1985. Soon after, Ochowicz found himself in need of a director for his grand adventure. "All of a sudden, a space opened up to do the Giro," said Neel. "It was natural. I had coached the national team in Europe. My junior team had done well. I spoke Italian, I had lived there. I knew the ropes."

It soon became apparent that Neel's concept of racing was more artful than scientific. As a teenager he had trained and groomed horses, and to him, racers were just that: thoroughbreds, to be worked, coddled, and occasionally chastised according to their own capabilities and temperaments. "Neel told us what to expect, and how to get our heads into it," said Hampsten. "He was phenomenal."

Michael Aisner, director of the Coors Classic, remembers that Neel was "quiet—he would walk up and whisper and provide inspiration. He had a wonderful way with racers. He could make them perform."

It was an approach that formed a useful contrast to Ochowicz—Sergeant Rock—with Neel placing intuition above hard-edged discipline. As would become clear on the roads of Italy, the fun-loving and slightly naïve 7-Elevens were not like other teams. And Neel, with his colorful and occasionally troubled background, was not like other directors.

Neel's racing experience, coupled with his powers of analysis, brought a new level of strategic intelligence to the team.

○○

While Neel could supply invaluable guidance from the team car, Ochowicz knew that he also needed a voice of experience in the peloton itself, among his riders. For this, he reached out to another freethinking Californian in the twilight of his career, Jonathan Boyer.

By his own admission, Boyer's best years seemed to be behind him. For the last several seasons, he had held tight to the notion that he was one of the world's best cyclists, and in many ways he had been, winning the Coors Classic in 1980, placing 10th in the 1982 world pro road championships, and 12th in the 1983 Tour de France. But in recent years, the sport seemed to have passed him by.

Growing up in the sleepy seaside village of Carmel, California,

Boyer started racing under the tutelage of Remo d'Agliano, an Italian restaurant owner who had been a successful amateur in the 1950s. D'Agliano liked what he saw in the 13-year-old. He seemed "intelligent," d'Agliano thought to himself; Boyer had a good position on the bike, but most importantly, he had the universal quality endemic to successful cyclists, which was that he knew how to suffer.

Pretty soon the pair was traveling to races with their bikes stuffed into d'Agliano's two-door Alfa Romeo. The older man would do the veterans race, and Boyer would race in the seniors. Frequently,

Boyer knew the people and the gritty dialect of the peloton. And he knew how to suffer.

both would win their classes. The ride home was resplendent with success, the Alfa wailing down the back roads, the man and the boy discussing tactics, training, and a day enjoyed in the sun.

Then, in an impetuous move that Boyer still does not completely understand himself, he decided to try his fortune in Europe. He spent the summer of 1973 working in French and Italian restaurants in Carmel, setting aside $350 for a plane ticket to Paris. Before going, he took an intensive French class at the local military language school. A few days after graduating high school, armed with only a plane ticket and the address of d'Agliano's friend in Paris, he set off on an adventure that would dictate the course of his life.

When he landed, he was so tired he collapsed on a lawn, and awoke just in time to see the gendarmes coming at him with a fire hose —they thought he was a transient. For the next several years, he lived the life of an itinerant bike racer, staying in fleabag hotels, jumping from team to team. "At the time I never thought twice about it," said Boyer. "But now I think: I was 17—how did I ever get the idea to do that?"

He adapted quickly, turning pro in 1977 for Lejeune BP. His position—and his attractiveness to teams—was enhanced by the novelty of being an American. It didn't hurt that his language skills were impeccable. "His French was perfect," said d'Agliano. "Like everything, he applied himself until it *was* perfect."

But by 1985, when Boyer was approached by Ochowicz, things had changed. Now a new generation of riders was coming up, achieving what he never thought possible: riding for an American team populated by American riders. Somehow, it didn't seem fair.

No one knew better than Boyer the hardship one could endure as an expatriate cyclist in Europe. The whole premise of his career had been about going overseas, paying dues. Now these young men of privilege were making their own foray to Europe, among their own kind and under the auspices of well-moneyed sponsors.

At the same time, Boyer knew he was the perfect mentor to

shepherd the boys through their grand adventure. Since his days of paying for French lessons in Monterey, he had become a veritable Tower of Babel, moving easily from the gutter French of the peloton to the restaurant parlance of Paris. He knew his way around a pack —when to move up, and when to sit tight. He knew the teams, who was going well, and who was a danger in a sprint. He knew the managers and race directors.

When he looked back at what he had undergone, he was proud of the road he had taken. Still, he did not wish similar hardships on others. "My nature has always been to help people out and not have them go through some of the learning processes I went through," he said. "The garbage of living in Europe—the food, accommodations, language—all that was easy for me."

And so Boyer accepted Ochowicz's offer, not as a contender, but as a mentor to much younger men who might gain glory at his expense.

oo

For all its financial resources, Southland was not willing to go it alone. Now, with the commitment to the Giro, Ochowicz needed a cosponsor, preferably a European one, to augment what the company had so generously supplied. He found one in Hoonved, a maker of industrial washing machines, owned by the charismatic businessman Dell'Oglio.

The sponsorship was as unlikely as the team itself. Neel said that Dell'Oglio tended to "go for oddball teams," a category in which the Americans were eminently qualified. Dell'Oglio, who Kiefel called "a cigar-smoking industrialist," was nonetheless a tremendous boon to the squad, providing a financial and psychological boost for the next five years. Neel said that the sponsorship was "valuable not so much for cash, but for enthusiasm. We got lavish attention. It was a great addition."

The infusion of Dell'Oglilo's money—about $50,000—was

crucial in helping supply the incidentals of a pro team, including transportation, hotels, and vehicles. But even with the added funds, said Ochowicz, "we were stretched as thin as you could get."

Only a few details remained. Ochowicz took care to fill out the team with riders who would furnish the greatest chance of success, including Phinney, Kiefel, Schuler, and Heiden. Now he had the strategic additions of Hampsten and Boyer. He had signed on the promising rider Chris Carmichael (who would, years later, become

Carmichael was one of several key additions that helped strengthen the team for its European foray.

Lance Armstrong's coach) and, through Neel, picked up Bob Roll, an eccentric but hardworking domestique.

In one final gesture of rebellion, Ochowicz hired a female *soigneur* named Shelley Verses. The very idea of a woman participating in that most intimate backroom ritual, during which towels can so readily drop from undressed men, was enough to send shock waves through the European cycling establishment.

It was becoming increasingly apparent that Ochowicz and his charges represented not just a new nationality, but a new culture of sport. They were strangers in a strange land. In a matter of weeks, his improbable, ragtag collection of racers would be toeing the line in Verona, Italy, for the greatest test of their athletic careers.

Thumbing his nose at tradition, Ochowicz hired Shelley Verses as the team's soigneur, shocking the Euro purists.

CHAPTER 14
The Kid from North Dakota

Ochowicz's stated goals for the team were to win a stage and get a rider in the top 20. But while the riders had grown in ability, organization, and sophistication, their reception in Europe was tepid at best. In part, they were victims of a previous American disaster. The year before, in 1984, pioneering pro John Eustice had fielded an American team in the Giro, with lackluster results. When the 7-Elevens showed up 12 months later, brimming with ambition, "the Italians were skeptical," said Kiefel with typical understatement.

The team's spirits were briefly buoyed in the opening stage when Phinney was 4th in a sprint finish. Then, just two days later, Hampsten attacked in the mountains, at one point gaining 30 seconds. As he crested the climb, it seemed he was observing himself from afar, a participant in a life he had only dreamed of. "When I went over the top, there were four ahead of me," he said, "LeMond, Hinault, Saronni, and Moser. It was weird to hear those four names announced, and then my own." Though the group was eventually reeled in, for Hampsten, the experience provided a tantalizing glimpse of what was possible. "It was my one shot to prove myself to the Europeans," he said, feeling philosophical. "It's a big trip, and there was no guarantee you would be invited back. So I tried to make the most of it."

Unfortunately, things soon turned calamitous. The next day began with slanting rain. Phinney's big toes had somehow become swollen and infected, requiring that pieces of his shoes be cut away. He almost didn't start. Even worse, the entire team was in declining health, with colds and bronchitis. Hampsten, spent from his effort the previous day, lost nine minutes and collapsed at the finish. If that weren't enough, a team car wouldn't start and had to be pushed.

In the United States, the squad had become accustomed to

quick and abundant wins. But, at the Giro, it was quite clear that things had changed. "In Europe, we were back at the bottom of the heap," said Schuler. Kiefel remembers that the races would typically start at a tourist's pace. At first, it seemed easy. The boys would just roll along and "eat a bunch of panini"—crude, doughy sandwiches that were the homemade predecessors to today's energy bars. Then, suddenly, the media helicopters would arrive, heralding the start of the real racing, as each team vied to get its jersey at the front of the pack where it would be seen by the cameras. "It would go from 30 kph to 50 kph," said Kiefel. "It would open up—it was so chaotic and painful. People would crash; there would just be this mountain of bikes."

Success in the U.S. did not prepare the team for the length of races in Europe. The 7-Elevens found themselves wondering whether they could keep up. Heiden pictured.

By the time the rest day arrived, the team was suffering from three colds, two cases of bronchitis, infected toes, and one broken collarbone (Bradley). At one point, even Neel, exhausted from all his ministrations, passed out.

By the second week, "we were pretty demoralized," said Kiefel, woefully.

∞

The European peloton is a cloistered society, steeped in tradition, infused with rites of passage and built on debts of pain and perseverance. From the perspective of the other teams, the 7-Elevens had paid no such debts, and as a result they were not very welcome. No sooner had the race gotten under way than they were demonized as crashers. "Whenever there was a shift in the peloton, or someone rubbed tires, Americans were always blamed," said Bradley.

At one point, another team director went so far as to chastise Ochowicz for his riders' etiquette—or lack of same—in the peloton. In the third stage, Phinney looked poised for a win, when an Italian rider tried to go between the American and the race fencing, crashing hard. The Italian's manager publicly accused Phinney of "hooking, attempted manslaughter, and just about everything else," according to *VeloNews*. Even the press gleefully joined in the condemnation before the stage winner, Saronni, said that this was ridiculous, and the affair was put to rest.

At times the antipathy was blatant and even dangerous. In one stage, Italian Roberto Conti grabbed Kiefel's brake cables, which has the same effect as someone steering your bike out from underneath you. "That's the most helpless feeling," said Kiefel, who miraculously stayed upright.

As the broadsides continued, Neel encouraged his riders to respond in kind to any transgressions. "To hell with them," he told his riders. He figured that Phinney, never one to be tangled with in a sprint, was more than capable of handling himself. "You're not going to shove around a Davis Phinney," he crowed. "Our guys weren't going to have it." Schuler took the mission as his own. When someone accused him of riding erratically, "I just turned and started screaming, 'Right now, let's go!' That was it—I didn't hear from him again. One by one, we earned their respect."

But if the team failed to be intimidated, it was at least in part owing to a state of blissful naïveté. Earlier that season Kiefel found himself jostling and bumping handlebars with "a little French guy." Not one to be easily unsettled, he pushed the rider back. It was only later that someone identified the offender as the unofficial boss of the peloton, Bernard Hinault. "I had no clue," said Kiefel.

Indeed, were it not for an element of obliviousness, the enormity of their task might have been overwhelming. "It was good not to be starstruck," said Kiefel. Instead, the team went blithely about

The team (here with American Alexi Grewal in his Panasonic-Raleigh kit) met a cold reception in Europe, in more ways than one.

its business, tilting against the European cycling establishment, threatening to topple it.

○○

Some of the team's behavior was deliberately contrary—Kiefel called it being "anti-Europe." They ate Mexican food at the team table, rather than the traditional pasta. Even worse, Boyer was a vegetarian, which the Italians regarded as tantamount to insanity for a calorie-starved bike rider doing 100-plus miles per day. Even their personal habits were different. Kiefel remembers that American team members didn't don their cycling shorts at the hotel each morning—they would wait until they got to the race. Meanwhile, the Italians would wear their cycling kit from the moment they rose in the morning. "We thought that was ludicrous," said Kiefel. At press functions, the 7-Elevens would dress in shorts and T-shirts, while the impeccable Italians wore matching team clothes.

Some of the criticism was warranted and even self-inflicted. En route to races, and despite Neel's considerable language skills, the team would routinely get lost and end up careening through the streets and driving on sidewalks in order to make it to the start on time. Some riders would arrive carsick from the madness. It all contributed to the general notion that the Americans were a little wacky. "They thought we were nuts," said Kiefel flatly.

Neel, who had ridden under similar conditions as an American interloper in the early 1970s, seemed to relish the way his boys were undermining the European hegemony. "We had a female *soigneur*. We played loud music. We ate Mexican food. We did things our way," he said. Roll, rapidly emerging as the team clown, delighted in the whole imbroglio, and began telling the press that the boys were Indians, living in tepees along the roadways.

○○

By the second week, the race seemed to be spinning out of control, an ongoing nightmare of crashes and illness, made even worse by an aura of thinly veiled disdain toward the American rookies. So before stage 15, a difficult, 203-km march to Perugia, Neel issued a mandate. He felt sure that a big break was going to occur and "no matter what," threatened Neel, the boys "were not to miss it." True to Neel's prediction, a big breakaway escaped halfway through the race. And true to his fears, the 7-Elevens missed it.

Neel was generally a calm and reasoned presence, but when he felt he was not being heeded, he could summon considerable vitriol. This was such a circumstance. He came alongside in the team car and, using some graphically precise language, exhorted them to chase. They dutifully nodded. But once Neel was out of earshot, the boys agreed that the very idea of chasing down such a powerful break was "crazy," according to Kiefel.

Fortunately, Moser, the previous year's overall winner, was also in the chase group, commanding it forward in his autocratic style. The 7-Elevens latched on, becoming the beneficiaries of this Italian march to the front.

Kiefel, riding securely in the pack, had just one job: to protect his team leader, Hampsten, keeping him out of the wind and near the front, where the risk of a crash was minimal. So when the group finally caught and reabsorbed the breakaway, Kiefel sat up in relief, his job done. But a moment later, several riders attacked, and Kiefel found himself among them.

The small group soon turned mutinous, attacking each other, one after another: first Marino Lejarreta, a Spanish veteran who had won the Tour of Spain in 1982; and then Acacio Da Silva, a young Portuguese pro with a few wins to his name. "I thought, crap!" said a reluctant Kiefel. "It's my turn to attack."

Anonymity has its benefits, and at that moment, no one considered Kiefel to be a serious threat. "When I went, they were thinking, 'Who the hell is this American guy?' And they sat up."

Kiefel caught the one rider remaining off the front, former world road champion Gerrie Knetteman, who promptly jumped on his wheel. "I told him to pull through, and he gave me the international 'no' sign—a head nod," said Kiefel. "We turned onto a big boulevard, all dusty. I just started to pull. I kept waiting for him to come around." But no one—not Knetteman or anyone else—was coming around that day. "As I hit the finish line, all these flashbulbs were going off," said Kiefel. "There is a great picture of me going, 'Huh?'" He had won by a scant two seconds.

It was classic Kiefel—an understated victory that was, to all around him, an astounding display of pure talent and speed. Hampsten called the stage win "amazing. When everyone was going as fast as they could—in the final kilometers into Perugia, where all the Italians knew the finish—he dropped them all like a stone."

The day after his stage win in Perugia, Kiefel reads about his exploits in La Gazzetta dello Sport. *Left to right: Kiefel, Schuler, Carmichael (hidden), Heiden, Roll, Hampsten, Phinney, Boyer (back to camera).*

But it was more than just a stage win. For Kiefel, for Ochowicz, and for the entire, audacious adventure, their place in the peloton was forever changed that day. The win signaled, in one small but significant way, that the Americans had arrived. Even the self-effacing Kiefel seemed to recognize the magnitude of his breakthrough victory. "It was a big celebration, we had wine, and morale went way up," he said. "The difference was night and day. All of a sudden, we were invited to participate at the front. The Americans weren't schlocks anymore."

$\overline{oo}$

Despite such flashes of brilliance, evenings in the hotel still resembled a hospital ward, with riders wheezing, nursing wounds, and flirting with collapse. "I remember one day in the middle, I could barely get going," said Hampsten. Seeing this situation, Dell'Oglio, the team's omniscient benefactor, began insisting that Ochowicz needed a team doctor to help bring the boys back from their moribund state.

But medicine and science were not an easy sell in the 7-Eleven camp. In the early days the team had rebelled against "scientific" training of any sort. Consecutive, 600-mile weeks had been the foundation of their joyously uncomplicated regimen. If you had a cold, you took a couple of aspirin and rode through it. If you crashed, you got back on your bike and picked the gravel out of your wounds later. "What do we need a doctor for?" asked Ochowicz.

In the end, though, Dell'Oglio prevailed, using his connections to procure two doctors for the team, including a precocious and recently minted physician by the name of Massimo Testa. "He looked like he was about 12 years old," said Ochowicz. Initially, Testa was to have been overseen by the more experienced doctor. But the older man, evidently bored with the upstart Americans, summarily left the race, leaving the relatively green Testa in charge of matters. "Basically, I pulled the short straw," said Testa of his newfound position.

He was soon pressed into service. Hampsten had been throwing up and had diarrhea. Testa proposed an IV of simple electrolytes. But Hampsten, ever the purist, was having none of it. "Needles don't grow on trees," he scoffed, spurning any potions he suspected might contain unnatural ingredients.

If Neel was the team's horse trainer, guided by intuition and feeling, Testa was the antithesis, a rigorous disciple of science. He likened athletes to specimens, and the racecourse to a laboratory. Using all of his powers of scholarly persuasion, Testa patiently went to work on Hampsten to convince him of the legitimacy of the IV. "We had to speak to him for an hour," said Neel. "The guy was as pure as the driven snow." Eventually, Testa was able to administer the medicine, showing every vial to Hampsten along the way, ensuring him that there were no mystery substances. The next day, Hampsten finished in the same group as LeMond and Hinault, feeling refreshed and recovered.

With that one episode, Testa passed into the inner circle, as a doctor and a confidant. No longer "Massimo," he was now "Max" to the boys and welcomed without reservation. "After that, and throughout my career, I always worked with Testa," said Hampsten.

But one small matter remained: Testa's mentor, the older physician, had by now returned to the race. Testa, figuring he was about to be upstaged, prepared to leave and go back to his university to continue his medical studies. He went to say good-bye to his charges, many of whom had benefited from his ministrations. But they balked.

"We said, 'Forget it, we want you!'" said Hampsten. It was all the prodding Testa needed. He remained with the team, as its physician and trainer, throughout its history.

o͞o

At the urging of sponsor Dell'Oglio, Dr. Massimo Testa was brought into the fold as the team medic. Max, as he was immediately nicknamed, stayed with the team for the next five years.

Thanks to Testa's careful doctoring, Hampsten had been steadily gaining strength, so much so that he'd begun making noise about attacking. "I was starting to do really well in the mountains the final week," he said. "I had worked all my life to be here. So I thought, 'What the heck—I'll attack.'"

Initially, he targeted the mountainous 19th stage. But Neel had a plan: Hampsten should save himself, continue to rebuild his strength, and attack in the 20th stage, to the summit of Gran Paradiso.

Neel summoned his horse sense to further bolster Hampsten's confidence. As Neel saw it, his job was to take riders outside their comfort zones, persuading them, calmly and assuredly, to do the thing they could not imagine for themselves. "A lot of times that is your role—to convince people of their own ability," Neel said. "I told Andy, 'You can win. Every time there is a selection, you're in the first group. You're the best climber—you just don't know it. If you don't look back, and you go as hard as you can, you will win.'"

Most of all, he told Hampsten, he needed to attack early, at the foot of the climb.

"But I never do that," Hampsten complained.

"I know," said Neel. "That's exactly why you have to do it now." It was a short stage—just 58 km, or 36 miles—and it started late, providing an opportunity to ride the course in the morning and perform some reconnaissance. Boyer, who would so often counsel Hampsten in his early years as a pro, accompanied him on the morning ride, while Neel proffered advice from the team car.

Neel picked a spot, about a kilometer from the base of the climb, at a sharp bend. "He's giving me a big talk," said Hampsten. "'You should attack right here.' I looked at the curve and said, 'Okay, I will.'" To further eliminate any confusion, they also noted a building with some writing on the wall as a landmark.

While everyone else rode Murray bicycles in the familiar red, white, and green livery, Hampsten rode a Raleigh, indisputable evidence of his split allegiance. (His domestic sponsor was still Levi's-Raleigh.) His bike was prepared time-trial fashion, with superlight wheels and just one bottle cage to shave valuable grams. He also wore a one-piece skinsuit. To the tradition-bound European teams, this getup was further evidence of the Americans' contrary nature. "Some Europeans were laughing at me for wearing a one-piece in a road stage, where you would normally always wear a jersey," said Hampsten.

For a moment, things seemed to be going awry, when LeMond attacked before the climb. But Hampsten, showing newfound maturity, waited calmly for the field to bring LeMond back. Then, at the designated spot, Hampsten put his plan into action. "It was the perfect moment," he said. "I made a really solid attack—100 percent."

Neel, behind in the team car, remembers a report crackling over race radio: "It's unbelievable—this little climber is going off like a rocket." Kiefel, riding in the field, recalled the team cars going by him, and Neel yelling out the window, "Andy is off the front!"

With each pedal stroke, Hampsten could feel his strength growing. It was as if a door had opened on the switchbacks of the Gran Paradiso, and he was passing through it, a portal to everything he had worked toward and dreamed of since he was a precocious junior. "I was

Hampsten became a star, changing the whole team for the better.

hearing voices saying, 'You can't do this, you're just a kid from North Dakota.' But I just opened it up the whole way. It was beautiful."

He won by a minute. A picture shows the boyish Hampsten, riding with arms upraised across the finish. His expression was one of joy, but also of unabashed surprise, as if it couldn't possibly have been that easy.

To everyone, on that day, it seemed a star had been born. "It was really fun," Hampsten said, "my favorite victory ever. From that point on, it buried any doubt as to whether I was good enough to do all the things I was thinking about for the last five years. I never had an easy time as a pro, but that gave me confidence that if I stick to my plan and give it everything, then I can do well."

Kiefel, who crossed the line minutes later, looked up to see Hampsten on the podium like an apparition. All he could think of was that things were about to change for the team, for the better.

oo

The 7-Elevens had met their goals in spectacular fashion—but they were not done yet. Heiden, who never figured prominently in the squad's aspirations—other than as a superdomestique and publicity magnet—found himself in close contention for the InterGiro, a midrace sprint competition.

Heiden was a source of perverse fascination for the Europeans. Everyone had heard of the cycling Schwarzenegger, based on his exploits in Lake Placid, and they were happy to have him in the peloton. Legendary rider Urs Frueler had even taken Heiden under his wing, teaching him the finer points of sprinting in the big show.

Befitting his imposing stature, Heiden's riding style lacked all subtlety. Hampsten remembers the team making elaborate plans to lead the big man out, but Heiden had his own idea of how a sprint should be conducted. He would simply launch an all-out effort with 500 meters to go, a distance he may have likened to a lap of the track or a skating oval. It proved remarkably effective, and Hampsten recalls that by the end of the race, Heiden trailed the sprint competition by a few scant points to a 27-year-old Swiss rider, Robert Dill-Bundi.

Neel, ever the strategist, had an elaborate plan to capture the title once and for all. Because the peloton was by now familiar with Heiden's trademark 500 m sprint, Neel cautioned him against using it on the final day—they would be waiting for him. "No matter what," he told the big man, "don't attack in the final kilometer, because they'll be ready for you."

Toward the end of the race, the Malvor team was leading out their man, Dill-Bundi. Aware of the unfolding drama, 7-Eleven was intending to do the same for Heiden. But he was nowhere to be found. "He was the biggest guy in the peloton," said Hampsten. "Where's Eric? We thought maybe he stopped for ice cream or something."

Suddenly, as they passed under the 1-km banner, there was Heiden, streaking through in anger, ignoring Neel's advice, and using the same tactic that had served him so well throughout the race.

He won the sprint, and with it, the InterGiro competition.

"It was brilliant," said Hampsten.

$$\overline{oo}$$

Heiden's victory was a fitting capstone to a spectacular race, conducted in trademark 7-Eleven style, with ample missteps, punctuated by spectacular successes. The team hadn't just won two stages: They had won two stages at the end of the race, which to Kiefel signified their growing strength and recuperative powers.

"There are Italian teams that don't win stages for five years," Kiefel gloated. What's more, Hampsten had squeaked into the top 20 overall on the final day.

Ochowicz's joy was so abundant that he felt compelled to smoke a cigar in celebration. "He was ecstatic," said Hampsten. "He had taken the criterium boys to Europe."

CHAPTER 15
From First to Worst

With the team's successful foray into the 1985 Giro in the books, Ochowicz began laying out a plan to achieve the biggest coup of his young career. Brimming with confidence in his riders, his organization, and his support from Southland, he plotted his team's entry into nothing less than *la grande boucle* itself—the 1986 Tour de France. Heiden remembers the idea burning like an ember in his old friend. "Och had big aspirations," he said. "He wanted to take an American team to the Tour."

But from the outset, 1986 would proceed in typical 7-Eleven fashion—unimaginable glories accompanied by unthinkable disasters. In the early spring, the team departed for Europe to gain some pro racing experience and toughen themselves for the travails ahead. But they soon discovered the challenges of an expatriate lifestyle. Unlike other, more established teams, they didn't have a home base. "We were living basically in a brothel in Ghent," said

1986 would bring highs and lows. Assembled for Paris-Nice, from left: Boyer, Carmichael, Heiden, Kiefel, Phinney, Roll, Shapiro, Stieda, Grewal.

team member Alex Stieda. "You could rent it by the hour. There were mirrors on the ceiling. We were the laughing stock of the peloton."

A major part of the team's preparation was to have been the three-week Tour of Spain, or Vuelta a España, in those days held in late April. As the team began to assemble for the race, Ochowicz got a call from the U.S. State Department. President Reagan had decided to bomb Libya, and for safety reasons, all U.S. citizens were to leave the country immediately. "There was all this preparation, then nothing," said Stieda. "We had a huge party, went to the airport, and flew back." Faced with the urgent need to continue preparation for the Tour, the team had to fabricate suitable replacements. "We came back, did Redlands [a small stage race in California]—anything to prepare for the Tour," said team member Chris Carmichael. American races in general were woefully short compared with the daily race distances of the big European tours. It was a struggle just to get in enough miles. "If we could race past 200K and still feel good, that was magical—a sign of not being amateur," said Stieda.

While their training proceeded in its own haphazard way, an even bigger problem loomed: The team still had not been formally invited to the Tour. A year earlier, Dell'Oglio had arranged for Ochowicz to speak with Tour director Félix Lévitan for 15 minutes, which was tantamount to an audience with the Pope. But in the intervening months, no invitation had been forthcoming. After considerable lobbying, and with a scant two weeks to go, the 7-Elevens were added to the roster—the first American-based team in the 83-year history of the race.

Ochowicz launched into a flurry of logistical activity. To bolster his team lineup, he had added riders with European experience, including Americans Alexi Grewal and Doug Shapiro, and Raúl Alcalá, a promising competitor from Monterrey, Mexico. He attended to a hundred additional details, sorting travel, staff, and logistics. As the race start date loomed, he even found himself silk-

Alcalá, from Monterrey, Mexico, signed on for 1986 and immediately added more climbing strength to the team.

screening jerseys with the 7-Eleven logo on the Descente assembly line in Switzerland and then hauling the boxes to Paris for the start.

It was, from everyone's perspective, a characteristic leap into the unknown. Whatever the 7-Elevens lacked in preparation, they would, in typical fashion, make up for with enthusiasm.

For the team's historic debut, they had chosen one of the longer Tours at 23 stages and more than 4,000 kilometers (almost 2,500 miles). It was also to be one of the biggest, with 21 teams of 10 riders each. Of these, the very last *dossard*—number 210—would be affixed to the jersey of the eager and effervescent Canadian, Stieda.

∞

Stieda was one in a continuing series of Canadian riders who would be so important to the squad throughout its history. He grew up in Vancouver, British Columbia, where he'd ridden with Ron Hayman, a member of the original team. Together, they experienced the joyous and uncomplicated lives of young bike racers. For a while, the pair were part of a team sponsored by Roto-Rooter, an arrangement that had the further benefit of allowing them to earn money as plumbers in the winter.

After years on the Canadian national team, primarily as a track rider, Stieda was approached by Ochowicz in 1981. He found the irreverent and fun-loving 7-Elevens immediately to his liking. In his first race, in New York City, he remembered "driving the team van in Manhattan, shooting bottle rockets out the window on Fifth Avenue. I thought, if this is what it's all about, this is cool. . . . It was a whole side of cycling I'd not seen before."

For Stieda, the team's carefree attitude was equally applicable to the Tour of Texas or the Tour de France. On the morning of the prologue time trial, held in the southwestern Paris suburb of Boulogne-Billancourt, he relaxed by playing the harmonica and being a tourist. Armed with a camera in his back pocket, he took pictures of the Eiffel Tower and other landmarks.

"It was my first time at the Tour," he said. "There I was, in the heart of Paris. I thought, 'I'm going to stop and enjoy this.'"

He could not possibly have known what the next 24 hours would bring.

∞

With this wide-eyed perspective, and wearing his caboose number 210, Stieda warmed up on the circuit and noticed that it had "four corners, like a criterium course." At just 4.6 kilometers—less than 3 miles— the race would take a little more than five minutes, an elapsed time strikingly similar to the duration of an individual pursuit on the track, his specialty. It all seemed surprisingly familiar, and he felt his confidence growing.

Ironically, as the last numbered rider, he started first. That morning, Shelley Verses, the team's *soigneur*, had bleached several riders' hair blond, including Stieda's. Helmetless and looking all the world like a California surfer, he proceeded to scorch the course, finishing in just 5 minutes and 33 seconds.

"I had given it everything," he said. "I knew I had done the best I could have."

As the first rider, his name went immediately to the top of the leader board. Defying belief, it stayed there a surprisingly long time. Rider after rider completed the course, and tick, tick, Stieda's 5:33 clung to the top row. Eventually, some of the strongest teams' top riders recorded better times, but when the final results were in, Stieda had not only done the fastest time on the 7-Eleven team, but his name stood 21st overall in the race's daily general classification, or G.C. It was a remarkably high placing, and that night, as Stieda celebrated his race, he quietly began to think about ways to defend it.

o͞o

The next morning's race, at just 85 kilometers, or 53 miles, also had a familiar feel. "I thought, it's 85K, which was as far as any crit I'd done," said Stieda. "And there were time bonuses along the way. It was a classic North American-style race; just get away and get primes."

And since it all felt familiar, he decided to use familiar armaments. "I showed up at the starting line with what I needed to carry for 85K," he said. "Just a couple of water bottles." He also wore a one-piece skinsuit—clothing that, at the time, was considered heresy in the tradition-bound European peloton, where everyone wore full jerseys with pockets in the back for food and extra clothing. Phinney, ever conscious of the team's reputation, was sufficiently embarrassed that he put some space between himself and his teammate at the starting line.

Once under way, Stieda noticed that the "peloton was going slow, just watching each other and cruising." Armed with the confidence of his previous day's success, he began to hatch a plan. "Maybe I could just go up the road and they wouldn't chase," he thought. "Some guys ride up the road to pee, and they let them go. I thought, 'Hey, I'll do that.'"

At 22 kilometers, Stieda made his move. Carmichael remembers looking over and seeing him "attacking, wearing a skinsuit, with his hat turned the other way. Everyone is looking over, wondering, 'Who is that guy? Is he even in the race?'"

Indeed, Stieda saw his move as clandestine. "I just stayed in the saddle and went as hard as I could. If you had seen me from behind, you wouldn't think I was accelerating." Of course, he had one other great advantage, which was that no one was inclined to take a North American rider seriously in the world's most prestigious bike race. "They thought we were all American jokers," said Stieda. "I was out of sight, out of mind. Pretty soon I had three minutes, four minutes, five minutes."

Along the way there were several sprints for time bonuses. Stieda won each of them in turn, riding alone, subtracting a critical 36 seconds from his overall time.

Back in the field, the 7-Elevens found Stieda's escapade to be mildly entertaining and a positive start to their first Tour. But gradually, there was a collective epiphany. At one point Pierce turned to Heiden and said, "You know, if Alex stays out there for two or three more sprints, he stands a chance of getting the jersey, because he had a pretty good time trial. He's pretty far up there."

The very notion that a North American rider in the first full day of his first Tour de France could garner cycling's highest honor seemed entirely implausible—if not laughable.

"Eric looked at me and said, '*Yeah, right. . . .*'"

oo

Ochowicz, of course, immediately saw the developing possibilities. To get the race lead, he reasoned, "You have to do a good prologue. Then you have to have the opportunity to get a little time. If the combination works out, you get the jersey." And that's exactly what Stieda's escapade was leading to.

Meanwhile, Stieda was "burying himself," in his words, to stay off the front. Eventually, he was caught by a small group, including Australian star Phil Anderson. "He was a guy we looked up to, as someone who had broken through—an English-speaking guy," said Stieda. "He said, 'Alex, you're in the jersey.'" At that moment, the possibility of the *maillot jaune* was less consequential than the fact that "Phil Anderson was actually talking to me," said Stieda.

At the finish, Stieda was 5th out of a six-rider breakaway. "I remember just crossing the line and looking back, and there was the main field, just going full bore, a wall of riders, eight lanes wide."

In that moment, he became the first North American in history to possess the leader's yellow jersey in the Tour. His overall margin: just eight seconds.

oo

Throughout the stage, Stieda had given little thought to the fact that, in less than three hours, the squad would be toeing the line for the 56K team time trial. It was a rarity for the Tour—a two-stage day.

Stieda needed rest. But first, there was the traditional pomp and circumstance afforded to the leader of the Tour. Clearly, his overall time had earned him the yellow leader's jersey. What he did not know was that, by virtue of his bonus points throughout the stage, he was also the owner of the red jersey (for "Catch Sprints"), the white jersey (best newcomer), the polka-dot jersey (best climber), and the combination jersey (for standings in all categories, a jersey discontinued in 1989 and no longer awarded). For each, he ascended the podium and in turn donned the ceremonial jersey, was handed flowers, and was kissed by trophy girls. After each one, Stieda kept thinking, "They've run out of jerseys." Finally, it was time for yellow. As he dragged himself to the podium one final time, he was so tired that a photographer had to remind him to smile. "I was elated, but I was so exhausted," he said.

Stieda (left) with Ochowicz (right) on the podium, won five Tour de France jerseys in one day.

Elated but apprehensive, Stieda had to be reminded to smile. His concern proved well founded.

In those days, Tour riders did not enjoy the sanctuary of luxury hotels or motor homes. Instead, the peloton retired en masse to a local school, where they lay down on cots in an austere gymnasium. For Stieda, it was a fitful sleep, his mind racing with thoughts of the afternoon's stage.

"I had put out so much," he said. "I didn't realize how depleted I was." He was about to find out.

oo

The 7-Elevens had the thing they wanted most in the world—a prize emblematic of the pinnacle of the sport. It had been an unbelievable stroke of luck. And now, it would prove their undoing.

The team time trial is one of the most technical disciplines in cycling, with riders at the thin edge of exhaustion, arrayed nose to tail and striving to stay within inches of each other to ensure maximum draft. While many on the team were experienced in the discipline (Phinney and Kiefel had won an Olympic medal in the event in 1984), none of them had done a 10-man version, where the need for precision—and the risks of a crash—are exponentially greater. And, unlike more experienced teams, they had not pre-ridden the course. "We could have been better prepared," said Ochowicz in a remarkable understatement. Stieda was even more succinct. "We had no idea what we were doing."

As the team of the yellow jersey, the 7-Elevens started last. Just a day earlier, they had been nobodies. Now they were the toast of the cycling world. "It was heady stuff, with motorcycles all over the place and helicopters overhead," said Phinney.

At 18 kilometers, Phinney, following a lead motorcycle, led the hard-charging group into a downhill corner. What he didn't know was that there was a traffic island just around the bend. Kiefel remembers thinking that Phinney was "going way too fast. He was amped and excited." The first few riders made it through safely, but others, farther back, weren't so lucky. The unsuspecting Heiden was first to pile into the median. In an instant, riders and bikes were scattered like a yard sale.

From there, things went from bad to worse. Doug Shapiro, an experienced American rider who had won the 1984 Coors Classic and been brought onto the team by Ochowicz in 1986, was oblivious to the carnage behind. "He kept sprinting up the hill, thinking the rest of the team is on his wheel," said Kiefel. While team mechanic Richie Gilstrap was attending to broken bikes, the leading riders had to make a decision: Should they keep going, or wait for the rest of the team to catch up? "It was complete disarray," said Phinney. "We're just arguing among ourselves. That was going to be indicative of the day—it went from bad to worse as the race went on. Tempers started to flare."

Once back in formation, they found themselves in an open

Winner of the 1984 Coors Classic and key member of the Dutch Kwantum team in 1985, Shapiro brought domestic and European experience.

area with a strong crosswind, where it was critical to draft and maintain a close following distance. At one point, new team member Alexi Grewal, gold medal winner in the 1984 Olympic road race, went to the front. What happened next is subject to dispute—according to different accounts, he was either pedaling roughly, failed to position himself for optimum draft, or both. Whatever the case, Grewal and Shapiro were suddenly engaged in a shouting match at 30 mph. In the next instant, "Shapiro takes a bottle and wings it at Alexi's head," said Kiefel.

It had taken only a few hours for the 7-Elevens to resume their accustomed position as the comedic element of the peloton. Even worse, said Kiefel, "it was all on French TV."

∞

No sooner had the team assembled itself for the second time, than another, more serious problem was revealed—Stieda, in all the excitement, had forgotten to eat lunch. Spent from his effort that morning, the awards marathon, and the scrutiny of the world's cycling press, he began to unravel. "Alex was gassed," said Ochowicz.

The usual tactic in these circumstances is for the exhausted rider to drift to the back and enjoy a draft, leaving the bulk of the work to his teammates. But for Stieda, even this proved impossible. "With 15 or 20 kilometers to go, my legs are starting to go," he said. "I just can't hold the wheel in front. I'm getting gapped more, and digging in to get over the hills."

Seeing the impending embarrassment of the yellow jersey being dropped, Neel instructed the group to ease up. But even after slowing, "Alex just couldn't do it," said Pierce. The risk was not just that Stieda would lose precious minutes, but that he might finish outside the time limit and be eliminated from the race entirely. If that weren't bad enough, Heiden, Kiefel, and Alcalá all punctured.

While Stieda continued his trip through purgatory, the time check was getting worse for everyone. It wasn't just Stieda's fate that hung in the balance; if the team stayed with him, they might all be eliminated. (The rules stipulated that riders must finish within a percentage of the stage winner's time.) Seeing the impending disaster, Neel asked Carmichael and Pierce to drop back and provide an escort for the exhausted Stieda, allowing the others to ride ahead.

In the end the three were able to nurse each other to the line. Stieda, having lost the yellow jersey, just made the time limit. The team finished in 19th, tied for second to last. Suffering the ultimate

With 15 km to go in the afternoon time trial, Stieda had bonked and was in danger of elimination. But Carmichael and Pierce brought him in on time.

indignity, Kiefel noted that only the Colombians—never known for their time-trialing prowess—were slower. Stieda had been in the yellow jersey for a little more than three hours. To many, it had been the quintessential 7-Eleven experience: lofty heights, quickly followed by towering ineptitude and miscalculations. The whole thing was fantastic fodder for anyone wanting to resurrect the old charges of American incompetence.

One journalist had the audacity—or simply the candor—to ask if they had ever done a team time trial before. "I was so mad that I just gave him the cold shoulder," said a disgruntled Phinney. "But actually, we couldn't have done any worse if we'd tried. On the first day of the Tour, we go from having yellow, and everyone talking about us, to going to last place, with everyone laughing at us."

It was, said Stieda, "the worst thing we'd ever done." But the race wasn't over yet.

Stieda (right) with Ochowicz (left), made a sweep of the Tour de France's jerseys in one morning and lost them all in one afternoon.

As much as anyone, Phinney carried the mantle of the team. Having suffered the indignity of the previous day's race, he now set about resurrecting their reputation in the eyes of the peloton and the public.

The third stage, at 214 kilometers, or 133 miles, was the team's first experience with a lengthy road race in the Tour. They found it daunting—a quantum leap in intensity and competitiveness compared with anything they had experienced in the United States. It was a Darwinian atmosphere in which a breakaway, even if ill-fated, could justify a year's salary, and all manner of risks were taken for a moment in the sun. Just maintaining a position in the field was a never-ending dogfight. "There's so much tension in the race," Phinney moaned. "There's all this humanity on bikes, trying to squeeze in, and it makes it very hard to keep your place." He found he was "fighting, fighting, fighting." But for what? "You'd finally get to the front, and in a minute, you'd be at the back of the peloton again."

At one of these disheartening moments, another rider, Robert Dill-Bundi, came flying past. Seeing an opportunity to advance, Phinney thought, "Sweet—I'll just get on his wheel and take it to the front." But Dill-Bundi had other, more grandiose plans than merely moving up in the field. "He gets to the front, and doesn't pull off—he just puts it in a larger gear and keeps cranking," said Phinney, who had every intention of capitalizing on Dill-Bundi's unintentional gift. "All of a sudden, in short order, I've gone from the back to a breakaway."

At an intermediate sprint, Phinney accelerated to test himself. His spirits soared when he discovered that he was "easily the fastest guy in the group." He began optimistically plotting for the finish.

Just then, a Spanish rider attacked and managed to establish a gap. In that moment, Phinney's hope for a stage win seemed to evaporate. "All of a sudden, the whole mentality changed," he said. "I thought, 'Oh, I guess we're racing for second.'"

As he had predicted, Phinney easily won the bunch sprint. "I was so totally relaxed because we were only racing for second," he said. "I just chilled." From his perspective it had been a nice confidence builder—2nd place in his first Tour de France road stage.

What he didn't realize was that the Spanish rider who had gone off the front had punctured. Phinney and his breakaway companions had passed him on the roadside without realizing it.

"Right as I came across the line, [journalist] John Wilcockson said, 'You won! That was incredible!' I said, 'Yeah, I won the group sprint for second.' He said, 'No, you *won!*'"

It was a consummation of all Phinney had worked for. Ochowicz, beaming, called it "a great win—the beginning of the second phase of his career—his first real international win. That's a credential you can hang your hat on the rest of your life: a stage win in the Tour de France." But it was more than that. It had been, in the pantheon of the team's accomplishments, a miraculous three-day adventure. They had soared, fallen to the ground, and soared again. "It was maximum glory and maximum embarrassment," said Phinney. "We had the Europeans just shaking their heads."

o͞o

Thanks to Phinney's stage win, Ochowicz was once again holding his head high in the face of skeptics and detractors. Feeling magnanimous, he decided that his band of expatriates needed a dose of Americana to serve as motivation for the road ahead, in the form of some artery-choking junk food. "The first thing I did was to go to McDonald's and get a big sack of French fries, burgers, and milk shakes," he said. "I went around to all their rooms. They loved it."

And they needed fortification. The papers were calling the race the "tour of crashes"—and, unfortunately, many of them involved the 7-Elevens. Heiden and Pierce both required stitches from their get-offs in the team time trial. After his earlier glories, Phinney crashed heavily in stage 15 and was forced to withdraw with a wrist injury. In a dramatic televised moment, he was shown reclined in an ambulance, anguished over the indignity of having to abandon. "All I want to do right now is finish," he said tearfully.

Heiden, a source of all good things for the team, fell on a descent in stage 18, resulting in a concussion and hallucinations. For a moment he lay on the ground, inert and bleeding. TV footage shows Ochowicz looking on, not with the concern of a team director, but with the raw emotion that a father would exhibit toward a son. "It was, for all of us, a frightening moment," said *CBS Sports* commentator John Tesh. Heiden was forced to withdraw and would never again compete in the Tour.

While many of these events were tragic or poignant, others were purely embarrassing. At one point team member Shapiro glanced over at a TV camera, only to ride right into the back of Pedro Delgado—a future Tour winner—causing the Spaniard to crash, break his collarbone, and abandon the race.

The incendiary Grewal also proved to be a public relations liability. While he was capable of astounding performances when fueled by his own anger and iconoclastic nature, among the fraternal, fun-loving 7-Elevens, his rebellious personality was immediately problematic. He was a strict vegetarian and arrived in Europe carrying his own grains and cooking equipment. In the evenings, the smell of garlic and herbs would waft from his hotel room. From Neel's perspective, "he was starving to death."

Even worse, he failed two of the team's sacrosanct tests: "He didn't go drinking or chase girls," said Stieda. At one point in the Tour, Grewal was struggling during a climbing stage. Annoyed by a cameraman on a motorcycle who began to chronicle his every pedal stroke, he first waved off the intruder. When the journalist persisted, Grewal spat venomously at the camera. Combined with other transgressions later in the sea son, the incident would lead to his dismissal from the team.

You never knew which Grewal was going to show up each day: the gifted climber or the pouting iconoclast.

All these dramas were brought home to an American television audience by *CBS Sports*, providing an unprecedented window into the sport for an uninitiated but increasingly curious public back home. Under the creative hand of producer Dave Michaels and anchorman Tesh, the network televised five segments during the race, including same-day coverage of the final stage and American Greg LeMond's eventual ascent to the top step of the podium—the first American to win the world's most important cycling event. Tesh, with his emotional commentary and artfully composed music, brought the race to America in the most personal terms. The network would play a huge role in popularizing the race for years to come.

oo

By the final week, they'd lost Phinney, Heiden, Grewal, Shapiro, and Carmichael to fatigue, illness, or injury. "From then on, we were just trying to get to the finish," said Ochowicz. "It became survival."

Kiefel, despite having placed 2nd in stage 7, was vowing never to come back. "Five days before the end, I remember thinking I had to finish, because I was never going to ride this stinkin' race again," he said. "I told myself that to get to the finish." (He would, in fact, do the race another six times.)

For his part, Pierce's most enduring memory was that he "suffered like a miserable dog." The top-placed 7-Eleven rider was Bob Roll, at 63rd. Stieda, despite his spectacular blowup early in the race, managed to finish 120th. Other team finishers included Pierce, Kiefel, and the new acquisition Alcalá.

To apply salve to their wounds after the Paris finish, the team went to Café Pacifico, one of the few Mexican restaurants in the city. In typical 7-Eleven fashion, it was a small act of culinary defiance. "Everyone else was going to the Moulin Rouge for a big dinner, and we'd go to Café Pacifico," said Ochowicz. It would be the first of many such visits.

It was a race that most of the team remembers as a reckoning, a sobering end to the charmed and high-spirited life they had led until then. The team was in the big show now, and the old formulas no longer worked. "When we went to Europe, a lot of what we had done—our elitism—went out the window," said Phinney. "We were new kids trying to fake it."

But they were also learning by degree. They had endured the taunts, the jibes, and the rigors of the world's most famous bike race. They had earned yellow, if only for a few hours, and Phinney had won a stage. All things considered, it had been a glorious experience.

"I wouldn't rewrite it in any way," said Neel.

Hayman, one of the original team members, had watched the race on TV back home. He found himself in a state of utter disbelief at how far the team had come from the rowdy and raucous days of the Ranch Dog, back in 1981. "It was the vision of one person that did it," he said of his old friend Ochowicz. "One person who believed in it so strongly that he dragged everyone along with him. Before they knew it, they all believed it."

CHAPTER 16
Not Just Americans Anymore

In the fall of 1986, as Ochowicz considered the lessons of the just-completed season, he put an overarching goal at the top of his to-do list: "We need to get Andy back."

"Andy," of course, was Hampsten, and as Och saw it, the skinny racer from North Dakota was key to the team's continental success. It was one thing, Ochowicz realized, to survive the Tour de France. It was quite another to work for a leader. Like following a general into battle, fielding a strong number one could have a transformative effect. "If you don't have a G.C. rider, you lose motivation, you lose vision in the race," he said. "You're just pedaling to the finish." And Hampsten was the best G.C. prospect in North America.

Hampsten had merely been on loan to the team in 1985. At the 1986 Tour, while the 7-Elevens had been undergoing their rude baptism, Hampsten had ridden for the French La Vie Claire team of Bernard Hinault and the eventual winner, Greg LeMond. It had been a watershed race: Hampsten had placed 4th overall and won the white jersey of best young rider. But he had also experienced the poisonous atmosphere created between the two leaders, and he wanted no part of it. Hinault, after winning the Tour with LeMond's help in 1985, had promised to return the favor the following year. Instead, Hinault again rode for himself, and the two teammates spent the race in a state of bitter acrimony. For LeMond, it was an unforgivable act of betrayal. For Hampsten, it was simply "the blowup." From his perspective, the team director and owner had the power to remedy the situation, but they had done nothing, standing idly by as Hinault "reinvented the team plan."

"I had just ridden for La Vie Claire, supposedly the greatest team ever, and it was terrible," he reflected. "It put a really bad taste

The team may have started as a small, domestic undertaking, but by 1986 it included European pros, U.S. amateurs, track riders, women, juniors, and a host of support personnel.

in my mouth." Another Frenchman from the 1986 team, Jean-François Bernard, was poised to take leadership of La Vie Claire the following year. In the same way that Hinault had turned mutinous against LeMond, Hampsten began wondering if Bernard might turn against him if they faced a similar situation, Frenchman versus American. Despite having two years remaining in his contract, it was not a chance Hampsten was willing to take. "There was a lot of talk of Bernard being leader of that team," he said, "and I didn't want to be on a team with him as leader." And there was another reason; rejoining 7-Eleven, Hampsten emphasized, meant that "I didn't have to worry about the pressure to take drugs. That would have been a deal killer for me." The philosophy at 7-Eleven, he said, was very anti-drug, and that view married well with Hampsten's stance on the issue.

So Hampsten was ready for the 7-Elevens—but were they ready for him? He had watched the team's Tour debut with a mix of admiration and revulsion. "While appearing to be bumpkins, they won everything in the first two days of the Tour," he reflected. "But from my view as a team leader, they weren't a solid team; they struggled to the finish."

Hampsten knew everyone on the team, some of them like brothers. He had raced with them, trained with them, and even lived with them, in the athletic mecca of Boulder. And he knew enough to look beyond their foibles and frequent missteps. It would take some hard work, he reasoned, "but I had a hunch that they could rise to the level they needed to." He also had an abiding confidence in his old friend Neel, who had figured so prominently in his career-changing stage win in the 1985 Giro.

In sum, he figured it was "better to be with guys I trusted." La Vie Claire, for all its vaunted strength, had few riders Hampsten felt he could trust, and even fewer whom he could call friends. His true cycling buddies didn't wear the Mondrian-inspired pattern of the Vie Claire jersey; they were the guys in the red, white, and green of 7-Eleven. When Och called, he was ready.

Roll (right) was a stalwart teammate, supportive and protective of the more fragile Hampsten (left).

Not Just Americans Anymore | 217

○○

As Ochowicz pursued his dream, he was also measuring the team against a new, international standard. And for this, he needed international riders. He had already acquired Raúl Alcalá of Mexico, an earnest and amenable rider who had previously distinguished himself with his hard work in the 1986 Tour. And Canadian riders had been part of the team from the outset. But for 1987, Ochowicz would make his first foray into the European ranks, acquiring Jens Veggerby of Denmark and Dag Otto Lauritzen of Norway.

It was, to some, an unfortunate transition—a movement away from the groundbreaking and often heretical approach that had dominated the team's early days. Others viewed it as unavoidable, a requisite part of competing on a world stage. But in

The additions of Lauritzen of Norway (left front) and Veggerby of Denmark (right front) in 1987 made 7-Eleven a more complete team.

the end, as Och saw it, he had no choice. "I needed Euro guys," he said with an air of finality. "I just needed stronger riders."

In adding Lauritzen and Veggerby, Ochowicz had made a calculated incursion into the European ranks. "I felt comfortable with those two," he said. "They were Scandinavian, which is a little different from the heartland of Europe. They spoke perfect English, and they had a similar mind-set." Plus, while the team was becoming more international, there were still unwritten prerequisites for membership, including a certain rebelliousness—and they qualified. Veggerby's philosophy sounded every bit like a 7-Eleven credo: "I was fed up with living in Italy and racing on Italian teams," he said. "To me it was important, when you are traveling eight or nine months a year with the same guys, to have fun, and to trust them." He even invoked Heiden's favorite word, *buddies*. "You have to feel that you are buddies," he said. "That was one of the things I thought I could find with 7-Eleven."

Lauritzen, who had taken 3rd in the 1984 Olympic road race, also found himself chafing against the European establishment. "I wasn't too happy with my French team," he said. "You had to be super good to be a leader." The American team, on the other hand, was clearly different. "It was a little more relaxed, but still serious," he said. "A lot of people told me, 'You are stupid,'" he added of his move to 7-Eleven. "But I was excited to join an American team."

If either man harbored any doubts about choosing 7-Eleven, they were dispelled at an early season training camp in Santa Barbara. When Veggerby ordered water at dinner, Ochowicz insisted that, since he was from Denmark, he must have a beer. At that moment, Veggerby knew he had landed in the right place. "It was a big relief," he said. "The atmosphere was much more friendly and relaxed." At the camp, both men were also introduced to the time-honored 7-Eleven tradition of eating Mexican food. As they surveyed their plates of beans, rice, and tortillas, Lauritzen remembers that they initially "refused to eat the shit. But later, it became our favorite." Thus indoctrinated, and having completed a sacred rite of passage, they passed into the inner sanctum of the team.

Veggerby assumed a stalwart support role, willingly putting his nose in the wind for countless miles. Post-7-Eleven, he became a standout six-day track star.

The spring camps were a carefree respite from the pressures of the regular season, an opportunity to bond and reconnect. During the summer months the team was frequently scattered across two continents, so this was one of the few times the entire squad would be gathered in one place. And without the constant pressure of racing, the boys would loosen up. Whatever regrets they had from the previous year were now officially erased; all was fresh and full of possibility. With new "kit" (cycling clothing) and bikes, it all felt a little like Christmas. "In the spring, everyone was there," said Veggerby. "Every night it was a new restaurant, every day a new plan. We had massage, new bikes, good training. We were allowed to go to the cinema. It was just a good time for two or three weeks."

Camps were generally held in California, usually Santa Barbara or Santa Rosa. The idea was to log long hours in the saddle in relative sunshine. But the weather was more often fickle, and often downright evil, giving them a foretaste of the spring classics just weeks away.

The long training rides were not only for conditioning of the body; they were there to establish a pecking order. The boys would ride six to eight hours a day, and in that broad expanse of time many things would be revealed about a rider and his conditioning: his sense of humor, his capacity for suffering, his composure in the face of rude drivers and bad weather, his tolerance for the inevitable ennui of sitting in the saddle for eight hours, a length of time most of us equate with a day at the office. In this cauldron of sweat and effort, every imaginable personality trait would be laid bare to the scrutiny of teammates, the crystallization of the best and worst in a man.

Some were earnest in their approach, having studied the route the previous evening, and would be among the first to appear in the morning, pockets full of food, legs warm and lubricated with ointment. Others arrived at the team van in relative disarray, perpetually late, half dressed and oblivious to the team's destination. Once under way, a rider could see the route spread out before him; he knew what was to be extracted from it for his benefit and where it fit in the 5,000-mile mosaic of roads that made up his preseason training. If this was a day at the office, he was ready to impress the boss and gun for a promotion. He may have already done 500 miles that week, and the coming day would be good for six hours in the saddle, or about 100 more.

There would be many such weeks, thousands of miles and millions of pedal strokes. It was an astounding distance, enough to circumnavigate the globe in a few short years. The average automobile would be retired with such mileage. But they went about it happily.

By 1987, the 7-Elevens were firmly indoctrinated in the ways of the European peloton—and that meant learning to suffer. Here, Kiefel and Boyer get aid from the team car.

○○

The team's overarching goal may have been success on the European circuit, but they still had a American-based sponsor and were compelled to make a showing stateside. As a result, the squad was frequently divided during the regular season: Half of them would be in Europe, while the other half—what Southland sports marketing coordinator Sean Petty called the "hit squad"—would race in the United States. Inevitably, an unfortunate few would be forced to compete in both arenas. "In those years, we spent half our time flying back and forth," said Stieda, who remembers finishing the Tour of Texas on a Saturday and flying through the night to be on the starting line of Paris-Roubaix Sunday morning.

While the team was in America, the camaraderie even extended as far as members sharing their homes with their teammates, sometimes for months at a time. Veggerby, for instance, remembers bunking for long stretches at Schuler's house in Wisconsin. He may have been Danish, but at such times, Veggerby began to feel tho roughly American. He said, "Everyone opened up their houses. I was not used to that. It was an American thing. I was basically a member of the family." It was more than a kind gesture—it was the logical extension of the "team-as-family" concept that had its roots in the collegial Midwest racing culture and that formed the team's essential DNA. The 7-Elevens were, in essence, a more polished and professional version of the sports clubs that had spawned Pierce, Schuler, Bradley, and so many others on the roads and tracks of the Midwest.

In the United States, the boys would often win at will. Ochowicz smugly called it "pot hunting." But often, the team's confidence would spill over into cockiness. "Did we get rambunctious? Yes," admitted Nitz. "We would do a 'three-stack' as we called it—first, second, and third. We'd get a little arrogant when we did that."

Phinney's earned his nickname, "Cash Register," every time he returned to the U.S. Pictured in the Tour of Texas, 1987.

Other squads came to resent the power and deep pockets of the team, referring to them derogatively as "the Slurpees." Many competing riders were dependent on their winnings for a living and could only watch in dismay as the 7-Elevens—often freshly arrived from some European stage race—pillaged the prize list. Eventually, for teams from Löwenbräu to Levi's, beating the 7-Elevens began to displace other, more conventional goals. It wasn't necessarily about personal success, or making the next national team trip. The overarching objective was to slay Goliath, the boys in red, white, and green. The prospect of beating the 7-Elevens was irresistible, and it drove the domestic teams to outdo themselves. "They set the standard," remembers Tony Conforti, who raced against them through that era. "Everyone thought: How are we going to get them?" Nitz had a unique perspective; for years, he had been on the side of David, not Goliath, as a member of the GS Mengoni team. "When I came up against 7-Eleven, I knew it would be tough," he said. "I had to really be on my game to do battle with them."

In the end, the sport as a whole was the beneficiary of this special brand of warfare. It was a drama that was played out in towns large and small across America, for the better part of a decade, resulting in vast amounts of media coverage and spectator interest. Despite occasional feelings of resentment, few doubted that the power and prominence of the team was good for the sport.

o͞o

The 1987 season would be the team's most ambitious yet, and with the crucial roster additions in hand, Ochowicz and Neel felt their confidence growing. In Hampsten, they had their climber and team leader. In Phinney, they had their sprinter. They had ample support in the mountains from Pierce and Alcalá, and in flat and rolling terrain from Kiefel, Bradley, Boyer, Veggerby, and Lauritzen.

And in Bob Roll, they had a combination of self-sacrifice, consistency, and comic relief. He, more than anyone, seemed to capture the spirit of the evolving team—which, although it was becoming increasingly mainstream, still prided it self on its idiosyncrasies and rebelliousness.

During a training ride in Italy, Phinney remembers stopping for some fortification at a small café. The proprietor, honored by the presence of a pro team in his midst, innocently inquired, "Who's the captain?"

Smart, funny, and consistent, Roll was a hardworking domestique for Hampsten in big tours and a reliable foot soldier in spring classics.

Roll, fluent in Italian, didn't miss a beat. "*Tutti i capitani,*" he said. "We're all captains."

oo

Sadly, one person would not be along for the ride. Heiden, the catalyst for the whole grand adventure, finally succumbed to the pressures of the Stanford School of Medicine. No longer able to put in the miles required for a three-week stage race, he would retire from the team at season's end (though stay on in the role of medical assistant).

"Before my second year of med school, I had to hang it up," he said with an air of resignation. "I couldn't train anymore." In typical fashion, he downplayed his contribution over the past seven years. "Even at the end, I was not as smart a rider as I could have been," he mused. "I still had a lot of learning to do."

Others certainly would have disagreed. Heiden had been the magnet for sponsorship in 1980, but it was a disservice to credit him with that alone. He had been a race winner, a model of sacrifice, a guiding hand. His accomplishments were many. He had been part of the groundbreaking team that competed in the 1985 Giro, where he won a sprint competition. That same year, he'd stunningly won the U.S. professional road championship in Philadelphia, despite studying for medical exams, preparing Tour de France commentary, and attending his own graduation from Stanford in the weeks leading up to the race. In that race he had broken away for 50 miles in the company of a small group, catapulted his giant body over the fearsome Manayunk Wall hill climb that graced every lap, and won the sprint. For 7-Eleven, and for Ochowicz, the victory had been nothing short of poetic, as it meant that one of the most famous athletes in America would wear the stars and stripes jersey of national champion for the following season. And that year, 1986, he'd been part of the first-ever American foray into the Tour de France.

But these many accomplishments were now in the past. As the man with the gigantic thighs loped off to Stanford and his new life, he could console himself with the certain knowledge that none of this could have taken place without him.

o͞o

As they rolled into the season, Hampsten, having observed the team's missteps in 1986, had a hunch that the squad still was not fit enough. He began urging the boys to log more miles in training. "My big question is, you guys are going to be around to help me, right?" he asked them.

True to his fears, at the beginning of the 10-day Tour of Switzerland in mid-June, Hampsten found himself "covering dozens of attacks." That night, in a team meeting, he chastised his teammates. "We were asleep," he said. "We should have been fitter."

The boys, seeming contrite, soon had ample opportunity to show their new resolve. By the final week, Hampsten, who had won the same race in 1986 as a member of La Vie Claire, had a scant one-second lead over Peter Winnen of Holland. There was, however, a midstage bonus sprint that could provide precious seconds and catapult Winnen into the lead—and the overall victory.

Thwarting that possibility seemed easy enough. "All we had to do," said Ochowicz, "was cover Winnen."

But in the rolling chess game that constitutes a major stage race, nothing is ever as simple as it appears. Roll had been designated to outsprint the Dutchman, but, as he began his effort, he disastrously pulled his foot out of the pedal. ("He never was the smoothest rider," said Kiefel.)

In that moment, it fell to Kiefel—ever the reluctant hero—to salvage the day. "I just put my head down and sprinted as hard as I could," he said. Not only did he take the sprint, he had sufficient composure to glance over and see Winnen "with the biggest grin on his face—then I see the smile just melt away. That felt really good."

In taking the midrace sprint, Kiefel had deprived Winnen of the precious time bonus and preserved Hampsten's one-second overall margin, enabling him to win the race for the second consecutive year.

"It was not a [stage] win," said Neel after watching Kiefel snatch victory from the jaws of defeat. "But it was as important as any win we ever had."

CHAPTER 17
Best in Bordeaux

There is a certain freedom to doing a race for the first time. Liberated from expectations and precedent, there is license to call it a "learning experience." And so it had been at the Tour de France in 1986. But in 1987, things changed. "As the team evolved, we started shooting for higher goals," said Kiefel, "[We wanted to] be better pros and not be cowboys. We wanted to be really solid."

For Hampsten, it seemed that his win in the Tour of Switzerland, just a week earlier, had positioned him perfectly for the Tour de France. He was obviously fit. His teammates, at his urging, had stepped up their training and general aggression. He trusted them to be there when it counted. And he would surely need them. Having placed 4th in the previous year's Tour and won the white jersey of best young rider, all eyes were upon him.

But no sooner had the race gotten under way than there were ominous signs for Hampsten. The precocious Alcalá, nominally there to support his team leader, was riding almost effortlessly at the front, while Hampsten appeared hesitant. "Raúl would pull for miles, and by the time he pulled off, there would be only four or five guys left," observed Neel. Not only was he riding strongly, he seemed to have an innate sense of where he needed to be. "Tactically he was always in the right place," said Neel. "Andy wasn't always in the right place."

In stage 6, Alcalá placed second, while Hampsten finished another minute back. In the stage 10 time trial, Alcalá—despite crashing into a hay bale, breaking a finger, and getting a bike change—finished 29th, while Hampsten crossed the line a distant 43rd. Hampsten, who could be psychologically fragile, was beginning to harbor doubts about the road ahead, and who carried the mantle of team leader. "Raúl is very strong and dangerous," he confessed.

With seemingly effortless ease, Alcalá rode into the King of the Mountains jersey in the 1987 Tour, later trading it for the white jersey of best young rider.

By midrace—as if Hampsten needed any reminders of his teammate's prowess—Alcalá was prominently wearing the polka-dot jersey of best climber, having claimed it on the race's seventh stage. Hampsten, meanwhile, was 48th on G.C. after stage 10, already 11:24 behind the race leader. Even with the mountains to come, where Hampsten would normally shine, a top placing was looking more and more remote.

○○

Still, the team had not won a stage. Roll and Bradley had withdrawn, suffering from diarrhea and vomiting. Hampsten was wrestling with his own demons, trying to regain the confidence he had shown the previous year. And Ochowicz was beginning to wonder if a major victory would elude him.

After a particularly hard day across northern France, Phinney was commiserating about the state of affairs with Neel. The two were looking for a miracle, something that could elevate the team and set them off in a new, positive direction. "We need a result," Neel told Phinney plainly. "We need a stage."

Phinney had already been eyeing stage 12, which finished in Bordeaux. The flat, coastal town has long been considered a sprinter's showcase. The Tour had visited it more than 70 times, and winners included the likes of Merckx and Phinney's boyhood idol, Maertens. Anxious to add his name to the list, Phinney decided to take a leap of faith. "You can count on it," he assured Neel, brashly anticipating a victory.

"I don't know where those words came from," he would later recount. "But I actually predicted it."

When a racer looks back at his successes, there are those that exist in memory purely as struggle, an unending fight for inches. Then there are those that seem, above all else, to be gifts—fitting rewards for the hours of training and relentless pain of racing. For Phinney, this would be such a day.

After reabsorbing a dangerous breakaway with just a few kilometers remaining, the peloton did several short circuits of the town, which Phinney was glad to discover "reminded me of being in a criterium in America." He looked around and saw he was surrounded by the world's best sprinters, including Jean-Paul Van Poppel, eventual winner of the green jersey; and Teun Van Vliet, who had earlier won the Ghent-Wevelgem classic. Yet Phinney was unfazed. "It didn't matter who I was racing with," he said. "Coming out of the last corner, with 400 meters to go, I was in 6th place, and I just hit it."

The outcome surpassed even Phinney's brash prediction. "I

just went flying by everyone," he said. "There was no way possible I was going to lose the stage that day.

"It was the greatest race of my career for sure. I felt like a puppet master was controlling things the whole way."

Kiefel, seeing Phinney on the podium, felt an abiding pride. While he had been so critical to Phinney's success in the United States, Kiefel knew that in the cut and thrust of the European peloton, he could not always be there for his old friend. Increasingly, it would be up to Phinney to fend for himself. "That was the thing about Davis," said Kiefel. "I helped when I could. But at other times, he did it all alone. His win in Bordeaux—that was pure Davis. It was masterful."

Phinney took his second Tour stage win in Bordeaux, exploding out of a small pack of the world's best sprinters with 400 meters to go.

After the clamor from the stage win had settled down, Phinney reflected on the victory in a conversation with reporter Cheryl Lindstrom of VeloNews. "There are a billion people who have won one stage in the Tour de France," Phinney said, exaggerating to make his point. "But there's a much smaller list of people who have won two," he continued. "I feel much more comfortable there now. I feel like I'm one of the major players in the race, where last year I was just a spectator." Indeed, while the 7-Elevens were struggling in the race to move up on overall time, Phinney's ride and Alcalá's performance at least demonstrated that the team was far from done. More than that—it showed that they truly belonged in the race.

o͞o

Of all the 7-Elevens, Dag Otto Lauritzen had perhaps the shortest pedigree in cycling. He came to the sport late, after years as a Norwegian policeman and then a paratrooper in the army. While jumping from a plane in 1980, he became tangled in his parachute cord, spun wildly in the air, and passed out. He awoke to find himself hanging upside down, his leg severely broken. After three hours of surgery, the doctor told him he could never walk normally, much less ride a bike. The next year, he began cycling for therapy, and within a few seasons, he was winning Norwegian national championships, in his mid-20s.

Now part of the 7-Eleven team, Lauritzen was in good form, as shown by his wins earlier in the season at the Redlands Classic and the Grand Prix of Frankfurt. But in the Tour's mountainous stage 13, he blew up catastrophically, losing more than 14 minutes. "I was *fringale*," he said. "Sugar empty. They all said, 'The Tour is over for Dag Otto.'"

As a result, expectations were low for Lauritzen in stage 14, an epic day culminating at the 5,643-foot ski area of Luz Ardiden. But he soon found himself in a small group that included his

Lauritzen was a powerful all-rounder, but the Tour's climbs took their toll in 1987. He struck back to win the difficult stage to Luz Ardiden.

teammate Hampsten. "I felt really strong, and I said to Andy, 'What do you want me to do, work for you?' He said, 'You are flying. If you don't take any favorites with you, take your own chance.'"

It was one of those perfect days for Lauritzen, one where your cycling power seems bottomless, and on the final climb to Luz Ardiden, he overtook several breakaway riders and moved into the lead. With just a few kilometers remaining, Ochowicz came alongside in the team car and told him that a lone rider—Luis Herrera—was coming up fast. "I didn't dare turn around," said Lauritzen. "I just gave it everything." Lauritzen bore down and managed to hold off the Colombian by just seven seconds, and in doing so became the first Norwegian to ever win a stage of the Tour. "It was," said Lauritzen, "my best day as a bike rider."

In the space of just three days, the team had won two stages, and Hampsten had finished third on the stage that Lauritzen won. Even sweeter, Lauritzen's win had come on Bastille Day, a sure and highly visible sign of the team's arrival on French shores.

After losing 14 minutes on the previous stage, Lauritzen regained his strength and powered to a decisive win over the legendary Ardiden.

oo

Hampsten, meanwhile, was feeling increasingly mystified. Nothing was going according to plan. "I've finally accepted the fact that this race is bizarre and everything I learned last year doesn't mean anything," he said.

And where Hampsten faltered, his erstwhile lieutenant, Alcalá, continued to soar, placing second in stage 16. He had by now lost the polka-dot jersey of the best climber, but had managed to garner a replacement in the form of the white jersey of best young rider, which Hampsten had won the previous year.

Unfortunately, the good times didn't last. On the day of the fearsome Mont Ventoux time trial, Neel found Hampsten and Alcalá both collapsed in the hallway of their hotel. The pair had apparently eaten a bad meal. (Another team staying in the same hotel also became sick, prompting Neel to suspect someone had tampered with the food, but this was never proven.)

"I couldn't even warm up," said Hampsten. "I was falling asleep. I was walking back from lunch, and I passed out."

By the end of the day, Hampsten had lost more than six minutes in a stage that should have played to his strength. Afterward he stared blankly out the window of the team car, sipping tea, his head in a child's blanket. "I have nothing left," he said. Two days later, on the stage that included the famed climb of Alpe d'Huez, he lost 10 minutes. The next day, now suffering from bronchitis, he lost 18 more.

Bit by bit, day by day, the glories of 1986 were fading fast, and Hampsten found himself casting about for solutions. "I'll try to do things differently next year," he said wistfully. "But for me, the one year I've been planning on is down the drain."

○○

Though the team had by now won two stages, by the final day, Ochowicz had to accept that a good overall result would elude him. The 7-Elevens' Tour had included successes, surprises, and no small amount of tribulation. But the last week had been more of the latter. Phinney had become sick and dropped out after his stage win, as had Roll and Bradley earlier in the race. While Alcalá was 9th overall and secure in the white jersey, Hampsten had dropped to 16th. "It's been kind of a rough week," admitted Ochowicz.

Jeff Pierce suffered through the three-week ordeal as much as anyone, crashing early on and struggling on the climbs. Nonetheless, before the start of the race, he'd had strange intimations of success. Seeking counsel, he'd gone with ex-racers and 7-Eleven staffers Richard and Noël Dejonckheere to visit their father, known only as "Chief."

It was a strange meeting, grave and full of import. "He was an old guy, sitting on the bed," said Pierce. "It felt like talking to

The team was unable to put Hampsten in yellow, but Alcalá captured the white jersey at the 1987 Tour.

Marlon Brando." At one point the older man said something quietly in French, nodding his head toward Pierce. It was only later that he asked the Dejonckheeres what their father had told them. "He said," Richard responded, "that you will win a stage in the Tour de France."

○○

The Tour's final stage is as much ritual as race. Close to two hundred bikes echo and reverberate down the cobblestones of the Champs Élysées in Paris. More than 250,000 people press in upon the barricades. The city itself appears to exist in a state of suspended animation. On this day, for the traditional finish of the Tour, it seems the entire heritage of France is proudly trotted out for flamboyant display.

But for the majority of the peloton, the final stage is mere formality, as much relief as celebration. For the wearer of the yellow jersey, who generally rides into Paris surrounded by a protective phalanx of teammates, the goal is to avoid crashes at all costs. For the climbers, the goal is to arrive safely in midpack and be counted among the finishers. Only the sprinters see the day as an opportunity, and they will do almost anything to be able to throw their hands skyward in front of the throbbing, partisan crowd.

Pierce remembers Ochowicz giving a "little speech" before the start. "He said, 'No matter what, I'm proud of you. You have the white jersey, you won two stages—you looked like a team. Today, let's just go finish things off.' "

The 192-km stage finished with five circuits up and down the Champs Élysées in the heart of Paris. With two laps remaining, Pierce dutifully followed a small attack and found himself in a group of three riders. With a lap to go, the group had grown to a dozen. When he looked around at his breakaway companions, he liked what he saw. "I started to think, 'Hey, this could actually work.' I could beat half these guys. For sure, I could get top 10 in the stage."

At one point the group slowed slightly after reabsorbing an attack. Pierce, who had been racing since he was in his early teens, let his instincts take over. "I didn't even think about it," he said. "I just attacked as hard as I could."

The final kilometers of a race are governed by an exacting calculus of energy output, psychology, and pure guts. Pierce, at that moment, found himself in a situation "where we were close enough to the finish" that a solo victory seemed possible but "far enough that the sprinters think they will still catch." In that moment of complacency, all things become possible.

But when he looked back, Pierce saw a familiar competitor emerging from the pack: 1984 Olympic silver medalist Steve Bauer, a fearsome sprinter. "I could tell by his size and shape," said Pierce. "I thought, okay, Bauer is coming after me, and it's 1K to go, and it's the biggest stage in cycling. What do I do?"

The reflexive reaction in such circumstances is to simply go harder, putting more distance between you and your pursuer. But Pierce, summoning the savvy gained over 16 years of racing, elected to do the opposite. "I backed off," he said, figuring that "if I go as hard as possible, I'll blow. It was a very surreal experience, almost like I was a spectator, outside of myself, watching the whole thing develop."

In the end, his calculations were impeccable. At the very moment that Bauer caught him, Pierce jumped. Bauer, having expended all his energy to bridge the gap, was left helplessly behind. A photo shows a dejected Bauer, his head down, and Pierce "screaming my head off. It was not a staged or thought-out victory salute. It was a pure explosion of emotion."

Pierce put his head down on the Champs Élysées to take the team's third stage victory at the 1987 Tour. Alcalá pictured at right in the white jersey.

Pierce's stage win was an unexpected but ecstatic end to a race that had included the best and the worst of what the Tour could offer. One of Ochowicz's goals had been to place a rider in the top five; by that measure, they had come up short (Alcalá was the top-placed rider, at 9th.) On the bright side, however, the team had won three stages in the world's most important race, garnered plenty of screen time in CBS's coverage back in the United States, and had also earned the coveted white jersey. It was a time for celebration, and in their usual fashion, they headed off to Café Pacifico to celebrate their wins over plates of refried beans and drown their disappointments in glasses of Mexican beer.

Tour winner Stephen Roche (right) congratulates Pierce on the final podium in Paris. Perhaps no one was as surprised as Pierce himself.

The end of the Tour was also a time when the earliest members of the team began a gradual exodus, pulled away by conventional jobs, family, or just plain fatigue. Bradley was among these departures, leaving at the end of the 1987 season. In recent years he had felt a gradual ebb of motivation. Since he was a teenager, he'd always been propelled by a pure love of the sport, winning bushels of national championships. He had felt the same childlike euphoria in the early days of the 7-Elevens, when all was fresh and new. But now, with several seasons in Europe under his belt, it had all begun to seem like work. "It was a passion, since I was a kid," he said. "I just enjoyed going out and doing bike races. As a youngster, I couldn't wait for the finish. But when we started to have 'jobs'—to chase or lead out—the wind went out of my sails. I had lost my mental edge."

It was, in a larger sense, a loss of innocence. In their initial forays, the team had been fueled by their own excitement, achieving wild and unlikely success that was at least in part due to a blissful ignorance of what was or was not possible. It was a uniquely American attitude, bordering on cockiness. They had shocked the European establishment and relished every minute of it. Now, as seasoned racers preoccupied with making a place for themselves in the professional peloton, they had become the thing they had rebelled against. Kiefel called it "learning to play the game." They were operating within conventional boundaries, with a more conventional sense of what was possible. "We were more like a European team," said Kiefel, with a hint of sadness.

CHAPTER 18
Triumph on the Gavia

To the uninitiated, the pro race caravan can seem like barely controlled chaos. Hours in advance, promotional vehicles come through, harkening the arrival of the great spectacle. Comical vehicles, shaped like giant hot dogs, candy bars, and cans of soda pop, dispense treats and trinkets to the throngs by the roadside. Then come the marshals, and the race director, and the press motorcycles. Finally, the peloton passes in a flash, followed by as many as four dozen team cars, bristling with bikes and spare wheels. At the back of the field, an entire city's worth of services are dispensed at 30 miles per hour by adept doctors and mechanics in their own vehicles. Physical problems are diagnosed, small surgeries performed, derailleurs adjusted, and roadside counsel conferred upon flagging spirits.

As a rider, should you be so unfortunate as to get dropped, suffer a flat tire, or temporarily succumb to some other problem, you must deftly thread your way through the madness to regain the field. Where you were once coddled and protected by the race's many vehicles and officials, you are now left to your own devices as you draft your way forward from car to car. As you fight to regain the race, you have the same rights as the thick phalanx of cars and motorcycles that you share the road with, which is to say, none at all.

In mid-April of 1988, this is exactly where Davis Phinney found himself in the Belgian one-day classic, Liège-Bastogne-Liège. A large group—including 7-Eleven riders Hampsten, Stieda, Roll, and a newly enlisted American racer, Roy Knickman—tumbled to the pavement after hitting an unmarked construction trench. After getting replacement wheels, Phinney and Stieda set about regaining the field.

Phinney had become accustomed to riding through the densely packed caravan and even prided himself on his mastery. In a one-day race like Liège, you never knew when it would pay off to suffer through the long chase. If you should regain the field, and if you still had good legs, you could get a good result, or even win. And the tenacious Phinney, as much as anyone, was not one to settle for a back-of-the-pack finish in such circumstances.

"Most sprinters, when they get a flat, they get in the team car," said Neel. "But Davis is a warrior. He said no, 'I want to get back on.'" Phinney and Stieda, riding together, started to work their way up through the densely packed caravan, trading turns at the front.

Suddenly, Phinney could see the field just a few hundred meters ahead. He put his head down and made one last push to regain the peloton.

A team station wagon had stopped by the roadside to assist a rider. When Phinney looked up, it was too late. His front wheel went squarely into the car's bumper, stopping his bike abruptly. Phinney, meanwhile, continued his momentum over the handlebar and through the car's rear window, leading with the left side of his face. Stunned but conscious, he slid down the back of the car and fell on the street.

Stieda, one of the first to come across Phinney—by now prostrate in the road—was aghast at what he saw. Blood was everywhere—Phinney's face was entirely red. Before long a doctor arrived, and an ambulance. Without giving it a second thought, Stieda dropped out of the race and climbed in with his teammate for the long ride to the hospital.

With Phinney steadily losing blood, the ambulance driver proceeded to get lost, taking an extra 30 minutes. When they finally reached the hospital, Phinney was rushed into two hours of surgery in which his nose was realigned, and he received "so many stitches

Sprinting to rejoin the Liège-Bastogne-Liège peloton after a crash in 1988, Phinney rode straight into the back of the Isoglass team car. Ten days and more than 120 stitches later, he was back on his bike.

that they lost count. . . at least 120," said Phinney. He had also cut his arm open, requiring another 30 stitches and a cast.

He was "cut to shreds," said Neel, who also allowed himself a bit of black humor. The car, he noted, belonged to the Isoglass team, a maker of car windshields.

Every bike racer, it seems, is faced with "the big one"—an accident so severe that it casts a long shadow on his every move. "A crash like that really takes it out of you," Phinney admitted soon after. "I had a tremendous fear of riding again." As if he needed any further reminders, Phinney, once called one of Boulder's "sexiest athletes," now had long, disfiguring scars across his handsome face.

But in some ways, the horrific accident was more shocking to his followers than to Phinney himself. Despite the memory of a crash that no one—from riders, to coaches, to his by then significant fan following—could forget, and heedless of the gravity of his injuries, Phinney seemed to put the whole thing behind him with remarkable speed. He was racing again just 10 days later.

The team rallied its support for Hampsten's 1988 Giro campaign as never before. Phinney, his facial scars still covered with protective ointment, counsels the race leader on strategy.

○○

Phinney's gruesome accident aside, it had been a good spring for the team, perhaps their best ever. Kiefel had won the Tour of Tuscany and placed 3rd in the Belgian one-day classic, Ghent-Wevelgem. Roll and Phinney had both won stages in the weeklong Tour of Romandie in Switzerland.

In the meantime, Hampsten had decided to forgo the Tour of Switzerland, which he had won the two previous years; instead, he was going to return to the Giro d'Italia, the showcase of his earlier glories. At Neel's urging, he had spent the winter engaged in a sort of survivalist's boot camp. "In the dead of winter I went on long hikes, when it was snowy," Hampsten said. "He convinced me that in order to get a deeper foundation, that I should do any exercise—even hiking—for eight hours."

Hampsten had fortified himself, mentally and physically, for his most ambitious season ever, and the plan appeared to be working when he won a mountainous stage of Paris-Nice in March. "I went to the Giro with good results," he said. "I was just healthy. My body, in my later 20s, was able to take the workload."

As the Giro approached, Neel's wintry regimen and the mental toughness it engendered would pay off in ways that neither man could ever have imagined.

○○

The 7-Eleven team that entered the Giro in May 1988 was a different enterprise altogether than the happy collection of cowboys that had made its pro debut in the same race three years earlier. Back then, by broad admission, they had been in a state of blissful ignorance about the scale of their undertaking. Now, in striking contrast, Hampsten had studied the Giro like a college student preparing for an exam. And throughout his studies, one leg of the race loomed largest: stage 14, a 120K march across the Italian Alps that included the fearsome Gavia Pass, a 14K ascent with gut-wrenching grades of 16 percent. And if that weren't enough, for part of the climb, the road was entirely dirt.

Before the race, Hampsten had been counseled by Gianni Motta, an Italian cycling legend and bike maker who had memorably won the Giro with two stage victories in 1966. "You have to win this race, and you must do it on the Gavia," he counseled the American.

Then he added ominously, "You have no idea how hard that pass is. The Giro," he said, "will be won on the Gavia."

ōo

Hampsten went well from the outset, placing 13th in the prologue and 2nd in the first mountainous stage. Then, gaining strength and confidence all the while, he won stage 12 with remarkable ease, attacking in the final 3 kilometers. With the most important stage race of his career in the offing, Hampsten had sufficient composure to sit up, reach into his back pocket, and put on his Oakley sunglasses. For this, he earned a large cash bonus from the company—but lost precious seconds in the process.

He was unconcerned. "It was one of the few days where I just felt so good, I thought other people were playing a practical joke on me," he said. "I just rode away."

The Gavia was just two days away, and everything seemed to be falling into place. Suddenly, Hampsten—who was not usually prone to bluster—was talking like a champion. "I was flying," he said.

ōo

For the first weeks of the race, the sun had cast long shadows across the roads, the riders comfortable in their shorts and Lycra. Meanwhile, on the high passes, the snowplows had been doing their work, preparing for the passage of the great spectacle.

Hampsten had the presence of mind to don his sponsor's sunglasses and adjust his jersey just before capturing his stage 12 win at the Giro.

But the day before the Gavia, it became clear that severe weather—including snow—was in the offing. For Ochowicz and Neel, the world at that moment revolved around this particular stage, and they moved forward with military precision. Ochowicz started by visiting a local ski shop, astonishing the proprietor by buying 10 pairs of thick winter gloves—in May. The two men mapped out a plan that included two strategically positioned support cars. One, with Neel, would stay behind, with warm clothes and hot tea for each rider. Ochowicz, meanwhile, would take the other to position himself near the summit with a musette bag of warm clothes prepared for each rider for the long descent to the finish in Bormio.

For Hampsten, there was succor not only in the physical support, but in the simple fact that people would be there for him, like sentinels in the wilderness. "Psychologically, that was really important," he said. "Other teams simply weren't prepared." Suddenly, the American newcomers were looking like veterans of the high mountains.

Neel had his own menu of solutions, which included a mix of science and folk wisdom. First, in the morning, he had them all eat steak to fortify themselves against the cold. Then, in a move that would pay huge dividends, he had the *soigneurs* completely cover each rider with Vaseline as insulation against the weather. Only their faces were left bare, leaving them all feeling a little like Italian olives.

In his role as diviner of spirits and psychotherapist, Neel tried to calm the boys before embarking on what was clearly going to be an epic day. His ploy was to frame the horrific conditions as an opportunity. In doing so, he was suppressing his own, very real concerns about the stage and what might happen. "People are going to freak out," he warned them. At the same time, he knew Hampsten was in peak condition, and what might have been a small margin on a good day, he said, "would be magnified" by the conditions. "Our plan is good," he said, "so don't let weather ruin it."

Thus prepared, and hermetically sealed against the elements, the team went forth to uncertain fate.

o͞o

That morning, in the village of Chiesa Valmalenco, they had awoken to a mix of rain and snow. Seeing this, the boys, many of them from Boulder, knew immediately what it was going to be like on the high passes. "Half of us lived in Colorado, we all knew about snow," said Hampsten. "I grew up in North Dakota, so I knew perhaps more about riding in snow than most."

Hampsten, who spent the winter of 1988 building his strength in anticipation of an all-out assault on the Giro d'Italia, also had experience riding in snow.

When they reflected on the war plans that Neel and Ochowicz had put into place, they wondered why other teams weren't similarly girding for battle. How could the Americans know what others apparently did not? Hampsten's simple assessment was that the U.S. squad did the math. "We were going up to 2,600 meters, and we were at 600 meters at nine in morning, and it was snowing—snow turning into rain. So there would definitely be snow up there."

For a moment at the start, 7-Eleven's carefully assembled plan seemed in danger of being derailed when riders on the other teams threatened to boycott the stage. They were "grumbling and bitching, shouting, 'Let's not race,'" said Hampsten. Fortunately, the tempest passed. "It was nothing cohesive," Hampsten said, and with no organized resistance, the race commissaires soon had everyone toeing the starting line.

Once the race was under way, Neel and Ochowicz's meticulous preparation began to pay dividends. No sooner had Hampsten begun the climb, he said, than Neel "had riders bringing me tea every three minutes." Drinking hot tea on a bicycle is no simple exercise. The thin-walled plastic bottles would "kind of droop into my bottle cage," said Hampsten. "After three minutes, it was just right. After eight minutes, it was frozen."

Once on the Gavia, despite the horrific conditions, Hampsten felt his confidence growing. Bike racers read their fellow competitors like books, and what he saw spoke volumes. "I started looking at other people, looking at them in their faces—they were definitely suffering more than we were," he said. "And they were way more scared than I was."

Team doctor, Max Testa, who had grown up skiing in the area, had supplied a precise picture of the road ahead. After 6 kilometers, the course turned to dirt, on grades approaching 14 percent. Neel called it simply, "a goat path." But fortunately, he noted, "we were prepared for a goat path."

Grades of 16 percent, a dirt road, and heavy snowfall combined to make the 1988 ascent of the Gavia Pass one of the truly epic days in Giro history. Hampsten, in the lead, was well prepared.

The moment the pavement changed, Hampsten attacked. Unfortunately, "all my competitors were on my wheel, expecting I would do it."

"But it was the only stick I had. People were so worried about the weather, I thought I would attack from the very beginning."

At the same time, he had shrewdly decided to leave something in reserve. It would be simple enough to make it to the top, he thought, while he was generating his own heat—but the real race would occur on the frigid descent to Bormio. He had to remain coherent, and just as important, physically able to navigate the descent.

It was, in such fearsome conditions, a remarkably lucid realization.

oo

Neel himself could barely get up the mountain in a car. At one point he found himself stuck and had to enlist a fellow director, Peter Post, to extricate him. Ochowicz, meanwhile, gingerly made his way up the pass behind a snowplow. Once he got there, the snow was so deep he could hardly find a place to park.

At one point Hampsten decided to don a neck warmer and hat. Before putting them on, he reached up to brush water from his scalp and was astounded when "a snowball came off my head and rolled down my back . . . it had really accumulated."

Ochowicz, stationed near the summit, could see solitary riders coming toward him out of the whiteness, leaving little tire tracks behind. Johan van der Velde, a Dutch rider renowned for his climbing ability, was first to arrive, and he found little cause for celebration once he got there. At one point Neel, feeling magnanimous, had handed the suffering rider hot tea, which he promptly dropped on the ground. "He was frozen like a statue," said Neel. "He couldn't even hold the bottle." He would eventually lose the better part of an hour to the leaders.

oo

Hampsten followed a minute later and decided to take a rain jacket from Ochowicz, along with a musette bag filled with gloves and a bottle of hot tea. In any other circumstance, putting on the jacket would have been an easy task, but Hampsten's hands were nearly frozen. "My judgment had already lapsed," he said. "If I'd been smart, I would have stopped, put my foot down, and my hands through the sleeves."

In the brief time he wrestled with his garments, Hampsten

When Hampsten brushed himself off, "a snowball came off my head and rolled down my back," he recalled.

was caught by Eric Breukink, one of his chief competitors. It was now raining, which Hampsten interpreted as a good sign—it meant that the temperature had managed to eke above 32 degrees.

Together, the two started the long descent to the ski village of Bormio, through the fog, snow, and rain.

oo

The descent included moments of clarity, punctuated with abject fear. Success in the race—and survival, no less—started to occupy Hampsten's thoughts in equal proportions. "I was pretty worried about what was happening," he said. His main concern was that "if I get really hypothermic, I will fall over." There was also the ever-present temptation to crawl in the team car—if one could be found—or that perhaps he might "see the team hotel and just stop there and get in the hot tub."

Hampsten's judgment may have lapsed earlier in small ways, but he was coherent enough to realize that he had to keep his bike functioning. Cog by cog, the snow and slush had enveloped his bike's rear sprockets, turning the assembly into a frozen mass. "I knew I had to keep one gear working," he said. "I kept it in the 53x14 and pedaled the whole way down. I never stopped pedaling, so it never stopped working."

With Breukink still at his side, Hampsten found the descent to be a terrifying wilderness. "There was no lead car, no follow car, just us and the snow," he said. At one point the pair came upon a mechanic by the roadside in a state of near delirium. He was like a sentinel at the gates of hell, a visitor from the netherworld. "He was muttering and cursing, saying the race was abandoned," said Hampsten. When the two flashed past, "he shrieked, he was so surprised."

A person in a survival situation can have a variety of reactions, many of which are counterproductive. Hampsten had made his choice long before, which was to fight.

"It was the place where I was able to push myself the most," he would say, years later. "Everyone had to go places in their mind, just to get down the mountain."

o͞o

Nearly every rider involved has a story about that day, June 5, 1988. While Hampsten may have been the protagonist, a thousand dramas were being played out in the peloton, which extended for more than an hour behind.

His teammate Veggerby, while descending at 70 kph on snow and ice, in a moment of insanity, took his hands from the handlebar and began clapping himself to stay warm. "Someone in a service car was hammering on the horn, telling me to be careful," he said. "I thought he meant I should go faster. I was desperate and lucky. I was just going with no brain, no fear. It was a terrible day."

As the snow changed to rain, riders found their bodies had gone numb. Hampsten pictured leading.

Kiefel, meanwhile, found his hands had become useless clubs. "It got so cold—and we had down tube shifters—that I couldn't brake or shift," he said. "I'd just hit them with my fist."

Roll, never one for half measures, employed a unique survival tactic and spent the descent screaming at the top of his lungs.

From Lauritzen's perspective, back in the field, the race resembled an arctic wasteland. "I was all alone," he said. "No one else could see me from the front or back. I was just crying on the bike. If you went off the cliffs, no one would have seen you." He would eventually finish more than 21 minutes back, calling it "my worst nightmare on the bike . . . one of the hardest days in my life. I was a paracommander," he added, referring to a former stint with the Norwegian Army, "and I knew pain, but that day was terrible. It was lucky that riders didn't die."

○○

Hampsten's earlier calculation—to conserve energy for the descent—would now prove its value. Wearing the neck warmer and wool hat that Ochowicz had given him at the summit, he managed to stay with Breukink, the pair gaining more than four minutes on the field.

But with 18 kilometers to go, Breukink moved ahead, and Hampsten couldn't respond. "To him, it looked like I was asleep," Hampsten said. "I was so cold, I couldn't jump to get on his wheel," even though he thought "it might be warmer on his wheel."

But more important things were at stake than the stage win. Although Hampsten finished 2nd on the day, seven seconds back, he had captured the pink leader's jersey by 15 seconds over Breukink. The 3rd place finisher in the stage was more than four minutes behind. Van der Velde, who had been first to cross the summit of the Gavia, had cracked entirely, losing 47 minutes.

Hampsten crossed the line and was overcome with a wave of confusing and contradictory emotions. "I was in a rage, psychologically," he said. Before long he found his old friend Neel, who had kept the car running, with the heater on. Hampsten crawled in and asked to be alone.

Then he started to cry.

○○

For Hampsten, and many of his teammates, it had been a day spent on the threshold of life and death. No sooner had the leaders come across than the finish line was transformed into a triage unit, with hypothermic riders collapsing into the arms of *soigneurs* and managers.

Of all the 7-Elevens, Roll seemed to have placed himself in the most precarious position physically. Video footage shows him hyperventilating, a support person embracing him from behind, trying to shake him out of his torpor. "He was the worst one," said Neel. Added Kiefel, "That guy could suffer."

While Roll and others paid dearly to count themselves among the finishers, others may have taken a more expeditious route. Looming large over the day has been the persistent rumor that many riders simply got in their team cars and hitched a ride to the finish rather than face the epic conditions. Lauritzen, for one, was insistent on the point, saying that "there were 30 or 40 riders who got in the car— then they were on their bikes again at the finish."

Ochowicz and Neel were both unfazed by the apparent scandal. "I don't care if they did," said Neel of the scofflaws. What was far more important was that their man was wearing the maglia rosa, the pink jersey of the race leader, with seven stages remaining.

Erminio Dell'Oglio, the team's great sponsor and benefactor, was nearly prostrate with emotion at the sight of Hampsten in pink. The team doctor, Testa, had to treat him for palpitations.

"He had to stay home for rest of the race," said Lauritzen. "It was too hard for his heart."

oo

Hampsten, arguably in the best shape of his life, was not done putting his stamp on the race. Four days later was an 18-km time trial—all of it uphill.

To help gauge his effort, he looked to his old friend Testa, who had been monitoring his heart rate daily. Testa instructed him to hold a very painful 180 beats per minute on the steep part of the climb, where he stood to gain the most time. "My tactic was to get a good start, but hit the second half really hard," said Hampsten.

Neel, exercising his horse sense, sequestered Hampsten in a back alley before the start, where he rode stationary rollers and listened to music. "He was calm, in the right mind-set," said Neel. "He was in his own private Idaho."

Hampsten executed the race perfectly, leading at every checkpoint, winning the stage by 32 seconds, and extending his lead over his major competitors on G.C. It was the best time trial performance of his career. In winning, he'd entered into a twilight between pain and pleasure, which caused him to wax philosophical.

"It hurt so much," he said, "it felt like a meditation."

oo

The whole race—his greatest accomplishment until that time—served to inform the rest of his career. Thinking back on the pain he'd put himself through on the Gavia, he compared himself to people who had faced life-threatening circumstances in the course of their daily lives. In comparison, his travail seemed entirely artificial, yet still existential in nature.

"People that are in true hardship do that just to survive," he said. "It's not a natural instinct. For an athlete to be in a particular set of circumstances, and to ask that of our bodies—it's an artificial setting, and you're willing to do it that one time and really push the limits farther than they've ever been pushed before."

"I did make a deal after the Gavia," he said, "realizing how much my body and mind would give to me. I really respected it after that day. I really had to pick and choose when I would go again to that depth."

At the race's conclusion, the team went to Bergamo, and the Bar Augusto, a famed cycling bar and one of the team's traditional watering holes. By this time, Dell'Oglio had recovered from his health scare and returned to the race. Hampsten handed him the trophy. The older man cried like a baby.

oo

Hampsten's stunning win seemed to set him up perfectly for his life's goal, the Tour de France. He had shown himself to be one of the world's best climbers. He had won a time trial—not his usual forte. And perhaps most important, he'd demonstrated that he was robust enough to survive the rigors of a three-week race.

But from the start of the Tour, it was evident that the incredible form he'd shown in the Giro had left him. He faltered on L'Alpe d'Huez, a mountainous stage that should have played to his favor, finishing four minutes back. In another mountain stage, he finished nine minutes back. On several occasions his teammates were pressed into service, pacing him back to the field. "I just didn't have anything," he told *VeloNews* after falling behind yet again. "I have no excuses." Eventually, he would finish 15th, 26 minutes down.

There was some speculation that he had perhaps celebrated too much after his spectacular win in the Giro. In the brief interval between the two tours, he'd flown back to Colorado to be feted by a hometown crowd, then to Philadelphia for the U.S. professional road championship, then to France for a training camp. By the end of the Tour, he was vowing to do things differently next year, staying in Europe for more of the season. "Traveling really takes it out of me," he said, feeling defeated.

Worse, after winning three stages in 1987, the team itself came up empty-handed. For the Americans, it had been an eminently forgettable Tour.

o͞o

Since the team's inception, Colorado's Coors Classic had been 7-Eleven's domestic showcase, a place of relative ease after the rigors of European racing. "Coming back to America—to race in August—we couldn't ask for anything better," said Ochowicz. "A lot of our guys were from Colorado, and they loved the atmosphere. By then [1988] it had become an easy race to do."

The Coors was unique in America, an event that was longer and harder than most U.S. racing of the era, but still only distantly

Kiefel and his teammates had been brought to a new level of fitness thanks to extensive European racing. Returning to the U.S. for the Coors Classic was a welcome homecoming--and a chance to show their strength.

related to the European grand tours that were now the focus of the team. Distances were generally shorter—rarely over 100 miles—and there were plentiful inner-city criteriums, a form of racing that was relatively rare in Europe, where they mostly occurred after the major tours as a means for faithful domestiques to earn appearance money while riding in the shadows of their team leaders.

Aisner took special pride in chafing against the traditional racing establishment. "[The fact] that the sport was steeped in 100 years of history didn't matter to people, or really to me," he said with a hint of smugness. "We were an odd mishmash of things I put together for entertainment. But I made it work in the context of a stage race."

One thing was certain: The Coors provided welcome visibility for the Southland Corporation in the home market. The company's sponsorship of a European-based team had always seemed more of a magnanimous gesture than a calculated return on investment. Not so at the Coors, where the squad's dominance could actually help propel sales of Slurpees at the corner store.

Phinney had become nearly synonymous with the race. Over the years the Coors Classic had become his special canvas, a place where he could showcase his high-velocity racing style and his movie-star presence. But it was more than that; he was also a prodigal son—a product of the towns, the mountains, and the people of Colorado.

Aisner relied utterly on Phinney for the success of his race, and not just because of his commanding wins. He was also the protagonist in Aisner's carefully scripted drama. Aisner took perverse pride in the choreography of his race, arranging the dramatis personae in such a way that it would maximally frustrate Phinney. "My goal was to set him up where he could do well, then scour the world to find every good sprinter in the world to foil him," said Aisner. "That's why I brought the Russian and East German teams—to give Davis a rough time in the sprints."

It worked. Phinney's raw emotion and his facile nature in front of the camera made for great television. David Michaels, who would produce award-winning Tour de France coverage, found Phinney to be the perfect focal point for his broadcasts, and Aisner was only too happy to heighten the drama. "Whether he won or lost, he always gave great sound bites," Aisner said. It was what bike racing in America needed—high drama—and Phinney supplied it in spades.

Still, by 1988, the team had won the event only once overall.

Phinney, who was famously inspired to start competing while watching the race with his father at age 15, had by now won more stages than anyone in the history of the race. However, at a compact five foot nine and 160 pounds, he had never excelled in the mountains. And while the Coors had been his showcase for close to a decade, he had never placed higher than 9th overall.

But by 1988, his time in the European pro peloton had changed him fundamentally. While he had not achieved his goals in the Tour de France, two weeks earlier, simply having completed the race provided its own dividends. "Davis went to Europe, then he came back, and he could climb," was the simple summation of longtime racer Wayne Stetina.

For Ochowicz, who had faced manifold challenges in Europe, the Coors had the feeling of a working vacation. Other squads would surely have disagreed. For them, the Coors provided a highly visible opportunity to sling rocks at a giant. In particular, Alexi Grewal, who had been summarily fired from the team two years earlier, seemed supremely motivated to antagonize his former sponsor. Fueled by a simmering dislike of Ochowicz and his entire operation, he challenged the team at every opportunity, earning the designation of most aggressive rider and finishing 4th overall.

Nonetheless, Phinney took the leader's jersey in the opening stage, and over the next 10 days it passed back and forth between four 7-Elevens before coming to rest on Phinney's shoulders with four stages to go. By the end, the team had taken all three podium spots. And if that weren't enough, 7-Eleven rider Inga Thompson won the women's race. It was a fitting capstone in this, the final edition of the famed race, which had served as their domestic showcase since 1981.

For Phinney, donning the final leader's jersey in his hometown was a poignant milestone in a career that had started as a dumbstruck 15-year-old standing at the race fencing in Boulder Park. He was, by now, firmly on the other side of that fence.

"A lot of what I've done here," he said, "has to do with what I once thought I couldn't do."

As he thought back, he realized it was a statement that could just as easily have applied to the unlikely journey of the team itself.

7-Eleven's domestic dominance was cemented when Inga Thompson won the women's Coors Classic, and Phinney won the men's race. Inga pictured, 1986.

CHAPTER 19
Ten Days in Yellow

In the sponsorship negotiations leading up to the 1989 season, the 7-Eleven team gained perhaps its most famous ally: Eddy Merckx. Universally acclaimed as the greatest cyclist who ever lived, Merckx had ridden indomitably for more than a decade, winning nearly everything that could be won—often two, three, four, five times or more. The case for his historic standing was made largely on the fact that, unlike the riders of today, he could win anything, more or less at will. Merckx was all but unbeatable in one-day classics (he won Milan–San Remo 7 times in 10 tries, for example), three-week stage races (five Tours de France, five Giri d'Italia), time trials (including the Grand Prix des Nations in 1973), and off-season track races in Belgium, and he even set a one-hour record in 1972—the full continuum of suffering, in other words.

Now a bike maker with a factory near his home in Belgium, Merckx signed on as a 7-Eleven team sponsor for 1989. The relationship was as ironic as it was useful. Here were the 7-Eleven team riders, in many ways still considered neophytes, allied with the walking personification of the European cycling establishment.

Merckx's mere presence implied great things. Hampsten remembers being in a busy Colorado restaurant during the Coors Classic, when a hush suddenly fell over the tables. "We all looked around and thought, something was different in this room," said Hampsten. "I looked over, and there was Eddy Merckx."

And Merckx was no mere figurehead for 7-Eleven. Famous for his obsessive attention to bike fit and performance—he once had Italian frame builder Ugo De Rosa make five different bike frames in the week before Paris-Roubaix so that he could test each design over the race's famous cobblestones—Merckx became a guru to the team on all matters related to position and style. "He was definitely hands on," said Ochowicz. "He had a lot of design input." Merckx presented a heavier bike to Hampsten for the first races of the season and a lighter bike for summer climbing, and delivered a bomber of a bicycle to Bob Roll for his spring classics campaign. But beyond the pragmatic value of the bikes, he was—well, he was Eddy Merckx. From Ochowicz's perspective, the team had, quite simply, been ushered into the inner sanctum of the racing world, and Merckx's presence was motivation enough for his riders, a mystical conveyance of speed and prowess. "He brought another level of credibility," said Ochowicz.

Merckx's involvement went deeper than sponsorship. He fine-tuned each rider's fit and position.

Merckx, in turn, seemed to relish the relationship. In early 1989, the team staged a big party at the annual bicycle trade show in Long Beach, California, to celebrate their successes and their new acquisitions. Merckx, 43 years old and having gained more than a few postcareer pounds, decided to accompany the boys on a ride up the coast to their training camp in Santa Barbara. "It was one of my first experiences with Eddy," said Hampsten. "He was dropping us on all the climbs."

But what mattered most was that Merckx, an icon of traditional European cycling, was embracing *them*, the upstarts of cycling, the cowboys. In their mix of old and new, with riders from America and Europe and a worldview unlike any other cycling team on earth, they now had the heady endorsement of the greatest cyclist of all time. And in one month they would ring in the new season in the most traditional fashion, with the toughest of spring classics.

The world's greatest cyclist, Merckx (eighth from left), joined as team sponsor in 1989. His participation "brought another level of credibility," said Ochowicz.

Team directors play a highly visible and seemingly glorious role, proffering food, equipment, and advice to their star riders, often in the media's bright glare. What's less celebrated are the mind-numbing drives, hotel bookings, tangled logistics, and seemingly unending chores both large (buying the team cars) and small (stickering the team cars) that go along with the job.

In early April Mike Neel, having overseen the team at the Tour du Pays Basque in Spain, decided to make the long overnight drive to Paris-Roubaix, which started the next morning. Exhausted, he elected to catch a few winks in the back of the car while mechanic Mike Hanley did a stint behind the wheel. Sometime in the middle of the night, Hanley fell asleep. The car careened into a tractor trailer truck, becoming wedged underneath it. Hanley's thigh bone was broken in the crash. Neel, meanwhile, woke up two days later from a coma, having suffered a concussion and a fractured skull.

He went back to California to recover, then returned to his old duties at the Giro in May. But things weren't the same. Reeling from the aftereffects of his concussion, he abandoned halfway through. Once back home, he spent a lot of time in bed. "I was still out of it," he said. "I was like a zombie—I had no motivation." He took to wearing bright suspenders and would lapse into French in midsentence. "I thought that was normal," he told the *San Francisco Weekly* at the time.

Though he would nominally stay with the team through the end of the year, Neel would not return for the 1990 season. Yet Neel's effect on the team had been immediate and transformative. He had been a gentle force of change that brought them into the European establishment, while never quite leaving the comfort and convenience of the culture they had known. He and Ochowicz had brought with them the subtle and not-so-subtle symbolism of home—everything from familiar food to female *soigneurs*—small insurrections against the existing hegemony. As Neel himself was so fond of saying, "We did it our way."

But as the team became more successful and more international, there was less need to straddle this cultural divide. Even prior to Neel's planned departure, a seismic shift had already occurred. Ochowicz had hired a European director, Noël Dejonckheere. "The accident had nothing to do with the change," Ochowicz insisted. "For Mike, it was probably the right time."

Neel, an indefatigable workhorse, translator, font of cycling knowledge, and most of all, a diviner of spirits, ambled off to the remote backwoods of Fort Jones, California, and a life of relative seclusion, transitioning from a checkered past to an equally checkered future.

It was, in fact, the passing of an era. But while Och looked forward, it was also clear to everyone that Neel had been an integral and essential part of the team's success in Europe.

o͞o

Back in America, the team's traditional U.S. showcase, the Coors Classic, had ended its nine-year run in 1988, but a new stage race emerged to take its place in May 1989: the Tour de Trump. Sponsored by the New York real estate developer and future U.S. President Donald Trump, who owned two casinos in Atlantic City, New Jersey, and was busy building a third, the race offered a glittering $50,000 first prize and featured a host of international pro teams. "It was a big deal for us," said Ochowicz, noting that the race's 10-day schedule would take it through a series of major East Coast cities that were important markets for the 7-Eleven chain.

After a short prologue time trial in Albany, New York, and a 110-mile stage from Albany to New Paltz, New York, Lauritzen took the lead in a 40-mile stage-2 breakaway between New York City and Allentown, Pennsylvania. Lauritzen's win gave him a comfortable margin, but over the course of the next week, Eric Vanderaerden of Panasonic-Isostar, who had trailed Lauritzen by 3:49 after stage 2, won four stages, and by virtue of generous time bonuses put himself within reach of the overall victory.

"Our only defense was to throw Davis in there for higher finishes," said Ochowicz. The strategy worked. The ever-reliable Phinney won the final two road stages, denying Vanderaerden precious time. In a coup de grâce, Kiefel blazed to victory in the last-stage time trial down the Atlantic City boardwalk, riding one of the best time trials of his life on a special bike equipped with an early version of the time trial handlebars that would later become ubiquitous among professional cyclists. Lauritzen finished 4th on the

With the Coors Classic defunct, 7-Eleven's domestic race focus shifted to the Tour de Trump. Lauritzen captured the leader's jersey on the second stage and held it to the end.

24-mile course, sealing his overall victory. However, Vanderaerden did not have a good race, following a race motorcycle off course in a detour that ended his hopes once and for all (he finished 3rd on G.C.). It was a win that evoked memories of the team's past dominance on home soil, replete with clutch victories by the team's most famous protagonists, Phinney and Kiefel.

○○

While 7-Eleven had been blazing a trail in Europe for the better part of a decade, it seemed that wherever the team went, another American, Greg LeMond, had already been there. LeMond's rise had been meteoric. He turned pro in 1980—the same year the 7-Eleven team was being formulated—and immediately began winning European races. He was 2nd in the world pro road championship in 1982 and won it outright the year after that, becoming the first American to do so. In his first Tour de France, in 1984, he finished 3rd and won the white jersey of best young rider. The following year he was arguably the strongest rider in the Tour, but was forced to ride support for teammate and winner Bernard Hinault, finishing 2nd. But in 1986 he bettered his teammate, becoming the first American winner of the world's most famous bike race.

Compared with the 7-Elevens, he was a remarkable physical specimen who existed on another plane entirely, unaided by an American sponsor or the relative comfort of an American team. His success had not merely been a triumph of physical ability. LeMond was intelligent and voluble, willing to talk endlessly about his craft and his ambitions. He was generous in his praise of his fellow racers and was able to reconstruct the patterns and emotions of a race in great detail, to the delight of an American press that was just getting the hang of this bike-racing thing. Along the way, he became fluent in French, conquered a foreign culture, and endeared himself to a discerning public with his French-sounding name.

The 7-Eleven team members, in contrast, existed in their own microcosm, carrying their culture with them and purposefully surrounding themselves with an American support structure and the familiarity of their native language. But, inarguably, they had been successful in their own right. In tandem with LeMond, they had helped bring American cyclists to world prominence in just a few short years.

For some time, Ochowicz had wondered what a combination of these two monumental forces would bring. So in 1989, he set about orchestrating his greatest coup ever—the union of the best American team with the best American rider.

LeMond's stakes could not have been higher. While turkey hunting in California in April 1987, he had been accidentally shot in the back by his brother-in-law. The blast nearly killed him, and after hours of surgery his doctors had been forced to leave 37 shotgun pellets in his body, deeming them too dangerously close to vital organs to remove (two are still lodged in the lining around LeMond's heart). After sitting out the 1987 and 1988 seasons, LeMond roared back to form in spectacular fashion, winning the 1989 Tour de France by eight seconds over Frenchman Laurent Fignon on the final day in what remains the most astounding finish in Tour history. Confounding all expectations, LeMond then went on to win the 1989 world road championship in Chambéry, France, unleashing a violent sprint to beat Dimitri Konyshev of Russia and Sean Kelly of Ireland at the line.

LeMond, having experienced a series of unsettling and fickle team sponsorships in recent years, was keenly interested in riding with his old friends from the States. Hoping to close a deal, Ochowicz and Southland representative Gerard Bisceglia pursued LeMond around Europe as he competed in the lucrative post-Tour criterium circuit. LeMond, like many racers, had a penchant for driving fast, and at one point Ochowicz and Bisceglia found themselves in the backseat of LeMond's Mercedes, fielding staccato questions at more than 100 miles per hour.

By late July, it seemed everything was set. Ochowicz, anticipating consummation of the deal, went to Grenoble with his lawyer to meet with LeMond, who was staying there with his wife in preparation for the world championships.

But LeMond—affable but frequently mercenary—received a late offer from Zed, a children's clothing maker, to the tune of $5.7 million over three years. Although Ochowicz claimed to have a signed contract from LeMond, LeMond reneged. "After that," said

Following months of negotiations, the team had signed a contract with American superstar LeMond (pictured leading, with Hampsten behind) when a last-minute offer from France's Team Zed snatched him away.

Ochowicz, "we walked away." And with that, the best American cycling team in history lost the best American rider in history, gone in a puff of smoke not unlike the cartoonish one that would adorn the front of LeMond's bright blue Zed jersey the following spring.

It had been that close, but the missed deal with LeMond was not a complete loss for the team. During the hard-fought but ultimately unsuccessful negotiations, Ochowicz had shaken the money tree at Southland and found it was still bearing fruit. "They didn't pull the money back," he said of the reported $5 million, three-year contract that had been offered to LeMond.

Indeed, Och would use the money to make a pivotal addition, a compact and very rapid Canadian rider by the name of Steve Bauer.

Canadian powerhouse Bauer was a constant antagonist for the 7-Elevens until he finally joined the team.

○○

The signing of Bauer for the 1990 season was, in some ways, an immense irony. While riding for GS Mengoni in the 1980s, Bauer had been Phinney's chief nemesis on the American criterium circuit. And now he had been brought into the fold, with Phinney as his teammate. But Bauer immediately proved his worth to 7-Eleven in the famed Paris-Roubaix cobblestoned classic, finishing an agonizing one centimeter behind his breakaway companion, Eddy Planckaert of Panasonic.

Though Bauer had never been an accomplished climber, he had a particular knack for the Tour de France. As far back as 1986, he had seen his countryman, Alex Stieda, get the yellow jersey with

Bauer leads Eddy Planckaert at Paris-Roubaix in 1990. At the finish, it took judges 10 minutes to determine that Planckaert had won by millimeters.

a good prologue time trial and a fortuitous breakaway in the first road stage. "I said, 'Holy shit—that's how you do it!'" said Bauer. "I figured out [that if there's a] stage in the morning, no one wants to chase, because there's a team time trial in the afternoon."

"So from the gun, on those stages, I would make sure to cover everyone."

In 1988, while riding for Weinmann/La Suisse, he employed the formula to perfection, winning the first stage, taking 2nd in the team time trial, and eventually wearing the yellow jersey for five days and finishing 4th overall.

Now, in 1990, riding for 7-Eleven, he was primed to try the approach again.

When an Italian named Claudio Chiappucci attacked in the first stage, Bauer went after him, joined by two others. As Bauer had predicted, the lethargic field—seemingly preoccupied with thoughts of the team time trial—never mounted a serious chase. Meanwhile, said Bauer, "We were just going flat out, like a four-man team time trial—like it was for the world record." Though he finished last in the small group, by the finish they had put 10 minutes on the field. This, combined with Bauer's strong 19th place in the prologue, was enough to put him in yellow.

The next day's team time trial, as much as anything, spoke volumes about how far the team had come. Just four years earlier, Stieda had lost the jersey in a similar stage, with team members infamously crashing into one another and hurling water bottles in bitter acrimony.

This time, they were determined not to squander the great gift they now possessed. From the outset, sporting aerodynamic gear, they were flying in precise formation, looking like veterans of the pro peloton—which of course, by now, they were. They posted a solid ride, finishing 6th and adding a valuable eight seconds to Bauer's overall lead. In light of the 1986 debacle, it had been a remarkable

A strong prologue and an all-out effort in stage 1 put Bauer in yellow. The solid team time trial kept him there, and he held the jersey until stage 10.

reversal of fortune. "That's the best we've ever done in a team time trial," said Ochowicz, beaming.

Normally, in such circumstances, a nonclimber could hope to retain the lead for three days, maybe four. But when Bauer considered the broad expanse of days that spread out before him, he saw that there were no major climbs until the Alps, nine stages hence. It seemed possible that he could retain the jersey until then. After all, he was riding strongly, and, just as important, he had at his beck and call what was arguably the strongest 7-Eleven Tour team to date.

Indeed, it took until stage 10, a fearsome day of three major Alpine climbs, to force a surrender. Bauer, having lost the yellow jersey, would eventually finish 27th. And stingingly, for Ochowicz, Le Mond would win the race, recording his third and final Tour de France victory in that blue Team Zed jersey.

Nonetheless, it had been a remarkable Tour for the 7-Elevens. And the 10 days spent in yellow, with the attention of the world's sporting press upon them, could not have come at a better moment.

Putting the memories of the 1986 debacle to rest, the team supported Bauer's 1990 yellow jersey with a solid team time trial.

CHAPTER 20
Southland Bows Out

For more than 30 years, the Southland Corporation had been a fortress of retail growth and financial success. By the late 1980s, however, the company had fallen into a slow financial decline. In 1987, facing a hostile takeover, founders John and Jere Thompson had borrowed billions to buy back 7-Eleven stock and regain control of the company they had nurtured and expanded from a series of Dallas ice docks back in 1928. What they could never have predicted was the stock market crash of October 1987, which forced a precipitous rise in interest payments on the loan.

Hoping to salvage what remained, they began divesting whatever property was not critical to the business. "We were selling all kinds of things," said Jere Thompson. Foremost among the items they could no longer afford was a professional bike racing team. Despite the squad's obvious and continuing success, and its multimillion-dollar value as an international marketing vehicle, the cycling team had grown from a $200,000 investment in 1981 to a $3 million–plus expense in 1990.

The company's downward slide was unstoppable. Facing billions in debt, Southland declared bankruptcy. It had been a rapid and frightening free fall for a company that, just 10 years earlier, had been a darling of the financial world.

The Thompsons, who had famously asked, "What's a velodrome?" had taken the great leap of faith to back Ochowicz's grand adventure back in 1981. But bike racing was now the last thing on their minds. As Bauer was enjoying his time in yellow at the 1990 Tour de France, Ochowicz was informed that there would be no team for the following season.

He had, by now, seen countless sponsors come and go over

the years—supporters within the industry for bicycle equipment and supplies and outsiders like American Airlines that provided travel for the team—but had never had to deal with a departure of this magnitude. Among all the sponsorship changes for Team 7-Eleven, Southland Corporation had been the rock-solid firm that had underwritten Och's entire professional life, and indeed, his stature and standing in the world. The looming change involved no small amount of angst.

oo

Desperately casting about for solutions, at one point Ochowicz mentioned to his old racing pal, John Vande Velde, that he was seeking a new title sponsor. Vande Velde, initially nonplussed, "woke up at 3 a.m." one day with an idea. One of his Chicago area cycling buddies happened to be the spouse of Sheila Griffin, the worldwide advertising director for Motorola, an electronics company based in Schaumburg, Illinois. Motorola was riding high on revenue from a booming market in cell phones, an industry it had created with the introduction of the first mass-market portable telephone in 1983. With the phone money rolling in faster than it could be spent, perhaps Motorola had some sponsorship dollars tucked away for worldwide marketing.

At the urging of Vande Velde, Griffin reluctantly agreed to meet. Ochowicz, with rider Tom Schuler in tow, drove to Chicago, where "45 minutes turned into five hours," said Griffin. With her interest piqued, Griffin asked Ochowicz when he needed a decision. His answer was "two weeks." After that, explained Ochowicz, he would need to release his riders to other teams.

"But Jim," said Griffin, "no contract has ever gone through Motorola that fast."

While Griffin tried to expedite the contract, Ochowicz was growing increasingly desperate. For it wasn't just the team that was vulnerable—it was Ochowicz himself. Over the past months, seeking to insulate his riders from the full scale of the impending disaster, he had mortgaged his house to make salary payments. It was a burden he carried alone. "No one knew this stuff except me," he said. "I could have lost everything."

Fortunately—miraculously—on September 19, Motorola came through with its signature on the deal. Even for Ochowicz, no stranger to financial risk, it had been a harrowing ride. The roughly $2 million sponsorship agreement—the very salvation of the team—had taken exactly 19 days from start to finish. "The guys," said Ochowicz, "never knew it was that close." What the guys soon learned, though, was that they were and for the next six years would be the Motorola Cycling team.

oo

In late September, seeking to impress his new benefactors, Ochowicz invited Griffin and a handful of other Motorola execs to a race in Hamilton, Ontario. It would be one of the last events to feature the familiar colors of a famous convenience store. On this day in Hamilton, Ochowicz was pleased to see one of his riders, Frankie Andreu, riding aggressively at the front. Andreu, like so many 7-Eleven team members before him, was one of the Midwest brethren. Like Ochowicz, Andreu had started racing in his early teens on the velodromes and circuits of a hundred small towns scattered through the nation's heartland. And, like Ochowicz, he was now performing on a world stage. Resplendent in that famous jersey, Andreu won the race handily, continuing a long tradition of what could only be called domestic dominance by the 7-Elevens.

oo

The Motorola team's official press introduction in the autumn of 1990 was to take place in Milan, the day before the squad's racing debut in the one-day Italian classic, the Tour of Lombardy. Things started well, with a smiling Dag Otto Lauritzen showing off the new blue-and-red Motorola jersey while the team stood by in their warm-ups, but that turned out to be the high point of the event. The next day, on the way to the race, the team got mired in an enormous traffic jam. For a moment, it seemed certain they would miss their racing debut entirely. (In the end Ochowicz brandished an invitation from race director Vincenzo Torriani, which was tantamount to a papal decree, and the *polizia* waved the squad through.) The race, in front of Motorola executives, did not go well. Their best-placed rider was Sean Yates, well down the charts in an ignominious 55th place. "We did terribly," Ochowicz admitted.

Sean Yates of England was a stalwart rider for one-day races and major tours. He was one of the few who rode for both 7-Eleven and the new sponsor, Motorola.

Still, as he watched his fledgling Motorola team come across the line, Ochowicz could only wonder at the distance he had traveled since the halcyon days of 1981, when he had taken the great leap to start his grand enterprise. The Motorola sponsorship was yet another of the "levels" that Ochowicz was so fond of. From his days as a young bike racer in Milwaukee, to his epiphany in Inzell, Germany, to being a team director in the world's greatest bike race, the levels he had reached had all been intermediate summits on the way to some loftier height.

When the team had started 10 years and thousands of races earlier, it had been an obsession, a dream, a glimmer in Ochowicz's eye. From the beginning, the foundation of the squad had always been about remarkable athletic talent. Over the years Ochowicz patiently assembled a charismatic and gifted group of riders equally adept at dominating domestic criteriums or winning on a world stage. In Phinney, Ochowicz found a lightning-fast sprinter who quickly adapted his talents to the European pro peloton. In Kiefel, he had a preeminent lead-out man, an all-rounder, and a capable race winner. In Hampsten, he found a gifted climber just waiting to exercise his talents on the high passes of Europe. But the team also had remarkable depth, with riders like Pierce, Lauritzen, Nitz, Stieda, Bauer, Alcalá, Yates, and dozens of others capable of winning on a given day. They had been the first U.S.-based pro squad to race successfully in Europe, the first to win stages in a major tour, and the first to have worn the coveted yellow jersey of the Tour de France.

As for the Southland Corporation, the company's financial support had bestowed legitimacy on a sport that for too many years had scraped out a marginal existence on the fringes of American athletic culture. It helped spawn a new era of corporate, nonendemic sponsorship, lifting American bike racing out of a backwater, where elite racers struggled to find their next meal and lived out of the rattling confines of the family van. By the time Southland ended its

In building Team 7-Eleven, Ochowicz patiently assembled a gifted squad that competed at the highest levels on the world's stage and redefined the structure of professional cycling.

sponsorship in 1990, it had reached into every corner of the sport, sponsoring a successful women's road team, a duo of powerful men's and women's track teams, and several junior teams. It had helped back a wildly successful Los Angeles Olympics in 1984, several national race series, and the 1986 world cycling championships in Colorado Springs. With Southland's support, American bike racing had gone pro.

Ochowicz, always a quick study and a forthright negotiator, proved to be as adept in the boardroom as in the team car, brokering hundreds of deals large and small. He went on to become co-owner, president, and general manager of the BMC Racing Team, which won the 2011 Tour de France with Cadel Evans; and manager of the CCC pro team, before retiring in 2020.

The 7-Eleven team, in turn, had changed the cycling world. Indeed, in the end, the squad's cultural impact may have exceeded its athletic one, forever altering the landscape of professional cycling. The 7-Eleven team had taken a sport with a 100-year tradition—tied to the working classes of the continent—and fashioned it in their own image. Some of the changes were highly visible, as when they had introduced female *soigneurs* and American culture—for better or worse—to the pro peloton. But other innovations were more fundamental, altering the hidebound structure that had dominated and in some ways suppressed professional cycling for decades. The 7-Elevens operated under a new, more egalitarian style, where anyone was given license to win on a given day. Rather than building a team around a single leader, the team had multiple stars with strong personalities, all of whom were expected to be ready to think for themselves on the road, sacrifice for teammates for the better good, and be ready to assume leadership in the middle of a race whenever necessary. When the team's riders first appeared on the European racing scene, they had been derided as cowboys and blamed for every crash. Now, other teams looked to the 7-Elevens as a model of modern team structure.

Through it all, they had brought an element of levity to the peloton. At times, thanks to Bob Roll's antics, they were the source of humor; at other times, such as the implosion in the 1986 Tour, they were the unhappy object of sarcasm. In either case, they were hard to ignore.

In the end they had come of their own volition, forsaking lives of comfort and convenience to do the one thing they loved best in the world: ride their bicycles. And, they had done it all in the name of a stunningly appropriate icon of Americana, the corner convenience store.

As he reflected on all this that fall day in Italy, Ochowicz, teeming with pride over everything he had done and was yet to do, was positively beaming at the prospect of a new season.

Perhaps no other professional cycling squad has ever been as unified in goals, attitude, outlook, support, and success as Team 7-Eleven.

EPILOGUE

Dozens of athletes rode for 7-Eleven during the team's 10-year existence. The bonds that developed were strong, so much so that every four years, alumni gather in Mexico to swap stories and reminisce about their roles in America's seminal pro squad. Today, many of the riders are still connected to the sport as coaches, promoters, commentators, and bike shop owners.

Steve Bauer continued to ride for Jim Ochowicz as a member of the Motorola team through 1995. He retired from cycling in 1996 and founded Steve Bauer Bike Tours. He also serves as a professional team owner and director, including for Israel Premier Tech.

Jonathan "Jock" Boyer ended his pro career in 1987 but returned to competitive cycling and in 2006 won the Race Across America for the second time (he had first won in 1985). At one point he was convicted of lewd behavior with a minor and served a short jail sentence. In 2007 he moved to Rwanda, where he coached a Rwandan cycling team and worked with a relief agency to provide bicycles and aid to the people there. He now runs the Boyer YL Ranch in Savery, Wyoming, catering to cyclists and other outdoor enthusiasts. He is a U.S. Bicycling Hall of Fame inductee.

Jeff Bradley retired in 1987 and ran a bike shop in Davenport, Iowa.

Chris Carmichael became the USA Cycling National Coaching Director and then founded Carmichael Training Systems, a coaching business serving endurance athletes. He was awarded the US Olympic Committee Coach of the Year award and authored several books on endurance training. In 2022 he stepped down from the CEO role of CTS to focus on personal coaching, his family, and riding his bike. He is a U.S. Bicycling Hall of Fame inductee.

Mark Gorski assumed numerous roles with the U.S. Cycling Federation, including board member and national team director. In 1999 he became director of the U.S. Postal cycling team. He has also worked as a race director and promoter. He is a senior vice-president for a life science real estate developer and lives in Indian Wells, California. He is a U.S. Bicycling Hall of Fame inductee.

Alexi Grewal was dropped by the 7-Eleven team in 1986. He rode for the Coors Light team through 1993. After leaving cycling, he became a carpenter and furniture maker, but he returned to racing in 2011. He is a U.S. Bicycling Hall of Fame inductee.

Andy Hampsten stayed with the team after the sponsorship was assumed by Motorola in 1991. He won the Alpe d'Huez stage of the Tour de France, considered the unofficial world championship of climbing, in 1992 and finished 4th overall in the race (for the second time). He is still thought to be one of the best American climbers in history. Today he runs a bike company, Hampsten Cycles, with his brother Steve. He leads bicycle trips in Italy with his company, Cinghiale Cycling Tours. He frequently takes his tours up the Gavia Pass. Even today, he says, "I still get quite emotional there." He is a U.S. Bicycling Hall of Fame inductee.

Eric Heiden graduated from Stanford Medical School in 1991 and has served as doctor for the 7-Eleven and Motorola teams as well as for professional basketball teams and the U.S. Speedskating team. Today he practices medicine in Park City, Utah. Heiden and former 7-Eleven physician Massimo Testa coauthored the book Faster, Better, Stronger in 2008. He is a U.S. Bicycling Hall of Fame inductee.

Ron Kiefel rode for the Motorola, Coors Light, and Saturn professional teams after 7-Eleven, retiring after the 1995 season. He later owned and managed the bike shop his father started in 1973 in Wheat Ridge, Colorado. He helped develop an online community for cyclists, called Preem. He is a U.S. Bicycling Hall of Fame inductee.

Dag Otto Lauritzen rode for Ochowicz's Motorola team through 1992. He retired from cycling in 1994 to operate real estate offices and fitness centers. He serves as a journalist on the Tour de France, and started his own sports clothing line, DO2.

Mike Neel left his coaching position with the 7-Elevens in 1989, then moved from one coaching job to another, sometimes working construction to make ends meet. He married a 7-Eleven soigneur, April Wilburn, but they were later divorced. He is a U.S. Bicycling Hall of Fame inductee.

Jim Ochowicz continued to direct teams, including Motorola, BMC, and CCC. His BMC rider Cadel Evans won the Tour de France in 2011. Ochowicz was also an investment counselor for a major San Francisco financial firm, Thomas Weisel Partners. His daughter, Elli, is an Olympic speed skater. He is retired in Park City, Utah, and rides often. He is a U.S. Bicycling Hall of Fame inductee.

Sean Petty, who oversaw 7-Eleven sports marketing, went on to hold senior management positions at USA Cycling and managed national team programs, marketing, sponsorship, membership and international relations. He was team leader for USA's 2000 Olympic cycling team in Sydney and served in various capacities at 51 UCI World Championships including road, track, mountain bike and BMX. He is a member of the UCI Road Commission, and a U.S. Bicycling Hall of Fame inductee.

Davis Phinney rode for the Coors Light cycling team following his nine-year stint with 7-Eleven. He retired from competition after the 1993 season. He is still considered the winningest American rider in history. Following his cycling career, he worked in sports television as a commentator and hosted bicycle camps with his wife, Olympic gold medalist Connie Carpenter-Phinney. In 2000 he was diagnosed with Parkinson's disease. He started the Davis Phinney Foundation to help educate and inspire people living with Parkinson's. Phinney's son, Taylor, is a past multi-time world champion cyclist, now retired, who rode for Ochowicz's BMC team, among others. Davis Phinney is a U.S. Bicycling Hall of Fame inductee.

Bob Roll rode for the Motorola team in its inaugural year, 1991, then raced mountain bikes professionally through 1998. After retiring from competition, he became a columnist for VeloNews; wrote four cycling books; and currently contributes cycling commentary for Versus television, where he continues to be known for his offbeat sense of humor. Roll joined NBC Sports' cycling coverage as an analyst in 2012, and works on the Tour de France and other international cycling road races. Roll continues to ride road and mountain bicycles recreationally.

Tom Schuler founded Team Sports, a management company, after retiring from competitive cycling. He helped direct the Motorola team; directed Team Saturn; helped found the Volvo-Cannondale mountain bike team; and launched numerous other teams in cycling, triathlon, and other endurance sports. He is a U.S. Bicycling Hall of Fame inductee.

Alex Stieda runs a bike touring company, Alex Stieda Cycling; teaches cycling classes; and works in computer technology in Edmonton, Alberta. He also does commentary for the Global Cycling Network.

Jere Thompson, former president and CEO of the Southland Corporation, didn't know the difference between a velodrome and a palindrome when he took the great leap of faith to invest in the team in 1980. After retiring from 7-Eleven, Thompson became an enthusiastic bicycle rider, always wearing a 7-Eleven jersey.

Jens Veggerby rode for Ochowicz's Motorola team and retired from cycling in 1998 after being struck by a car and suffering numerous injuries. He runs an art gallery in Copenhagen, and a sports management and events company, Veggerby Sport & Culture.

Team reunion, 2010. Back row (left to right): Ochowicz, Phinney, Heiden, Kiefel, Pierce. Kneeling: Shapiro, Schuler.

Team Reunion, 2015. Back row (left to right): Roll, Phinney, Veggerby, Shapiro, McKinley, Petty, Hayman, Knickman, Van Haute, Kiefel, Carmichael. Front row (left to right): Schuler, Lauritzen, Ochowicz, Stieda, Bradley, Demgen, Hampsten.

Team Reunion, 2022. Back row (left to right): Matush, Testa, Bradley, Kiefel, Boyer, Heiden, Weaver, Van Haute, Craven, Lauritzen, Petty. Front row (left to right): Pierce, Schuler, Bauer, Veggerby, Carmichael, Ochowicz, Phinney, Demgen, Hampsten. Kneeling: Shapirio.

SENIOR TEAM ROSTERS

1981 Jeff Bradley, Greg Demgen, Ron Hayman, Eric Heiden, Tom Schuler, Danny Van Haute, Roger Young

1982 *Men*: Jeff Bradley, Greg Demgen, Matt Francis, Mark Gorski, Ron Hayman, Eric Heiden, Ron Kiefel, Davis Phinney, Tom Schuler, Alex Stieda, Danny Van Haute, Roger Young; *Women*: Jacque Bradley, Sarah Docter, Rebecca Twigg

1983 *Men*: Jeff Bradley, Greg Demgen, Matt Francis, Mark Gorski, Ron Hayman, Eric Heiden, Ron Kiefel, Davis Phinney, Tom Schuler, Alex Stieda, Andy Weaver; *Women*: Betsy Davis, Peggy Maass, Cindy Olavarri, Rebecca Twigg

1984 *Men*: Jeff Bradley, Mark Gorski, Eric Heiden, Ron Kiefel, Kit Kyle, Leonard Nitz, Rory O'Reilly, Davis Phinney, Tom Schuler, Alex Stieda, Andy Weaver; *Women*: Betsy Davis, Peggy Maass, Cindy Olavarri, Rebecca Twigg

1985 *Men*: Frankie Andreu, Scott Berryman, Jeff Bradley, Chris Carmichael, Curt Harnett, Eric Heiden, Ron Kiefel, Kit Kyle, David Lettieri, Robert Mathis, Leonard Nitz, Davis Phinney, Tom Schuler, Alex Stieda; *Women*: Kelly Kittredge, Peggy Maass, Julie Olson, Connie Paraskevin, Laura Peycke, Rebecca Twigg

1986 *Men*: Frankie Andreu, Jeff Bradley, Chris Carmichael, Alexi Grewal, Curt Harnett, Eric Heiden, Ron Kiefel, David Lettieri, Robert Mathis, Leonard Nitz, Davis Phinney, Bob Roll, Tom Schuler, Russell Scott, Doug Shapiro, Alex Stieda; *Women*: Connie Paraskevin, Laura Peycke, Muriel Sharp, Inga Thompson, Rebecca Twigg

1987 *Men*: Raúl Alcalá, Frankie Andreu, Jonathan Boyer, Jeff Bradley, Chris Carmichael, Kenny Christoff, Andy Hampsten, Eric Heiden, Ron Kiefel, Dag Otto Lauritzen, Robert Mathis, Scott McKinley, Leonard Nitz, Davis Phinney, Jeff Pierce, Bob

Roll, Tom Schuler, Doug Shapiro, Stefan Spielman, Alex Stieda, Jens Veggerby; *Women*: Bunki Bankaitis-Davis, Inga Thompson, Jill Koval, Kathi Riggert, Tricia Walters

1988 *Men*: Raúl Alcalá, Norm Alvis, Frankie Andreu, Chris Carmichael, Andy Hampsten, Eric Heiden, Ron Kiefel, Roy Knickman, Dag Otto Lauritzen, Tommy Matush, Scott McKinley, Leonard Nitz, Davis Phinney, Jeff Pierce, Bob Roll, Tom Schuler, Doug Shapiro, Stefan Spielman, Alex Stieda, Jens Veggerby, Brian Walton; *Women*: Bunki Bankaitis-Davis, Inga Thompson, Sue Ehlers, Kathi Riggert, Tricia Walters

1989 *Men*: Norm Alvis, Frankie Andreu, John Brady, Nathan Dahlberg, Andy Hampsten, Eric Heiden, Ron Kiefel, Roy Knickman, Dag Otto Lauritzen, Tommy Matush, Scott McKinley, Davis Phinney, Jeff Pierce, Bob Roll, Tom Schuler, Stefan Spielman, Alex Stieda, Jens Veggerby, Brian Walton, Sean Yates, Gerhard Zadrobilek; *Women*: Bunki Bankaitis-Davis, Deirdre Demet, Phyllis Hines, Leslee Schenk, Inga Thompson

1990 Norm Alvis, Frankie Andreu, Steve Bauer, John Brady, Thomas Craven, Nathan Dahlberg, Andy Hampsten, Eric Heiden, Ron Kiefel, Roy Knickman, Dag Otto Lauritzen, Tommy Matush, Scott McKinley, Davis Phinney, Jeff Pierce, Bob Roll, Tom Schuler, John Tomac, Jens Veggerby, Brian Walton, Sean Yates, Urs Zimmerman

NOTES

Chapter 1

P. 1 no professional events for them: *VeloNews*, April 25, 1980, p. 1.
P. 1 you could become a pro cyclist: Interview with Jack Simes (pro located in Allentown), *VeloNews*, May 23, 1980, p. 1.
P. 3 in downtown Boulder: Carpenter/Phinney Bike Camp website, Davis Phinney biography, http://www.bikecamp.com/about.davis.html.
P. 4 Pan American Games and world championships: U.S. Bicycling Hall of Fame website, http://www.usbhof.org.
P. 4 the view of their native country: Wikipedia website, U.S. Bicycling Hall of Fame, http://en.wikipedia.org/wiki/United_States_Bicycling_Hall_of_Fame.

Chapter 2

P. 7 between Albany and Montreal: Official website of the Olympic movement, http://www.vancouver2010.com/img/00/05/08/legaciesofthegames-lakeplacid_56d-cY.pdf.
P. 7 worth a try: Official website of the Olympic movement, http://www.olympic.org/en/content/Olympic-Athletes/All-Athletes/Athletes-HA-to-HM/-Eric-Heiden-/.
P. 7 lap after lap: ESPN website, Eric Heiden was a reluctant hero, ESPN.com.
P. 8 almost half a second: Answers.com website, Eric Heiden, http://www.answers.com/topic/eric-heiden; Official website of the Olympic movement, http://www.olympic.org/en/content/Olympic-Athletes/All-Athletes/Athletes-HA-to-HM/-Eric-Heiden-/.
P. 8 to cheer them on: Answers.com website, Eric Heiden, http://www.answers.com/topic/eric-heiden.
P. 8 Miracle on Ice: Wikipedia website, Miracle on Ice, http://en.wikipedia.org/wiki/Miracle_on_Ice.
P. 9 headed for the rink: Universal Sports website, http://www.universalsports.com/news/article/newsid+330127.html; Snyderemarks website, Eric Heiden 25: An exclusive interview, http://snyderemarks.com/eric-heiden-25-an-exclusive-interview/.
P. 9 margin of six seconds:Official website of the Olympic movement, http://www.olympic.org/en/content/Olympic-Athletes/All-Athletes/Athletes-HA-to-HM/-Eric-Heiden-/.
P. 9 at those Games: Wikipedia website, 1980 Winter Olympics, http://en.wikipedia.org/wiki/1980_Winter_Olympics.
P. 9 *Sports Illustrated* and *Time*: *Sports Illustrated* website, February 25, 1980, cover page, http://sportsillustrated.cnn.com/vault/cover/fea-tured/8680/index.htm; *Time* website, February 11, 1980, cover page, http://www.time.com/time/covers/0,16641,19800211,00.html.
P. 9 Kris Kristofferson's daughter: Geoff Drake, interview with Roger Young; SFGate website, Lance tale, crashes stir Tour frenzy, http://articles.sfgate.com/2005-07-09/bay-area/17381685_1_bike-lance-armstrong-spandex-shorts.

P. 9   fame and publicity: Wikipedia website, Speed skating at the 1980 Winter Olympics, http://en.wikipedia.org/wiki/Speed_skating_at_the_1980_Winter_Olympics.

P. 10   as a junior: Answers.com website, Eric Heiden, http://www.answers.com/topic/eric-heiden; Wikipedia website, Eric Heiden, http://en.wikipedia.org/wiki/Eric_Heiden.

P. 10   into a European sport: Wikipedia website, Eric Heiden, http://en.wikipedia.org/wiki/Eric_Heiden.

P. 11   several days per week: Yellow Jersey website, http://www.yellowjersey.org/613.html.

P. 13   of rippling muscle: *VeloNews*, May 22, 1981; *Washington Post* website, Heiden's View of His Success: What's the Fuss? February 24, 1980, p A1, http://www.washingtonpost.com/wp-srv/sports/longterm/olympics1998/history/memories/80-heidreact.htm.

P. 13   recognizable limp: *Washington Post* website, Heiden's View of His Success: What's the Fuss? February 24, 1980, p A1, http://www.washingtonpost.com/wp-srv/sports/longterm/olympics1998/history/memories/80-heidreact.htm.

P. 18   in the parking lot: Velodromes of the World website, Velodromes of the World—United States http://globadome.com/six/velodromes/unit.html.

P. 20   champions of the day: International Cycle Sport website, Coureur Sporting Cyclist, http://www.internationalcyclesport.com/html/coureur_sporting_cyclist.html; Wikipedia website.

P. 24   achieve the best time: Wikipedia website, Pan American Games, http://en.wikipedia.org/wiki/Pan_American_Games.

P. 26   won a bronze medal: Wikipedia website, Cycling at the 1971 Pan American Games, http://en.wikipedia.org/wiki/Cycling_at_the_1971_Pan_American_Games#Men.27s_4.000m_Individual_Pursuit_.28Track.29.

P. 26   Vande Velde and company: Wikipedia website, UCI Track Cycling World Championships, http://en.wikipedia.org/wiki/UCI_Track_Cycling_World_Championships.

P. 27   Munich Massacre: About.com website, History of the Olympics, http://history1900s.about.com/od/fadsfashion/a/olympics1972.htm.

P. 35   started in 1888: Wolverine Sports Club website, WSC History, http://www.wolverinesportsclub.com/WSC_History.html.

Chapter 3

P. 37   after the Olympics: *Washington Post* website, Heiden's View of His Success: What's the Fuss? February 24, 1980, p A1, http://www.washingtonpost.com/wp-srv/sports/longterm/olympics1998/history/memories/80-heidreact.htm.

P. 37   as a learning experience: Geoff Drake interview with Eric Heiden. p. 42 to do it," he said: *VeloNews*, May 22, 1981.

P. 38   among others: *VeloNews*, June 13, 1980.

P. 38   Heiden's presence alone: *VeloNews*, May 22, 1981.

P. 39   said another: *New York Times* website, No Gold for Heiden in Bike Race, May 26, 1980, http://select.nytimes.com/gst/abstract.html?res

	=F10F15FF3B5C12728DDDAE0A94DD405B8084F1D3&scp =1&sq=%22heiden%20fails%20again%22&st=cse; Heiden Fails Again As Bauer Wins Race, May 27, 1980, http://select.nytimes.com/gst/ abstract.html?res=F10F15FF3B5C12728DDDAE0A94DD405 B8084F1D3&scp=1&sq=%22heiden%20fails%20again%22&st=cse.
P. 39	trials in San Diego: *VeloNews*, June 13, 1980.
P. 39	2nd in the kilometer: *VeloNews*, June 13, 1980.
P. 39	a party to prove it: *VeloNews*, June 13, 1980.
P. 42	in August 1980: *VeloNews*, July 11, 1980, calendar.
P. 46	wherever he went: *VeloNews*, June 13, 1980.
P. 46	put him through school: *VeloNews*, October 10, 1980.
P. 47	or something like that: *VeloNews*, October 10, 1980.

Chapter 4

P. 49	7,000 stores by 1981: Southland press materials and *VeloNews*, April 23, 1982.
P. 49	16 countries: 7-Eleven website, Fun Facts, http://corp.7-eleven.com/ AboutUs/FunFacts/tabid/77/Default.aspx.
P. 50	thirst of a nation: 4.7 billion in 1980, according to Southland press materials.
P. 50	enlarged to 64 ounces: 7-Eleven website, Fun Facts, http://corp.7-eleven.com/AboutUs/FunFacts/tabid/77/Default.aspx.
P. 50	life of the company: 7-Eleven website, Fun Facts, http://corp.7-eleven.com/AboutUs/FunFacts/tabid/77/Default.aspx.
P. 50	your typical market: 7-Eleven website, Fun Facts, http://corp.7-eleven.com/AboutUs/FunFacts/tabid/77/Default.aspx.
P. 51	international store was opened in 1980: FundingUniverse website, 7-Eleven, Inc., http://www.fundinguniverse.com/company-histories/7 Eleven-Inc-Company-History.html; 7-Eleven website, Milestones, http:// corp.7-eleven.com/AboutUs/Milestones/tabid/76/Default.aspx.
P. 51	Games in Los Angeles: *Time* website, January 7, 1985, Person of the Year, Peter Ueberroth, http://www.time.com/time/subscriber/personof theyear/archive/stories/1984.html.
P. 52	"Man of the Year" in 1984: Wikipedia website, 1984 Summer Olympics, http://en.wikipedia.org/wiki/1984_Summer_Olympics; *Time* website, January 7, 1985, Person of the Year, Peter Ueberroth, http://www.time.com/ time/subscriber/personoftheyear/archive/stories/1984.html.
P. 54	had 7,000 stores: *VeloNews*, April 23, 1982.
P. 55	of the L.A. Olympics: *VeloNews*, April 23, 1982.
P. 56	people to the game: Ultimate Soccer Coaching website, Signature Moves of Famous Soccer Players, http://www.ultimatesoccer coaching.com/signature-moves-of-famous-soccer-players/.
P. 56	firm, Sports Mondial: *VeloNews*, April 23, 1982.
P. 57	John) and Roger Winter: All Business website, John P. Thompson, Industry Pioneer, Has Died at 77, http://www.allbusiness.com/retail -trade/food-stores/4477547-1.html.
P. 61	then living in Chicago: Geoff Drake interview with Tom Schuler.
P. 63	ever met in his life: Geoff Drake interview with Gerard Bisceglia.

Chapter 5

P. 68 de facto elder statesmen: Sports Reference website, SR/Olympic Sports, Roger Young, http://www.sports-reference.com/olympics/ athletes/yo/roger-young-1.html.
P. 69 one of four children: Geoff Drake interview with Roger Young.
P. 69 with cancer and died: Geoff Drake interview with Roger Young.
P. 71 venue and press events: Geoff Drake interviews with Roger Young and Danny Van Haute.
P. 71 Montreal Olympics: Geoff Drake interview with Danny Van Haute.
P. 73 under another sponsor: Geoff Drake interview with Tom Schuler.
P. 74 Olympic team as an alternate: Geoff Drake interview with Tom Schuler.
P. 74 Michigan in 1979: Geoff Drake interview with Tom Schuler.
P. 74 On the AMF team: Geoff Drake interview with Tom Schuler.
P. 75 for a pro team, Safir-Ludo: Wikipedia website, Ron Hayman, http://en.wikipedia.org/wiki/Ron_Hayman.
P. 79 with a surfeit of possibilities: *VeloNews*, September 12, 1980.
P. 81 in the Smithsonian Institution: SFGate.com website, September 22, 2002, PROFILE / Eric Heiden, Olympic gold medalist / From skates to scalpel / Five-time gold medalist says career in medicine is his greatest achievement, http://articles.sfgate.com/2002-09-22/living/17562623_1_olympics-heiden-olympic-history-gold-medals.

Chapter 6

P. 84 career in medicine: Interview with Roger Young, *VeloNews*, May 22, 1981.
P. 87 typical ingenuousness: *VeloNews*, May 22, 1981.
P. 89 more than a little attitude: *VeloNews*, April 10, 1981, *VeloNews*, May 8, 1981.
P. 90 all of them former Olympians: *VeloNews*, November 13, 1981; Sports Reference website, SR/Olympic Sports, Hugh Walton, http://www.sports-reference.com/olympics/athletes/wa/hugh-walton-1.html; Sports Reference website, SR/Olympic Sports, Wayne Stetina, http://www.sports-reference.com/olympics/athletes/st/wayne-stetina-1.html; Wikipedia website, Dale Stetina, http://en.wikipedia.org/wiki/Dale_Stetina.
P. 91 irritating the 7-Elevens: Spokepost.com website, November 30, 2006, Wayne Stetina Interview, http://spokepost.com/news/story/1666/.
P. 91 Boston to Manhattan Beach: *VeloNews*, June 26, 1981.
P. 91 and sponsorship magnet: *VeloNews*, June 26, 1981.
P. 96 bidding in the wider world: *VeloNews*, April 23, 1982.
P. 97 350 stores in his region: Geoff Drake interview with Gerard Bisceglia.
P. 97 classic movie *Breaking Away*: Internet Movie Database, *Breaking Away*, 1979, http://www.imdb.com/title/tt0078902/.
P. 97 the "great whoopee": *Sports Illustrated* website, March 3, 1980, The Big Whoopee, http://sportsillustrated.cnn.com/vault/article/magazine/MAG1123215/index.htm.
P. 98 in a remarkable understatement: *VeloNews*, October 10, 1981, quoting from the *New York Times*.
P. 100 in a motorpacer Carlton Verbist: Pro Cycling News website, May 3, 2004, Jelly Belly presented by Aramark Camp and Presentation, http://www.dailypeloton.com/displayarticle.asp?pk=6113.
P. 103 Americans Need Discipline: *VeloNews*, December 11, 1981.

Chapter 7

P.104 defined the sport in Europe: *VeloNews* website, April 29, 2005, In-side Cycling: Aisner and the Coors Classic, http://velonews.com-petitor.com/2005/04/news/inside-cycling-aisner-and-the-coors-classic_7960.
P.105 into the team van: Geoff Drake interview with Greg Demgen.
P.106 increasingly international flavor: *VeloNews*, July 24, 1981.
P.106 by almost five minutes: *VeloNews*, July 24, 1981.
P.106 women's event that year: *VeloNews*, August 27, 1980; Geoff Drake interview with Ron Hayman.
P.107 season with a flourish: *VeloNews*, November 13, 1981.
P.107 race in Charlottesville, Virginia: *VeloNews*, November 13, 1981.
P.108 7-Eleven spoils of $25,000: *VeloNews*, November 13, 1981.
P.108 she had also won in 1973 and 1976: *VeloNews*, September 11, 1981.
P.108 seven tracks in North America: *VeloNews*, November 13, 1981.

Chapter 8

P.110 winner George Mount: *Sports Illustrated* website, July 24, 1978, The ZingerWasaRealHumdinger,http://sportsillustrated.cnn.com/vault/article/magazine/MAG1093897/index.htm.
P.111 double-butted spokes: Geoff Drake interview with Davis Phinney.
P.118 a big presence on the bike: 7-Eleven press materials.
P.120 "10 Sexiest Male Athletes": *VeloNews*, November 12, 1982.

Chapter 9

P.122 he had been feeling: Geoff Drake interview with Ron Kiefel.
P.122 Poland and Czechoslovakia: Geoff Drake interview with Eugene Kiefel.
P.123 from the age of 13: Geoff Drake interview with Ron Kiefel.
P.123 run by his son, Ron Kiefel: Wheat Ridge Cyclery website, WRC History, Colorado's Largest Single Bike Shop, http://ridewrc.com/articles/wrc-history-pg44.htm.
P.123 a unicycle to get there: Geoff Drake interview with Eugene Kiefel.
P.124 Denver Tech Center: Geoff Drake interview with Eugene Kiefel.

Chapter 10

P.133 7-Eleven/Bicycling Magazine Grand Prix: *VeloNews*, April 23, 1982.
P.133 couldn't go 50/50 anymore: *VeloNews*, February 12, 1982.
P.133 same trajectory indefinitely: *VeloNews*, February 12, 1982.
P.135 Gorski, a powerful sprinter: Geoff Drake interview with Mark Gorski.
P.135 broke his collarbone: Geoff Drake interview with Mark Gorski.
P.135 team member Jeff Bradley: *VeloNews*, April 23, 1982; *VeloNews*, February 12.
P.136 was a godsend: 7-Eleven press guide.
P.138 princely sum of $500: Roger Young e-mail.
P.139 Instant air conditioning: Geoff Drake interview with Alex Stieda.
P.141 6 of the top 10 places: *VeloNews*, April 9, 1982.

Chapter 11

P. 147 Moscow Games four years earlier: *VeloNews*, May 25, 1984.
P. 147 would have faced in L.A.: *VeloNews*, June 22, 1984.
P. 147 left alone by the politicians: *VeloNews*, June 22, 1984.
P. 148 other side of the Iron Curtain: *VeloNews*, May 25, 1984.
P. 148 American rival, Nelson Vails: *VeloNews*, July 27, 1984.
P. 148 four East bloc riders: *VeloNews*, September 23, 1983.
P. 148 Lutz Hesslich of East Germany: *VeloNews* June 22, 1984.
P. 148 for the absence of the Easterners: *VeloNews*, June 22, 1984.
P. 151 age of cycling, it was now: *VeloNews*, July 13, 1984.
P. 151 foretold the coming landslide: *VeloNews*, August 24, 1984.
P. 152 *ABC Sports*, *Sports Illustrated*, *Time*, and *Newsweek*: *VeloNews*, August 24, 1984.
P. 153 0.04 off the Olympic record: *VeloNews*, August 24, 1984.

Chapter 12

P. 158 a little more palatable: 7-Eleven website, Accomplishments & Milestones, http://corp.7-eleven.com/AboutUs/Milestones/tabid/76/De-fault.aspx.
P. 160 season opener in Italy: Trofeo Laigueglia website, Internazionale per Professionisti, Sabato 19 Febbraio 2011, http://www.trofeolaigueglia.it albo.htm.
P. 160 of the Étoile de Bessèges: *VeloNews*, March 8, 1985.
P. 160 offered a new opportunity: *VeloNews*, March 8, 1985.
P. 160 comprised two large loops: *VeloNews*, March 8, 1985.
P. 162 Italian national road champion: *VeloNews*, April 26, 1985.
P. 162 won the worlds and the Giro: Wikipedia website, Giuseppe Saronni, http://en.wikipedia.org/wiki/Giuseppe_Saronni.
P. 166 won handily by Phinney: *VeloNews*, April 26, 1985.
P. 167 to England for the summer: Cycling Forums website, Andy Hampsten Interview, http://www.cyclingforums.com/forum/thread/430967/andy-hampsten-interview.

Chapter 13

P. 172 California, antiwar protests: May 1992 *Bicycling*, Geoff Drake profile.
P. 173 won by Freddy Maertens: Wikipedia website, UCI Road World Championships—Men's Road Race, http://en.wikipedia.org/wiki/UCI_Road_World_Championships_%E2%80%93_Men's_road_race.
P. 173 and his marriage were in tatters: *SFWeekly* website, April 28, 1999, Road to Redemption, http://www.sfweekly.com/1999-04-28/news/road-to-redemption/3/.
P. 173 capabilities and temperaments: May 1992 *Bicycling*, Geoff Drake profile.
P. 174 1983 Tour de France: *VeloNews*, October 8, 1982; *VeloNews*, August 26, 1983.
P. 175 saw in the 13-year-old: Geoff Drake interview with Remo d'Agliano.

Chapter 14

P. 180   with lackluster results: *VeloNews*, September 14, 1984.
P. 181   4th in a sprint finish: *VeloNews*, June 28, 1985.
P. 182   all his ministrations, passed out: *VeloNews*, June 28, 1985.
P. 184   living in tepees along the roadways: *Los Angeles Times* website, March 24, 1992, U.S. Provides a Roll Model for Cyclists, http://articles.latimes.com/1992-03-24/sports/sp-4264_1.
P. 185   a few wins to his name: Wikipedia website, Marino Lejarreta, http://en.wikipedia.org/wiki/Marino_Lejarreta; Wikipedia website, Acácio da Silva, http://en.wikipedia.org/wiki/Ac%C3%A1cio_da_Silva.
P. 190   attacked before the climb: *VeloNews*, June 28, 1985.
P. 192   sprinting in the big show: Information from Ron Kiefel.

Chapter 15

P. 195   team member Chris Carmichael: *VeloNews*, June 27 1986.
P. 196   21 teams of 10 riders each: Le Tour France website, Jacques Anquetil, http://www.letour.fr/2009/TDF/COURSE/docs/guide_touristique_2010_histoire_3.pdf.
P. 197   and other landmarks: Geoff Drake interview with Alex Stieda.
P. 198   felt his confidence growing: *VeloNews*, August 22, 1986.
P. 198   blond, including Stieda's: Geoff Drake interview with Shelley Verses.
P. 203   exponentially greater: *VeloNews*, August 24, 1984.

Chapter 16

P. 224   Boyer, Veggerby, and Lauritzen: 1987 press kit.
P. 226   leading up to the race: *Sports Illustrated* website, SI Vault, July 1, 1985, Now Eric's Hell on Wheels, Too, http://sportsillustrated.cnn.com/vault/article/magazine/MAG1119619/index.htm.
P. 226   and won the sprint: *VeloNews*, July 12, 1985.
P. 227   Peter Winnen of Holland: *VeloNews*, July 11, 1986; *VeloNews*, July 10, 1987.

Chapter 17

P. 228   a distant 43rd: *VeloNews*, August 14, 1987.
P. 230   boyhood idol, Maertens: Le Tour France website, Le Tour en chiffres, Les vainqueurs d'étapes, http://www.letour.fr/2009/TDF/COURSE/docs/guide_touristique_2010_histoire_8.pdf.
P. 230   Ghent-Wevelgem classic: Tour de France archives; http://www.gent-wevelgem.be/en/history/record-of-honour/.
P. 232   to make his point: *VeloNews*, August 28, 1987, p. 9.
P. 232   was in good form: Enotes website, Dag Otto Lauritzen, http://www.enotes.com/topic/Dag_Otto_Lauritzen; Wikipedia website, Exchborn–Frankfurt City Loop, http://en.wikipedia.org/wiki/Rund_um_den_Henniger_Turm.
P. 233   teammate Hampsten: Wikipedia website, Luz Ardiden, http://en.wikipedia.org/wiki/Luz_Ardiden; Le Tour France website, Le Tour et ses

sommets; http://www.letour.fr/2009/TDF/COURSEdocs/guide_touristique_2010_histoire_6.pdf.
P.233 on French shores: Timeanddate.com website, Bastille Day in France, http://www.timeanddate.com/holidays/france/bastille-day.
P.235 was never proven: Geoff Drake interview with Mike Neel.

Chapter 18

P.241 Liège-Bastogne-Liège: *VeloNews*, May 13, 1988.
P.242 regain the peloton: *VeloNews*, June 10, 1988; Geoff Drake interview with Davis Phinney.
P.245 Romandie in Switzerland: *VeloNews*, May 27, 1988.
P.246 road was entirely dirt: *VeloNews*, July 8, 1988.
P.246 two stage victories in 1966: Wikipedia website, Gianni Motta, http://en.widipedia.org/wiki/Gianni_Motta; Gianni Motta official website, Gianni Motta Biography, http://www.giannimotta.it/biografia/inizi.php.
P.256 losing 47 minutes: *VeloNews*, velonews.com, May 24, 2008, Andy Hampsten and the 1988 Pink Jersey, Part 1, http://velonews.competitor.com/2008/05/road/andy-hampsten-and-the-1988-pink-jersey-part-1_76639.
P.259 for a training camp: *VeloNews*, July 8, 1988.
P.262 excelled in the mountains: Press guides.
P.262 higher than 9th overall: *VeloNews*, September 9, 1988.
P.262 finishing 4th overall: *VeloNews*, Septembe*f*r 9, 1988.

Chapter 19

P.266 their new acquisitions: *VeloNews*, February 10, 1989.
P.266 on all the climbs: Geoff Drake interview with Andy Hampsten; *VeloNews*, March 31, 1989.
P.267 started the next morning: *VeloNews*, April 28, 1989.
P.267 *San Francisco Weekly* at the time: *SFWeekly* website, April 28, 1999, Road to Redemption, http://www.sfweekly.com/1999-04-28/news/road-to-redemption/4/.
P.271 post-Tour criterium circuit: *VeloNews*, September 22, 1989.
P.272 over three years: *New York Times* website, September 3, 1989, Sports People.
P.275 five days and finishing 4th overall: *VeloNews*, August 12, 1988; Wikipedia website, Steve Bauer, http://en.wikipedia.org/wiki/Steve_Bauer.
P.275 try the approach again: *VeloNews*, July 23, 1990.
P.277 force a surrender: *VeloNews*, August 6, 1990.

Chapter 20

P.278 docks back in 1928: *VeloNews*, August 6, 1990.
P.280 race in Hamilton, Ontario: *VeloNews*, October 22, 1990.

PHOTOGRAPHY CREDITS

Robert F. George:
12, 34, 67, 72, 78, 79, 82, 95, 109, 117, 125, 136, 153, 166

Tom Moran:
43, 55, 62, 65

Jim Ochowicz:
17, 22, 25, 85, 88, 90, 137, 164, 172, 186, 194, 216, 285, 291 (top and bottom)

John Pierce, PhotoSport International:
31, 58, 74, 99, 127, 131, 134, 140, 145, 151, 161, 168, 174, 178, 184, 189, 196, 201, 202, 204, 206, 207, 211, 215, 223, 239, 260, 263, 265, 266, 269, 273, 281, 283, 290

Cor Vos:
70, 105, 247, 249, 251, 253, 255, 272

Graham Watson:
44, 76, 112, 120, 130, 175, 181, 183, 191, 217, 219, 221, 225, 229, 231, 233, 234, 236, 238, 243, 244, 274, 276, 277

INDEX

Photographs are indicated by page numbers in italics.

ABC Sports, Olympic cycling coverage, 152
aerobic metabolism, 32
Aisner, Michael
  with Anquetil, *105*
  comments on team members, 37, 46, 119, 132, 173
  and Coors Classic, 106, 261
  on obscurity of cycling as sport, 53–54
  Russian team in Coors Classic, 106
Alcalá, Raúl, team member, *196*, 212, 217, 224, 229–235, *229*, *236*, *238*
Alex Stieda Cycling, 289
Algeri, Vittorio, 162
Alpe d'Huez, France, 235, 259
American Machine and Foundry sports conglomerate, 11
American versus European sports culture/racing, 3–6, 21–22, 66–67
AMF Wheel Goods team, 11, 37–38
anaerobic metabolism, 32
analytical confidence, 35
Anderson, Phil, 200
Anderson, Terry, team member, *88*
Andreu, Frankie, team member, 280
animosity from other teams, 92–93, 181–186
Anquetil, Jacques, 20, *105*
anti-drug policy, 215
anti-Europe behavior, 184
Ariden, Luz, 232–233, *233*, *234*
Armstrong, Lance, 178
asterisked athletic records, 147–148, 152–153
Bastille Day, 233
Bauer, Steve, team member, 90–91, 238, *273*, 274–277, *274*, *276*, *277*, 286, *291*
Bernard, Jean-François, 214–215
bicycle trade show party, 266

Bicycling magazine, 108
Bisbee, Arizona, national road championships (1980), 42
Bisceglia, Gerard, 63, 97–98, 271
Blanchford, Sally, 19
BMC Racing Team, 284, 288, 289
body fat percentage, 12–13, 32
Bormio, Italy, 248
Borysewicz, Eddie "Eddie B.," 148–150, 167
Boulder, Colorado residents, weather knowledge, 248–249
Boulder High School, 111–113, 119
Boyer, Jonathan "Jock"
  in Coors Classic (1981), 106
  cycling in Europe, 4
  early cycling experience, 174–176
  life after Team 7-Eleven, 286, *291*
  Paris-Nice opener (1986), *202*
  Team 7-Eleven role, *166*, 174–177, *175*, *186*, *221*, 224
  as vegetarian, 184
  U.S. Bicycling Halle of Fame inductee, 286
Bradley, Debbie, 33
Bradley, Jacque, 33, 135, *136*
Bradley, Jeff
  on Coors Classic, 104
  on cycling versus skating, 36
  departure from team, 240
  life after Team 7-Eleven, 286, *291*
  Mohawk placing (1981), 108
  on Ochowicz as rider, 100–101
  as original team member, 33, 78–80, *85*, *88*
  at La Primavera, 79, *79*, 89, *90*
  Team 7-Eleven role (1987), 224
  Tour de France (1987), 229, 235
  Tour de Texas (1984), *34*
Breaking Away (film), 97, 113
Breckenridge, Colorado, training

Index

for Coors Classic, 105
Breukink, Eric, 253–256
brothel ashore base, Ghent, 194
Brown Deer Park Velodrome, 16, 33
Café Pacifico, Paris, 212, 239
Canadian cyclists, 75
caravan negotiation for trailing cyclists, 241–242
Carlson, Rockey & Associates, 96
Carmichael, Chris, team member, 178, *178*, *186*, *194*, 195, 199, 205, 212, 286–287, *291*
Carmichael Training Systems, 286
Carpenter-Phinney, Connie, 88, 110, 151, 289
Carroll, Dan, *22*
Carson, Johnny, 46, 99
Carter, Jimmy, 39
categories, racing, 5
CBS Sports, 210–211, 239
Champs Élysées, Paris, 236–237, *238*
Charlottesville, Virginia race (1981), 107
Chauner, Dave, *25*, 26–27
Chew, Tom, on Phinney, 121
Chiappucci, Claudi, 275
Chicago, Illinois, road racing, 33
Chiesa Valmalenco, Italy, 248
Cinghiale Cycling Tours, 287
Colorado junior state road championships (1976), 125
Colorado Springs, Colorado, Olympic training facility, 148
Comfort, Tony, *See* Conforti, Antonio
Conforti, Antonio (Tony Comfort), 113–116, 224
Conti, Roberto, 182
Coors Classic, 104–106, *105*, 111, 130, 167, 174, 259–263, *260*
Coors Light team, 287–289
Coppi, Fausto, 20
Coureur Sporting Cyclist magazine, 20
crashing, 118, 124, 135, 182, 203, 209–210, 228, 237, 242–244, *243*
criteriums (crits), 37, 67–69, 89, 91, 106, 141, 167, 169–179, 260

cycling versus skating, preference for, 35–36
cyclist's life in U.S., (ca. 1980), 1–2, 33–34
Da Silva, Acacio, 185
d'Agliano, Remo, 174–176
Davis Phinney Foundation for Parkinson's disease, 289
de Latour, René, 20
De Rosa, Ugo, 264
De Telegraaf (Holland newspaper), 43
Dejonckheere, "Chief," 235
Dejonckheere, Noël, 159, 235, 268
Dejonckheere, Richard, 159, 235
Delgado, Pedro, 210
Dell'Oglio, Erminio, 164, *164*, *166*, 177–178, 187, 195, 257–258
Demgen, Greg
  on animosity from other teams, 93–94
  comments on team members, 87, 92, 103, 109
  in Coors Classic (1981), 106
  departure from team, 143
  at La Primavera, *90*
  life after Team 7-Eleven, *291*
  nicknamed "Doughboy," 100
  original team member, 77–78, *85*
  on training camp, 84
  as young race, *78*
Denver Post newspaper, on Phinney, 120
Descente apparel company, 81, 195–196,
Detroit, Michigan, road racing, 33
Dill-Bundi, Robert, 193, 208
Docter, Sarah, 135
domestic teams' attitude toward Team 7-Eleven, 223–224
domestiques/superdomestiques, 178, 192, *225*, 260
Donaghy, Bruce, 90, 107
Dorgan, Toy, 119
dossard, 196
drafting, 24, 96, 202–205, 241
Duker, Peter, 29
Dutch junior skating team, 20–21
East Germans in Coors Classic, 261

Eastern bloc boycott of 1984 Olympics, 147
Eastern European athletic teams' lack of freedom, 26–27
elite families of skating/cycling, 35
Emery, Brent, at Primavera, *79*
endemic/nonendemic sponsorships, 46
Étoile de Bessèges race, 159–160
European versus American sports culture/racing, 3–6, 21–23, 66–68
Eustice, John, 180
Evans, Cadel, 284, 288
Faster, Better, Stronger (Heiden and Testa), 287
Fatka, Michael, 170
fear of riding after accident, 243
female *soigneurs*, 179, *179*, 184, *267, 284*
food poisoning question, Tour de France (1987), 234
friction from Phinney's domination, 142
Fureter, Urs, 192
Gavia Pass (1988), 246, 250–256, *251, 253, 255*
general classification, *See* G.C. riders
G.C. (general classification) riders, 214
Ghent, Belgium, 14, 194
Ghent-Wevelgem classic, 230, 245
Gilstrap, Richard, 82, 136–137, *137*, 203
Gimondi, Felice, 56, 114
Giro d'Italia (1985)
  breakaway strategy, 163–166, 180–181, 185–187
  Hampsten stage win, 189–192, initial thoughts about, 193
  sponsorship and support, 163–165, 177–178
  team recruitment for, 165–177
Giro d'Italia (1988), *244*, 245–246, 257–258, *See* Gavia Pass (1988)
goals, obsessing on, 115–116
Gorski, Mark
  comments on team members, 135, 150
  life after Team 7-Eleven, 287
  Olympics (1984), 146–148, *153*
  on Ranch Dog, 138–139
  as team member, 135–136
  U.S. Cycling Federation, 287
  U.S. Postal cycling team director, 287
Gran Paradiso, Italy, 189–191
Grand Prix of Frankfurt, 232
grand tours, European, 4, 260
Great Mohawk Cycling Classic (1981), 107
Grewal, Alexi
  dismissal and resentment, 210, 262
  in Europe, *183*
  life after Team 7-Eleven, 287
  Paris-Nice opener (1986), *194*
  personality and demeanor, *211*
  Tour de France (1986), 195, 204–205, 212
  U.S. Bicycling Hall of Fame inductee, 287
Griffin, Sheila, 279
GS Mengoni team, 90–91, 224, 274
Hamilton, Ontario race, 280
Hampsten, Andy
  anti-drug policy, 215
  comments on team members, 167, 173, 264
  and Coors Classic, 167
  first rider treated by Testa, 188
  Gavia Pass ordeal (1988), *251*
  as G.C. rider, 214
  Giro d'Italia (1985), 180, 189–193
  Giro d'Italia (1988), *244*, 245–250, *249*, 254–258, *251, 255*
  La Vie Claire team, 214–215
  Levi's-Raleigh team, 166
  Liège-Bastogne-Liège accident, 241
  life after Team 7-Eleven, 287, *291*
  Oakley sunglasses sponsorship, *247*
  as strong climber, 167–169, *168*

Index

as team member, 170, *186*, *191*, 215–216, *216*, *272*
Team 7-Eleven role (1987), 224
Tour de France (1987), 229–230, 232–235
Tour de France (1988), 258–259
Tour de France (1992), 287
Tour of Switzerland (1987), 227
U.S. Bicycling Hall of Fame inductee, 287
Hampsten, Steve, 287
Hampsten Cycles, 287
Hanley, Mike, 267
hardships facing aspirin cyclists, 1–2, 6
Hayman, Ron
 on Charlottesville race (1981), 107
 comments on team members, 7–8, 100, 142, 213
 Coors Classic (1981), 105
 La Primavera, 89, *90*
 life after Team 7-Eleven, *291*
 Löwenbräu Grand Prix placing, 91
 Mohawk win (1981), 108
 move to Mengoni team, 142
 nicknamed "Skin," 100
 original team member, *65*, 75–76, *76*, *85*, *88*
 as team leader, 92–93
 as team member, *109*
Heid, Jack, 4, 59
Heiden, Beth, 9, 106
Heiden, Eric
 as advantage to team success, 59–60
 body type as cycling disadvantage, 11–12
 cycling career review, 225–226
 early cycling experience, 11
 early skating career, 10
 future after racing, thoughts on, 144
 generosity toward buddies, 46
 Giro d'Italia (1985), *166*, 192–193
 La Primavera, *90*
 life after Team 7-Eleven, 287, *290*, *291*
 love of competition, 11, *12*
 Löwenbräu Grand Prix, 91
 Midwestern work ethic, 10
 nicknamed "Gomer," 8, 99
 on Ochowicz and Tour de France, 194
 Olympics (1980), 7–9, 39
 original team member, *58*, *67*, *85*, 157
 pain tolerance, 11, 33, 39
 Paris-Nice opener (1986), *194*
 personality and demeanor, 7–10, 98
 pro-am cycling team concept, 40–42
 as pro cyclist, *44*
 promotion of cycling, 98, *99*
 racing for showers while training, 86
 Ranch Dog ventilation, 139
 represented by Kaminsky, 37
 retirement as cyclist, 226
 Schwinn sponsorship, 46
 spotlight more on team, 96–97
 as team member, *181*, *186*
 as television commentator, *38*, 46
 Tour de France (1986), 203, 210, 212
 U.S. Bicycling Hall of Fame inductee, 287
Heiden, Jack, 11
Herrera, Luis, 223
Hesslich, Lutz, 148, 152
Hiltner, Mike, *25*
Hinault, Bernard, 180, 183, 188, 214–215, 270
hit squad, 222
Holum, Dianne, 9
Hoonved washing machine company, *164*, 177
Howard, John, 4
Huebner, Michael, 148
Hughes, Dale, 32, 36
hypothermia, 253, 256
incompetence, reputation for, 206
Innsbruck, Austria, Olympics (1976), 28

InterGiro, 192–193
International Olympic Committee
 ruling on athletes per nation
 (1984), 148
Inzell, Germany, World Sprint
 Championships, 20–22, *22*
Isoglass team, 243, *243*
jersey design, *58*, 81
Jonland, Gary, *22*
Junge, Bob, 123–124
Kaminsky, Art, 38, 43–44
Kelly, Sean, 114, 271
Kenosha, Wisconsin, velodrome
 racing, 33
Kiefel, Eugene, 122–123
Kiefel, Ron
 changes in team persona, 240
 Coors Classic (1986), *131*
 competition with Phinney, 125–126
 conflict with Conti, 182
 cycling ambition as teen, 3
 in Denver Tech Center
  competition, 123–124
 early cycling experience, 122–123
 on European racing, 160–163,
  161, *221*, *260*
 on evolving professional attitudes,
  228
 first European win, 163
 future after racing, thoughts on,
  144
 Gavia Pass (1988), 255
 Ghent-Wevelgem classic (1988)
  placing, 245
 Giro d'Italia (1985), *166*, 181,
  185–186, 193
 and Hinault, 183
 on Italian skepticism of Team 7-
  Eleven, 180
 life after Team 7-Eleven, 288, *290*,
  291
 nicknamed "Wookiee," 122
 Olympics (1984), 150, 203–204
 original team member, *88*, *127*,
  157, 224
 Paris-Nice opener (1986), *194*
 personality and demeanor, 122–123, *127*, 131
 and Phinney, 128–129, *130*, 132,
  140, 231
 strong uphill finisher, 124, *125*
 Team 7-Eleven role (1987), 224
 as team member, *140*, *186*
 Tour de France (1986), 212
 Tour de Trump (1989), 269–270
 Tour of Switzerland (1987), 227
 Tour of Tuscany (1988), 245
 U.S. Bicycling Hall of Fame
  inductee, 288
kit (cycling clothing), 184, 220
Knetteman, Gerrie, 186
Knickman, Roy, team member, 241,
 291
Konyshev, Dimitri, 271
Krott, Herman, 103
La Gazzetta dello Sport magazine, 2,
 165, *186*
La Primavera race, 89
La Vie Claire team, 214–216, 227
Lake Placid, New York, 7, 15, 28, 71,
 76, 81
Lanigan, Bill, *22*
Lauritzen, Dag Otto
 as first Norwegian to win Tour de
  France stage, 233, *233*, *234*
 first to wear Motorola jersey, 281
 Gavia Pass (1988), 255–257
 Grand Prix of Frankfurt win, 232
 life after Team 7-Eleven, 288, *291*
 parachute accident cycling
  therapy, 232
 Redlands Classic win, 232
 team member, 217–218, *217*
 Team 7-Eleven role (1987), 224,
  282
 Tour de France (1987), 232–233
 Tour de Trump (1989), 268–270,
  269
LeBombard, Lyle, 16–17
LeBombard, Wayne, 16–18
Lejarreta, Marino, 185
Lejeune BP team, 176
LeMond, Greg, 78, 106, 156, 159,
 180, 188, 190, 211–212, 214–215, 270–273, *272*
Lévitan, Félix, 195
Liège-Bastogne-Liège classic, 241,

Index

243

life levels, philosophy of, 282
Lindstrom, Cheryl, 232
Los Angeles Olympic Velodrome, 48, 54–55, *55*, 146
Löwenbräu Grand Prix criterium series, 91, 93
Lyman, Greg, *22*
Madison, Wisconsin, 10, 33
Madison Speed Skating Club, 10
Madison Square Garden track races, 3–4
Maertens, Freddy, 114–115, 160, 173
maillot jaune, See yellow jersey
maximal oxygen uptake (VO_2 max), 32
McElmury, Audrey, 4
Mengoni, Fred, 142
Merckx, Eddy, 27, 56, 114, 160, 173, 230, 264–266, *265*, *266*
Mexican food as team tradition, 184, 212, 218–219, 239
Michaels, Dave, 211, 261
Midwestern work ethic, 10, 40
Milwaukee, Wisconsin, 15, 33
Miracle on Ice, 8
Miroir du Cyclisme magazine, 2, 114
Mont Ventoux time trial, 234
Moser, Francesco, 115, 163
Motorola Corporation/team, 279–282, 286–289
Motta, Gianni, 246
Mount, George, 4
Mulica, Dave, *25*
Munich Massacre, 27
Murray bicycles, 190
muscle development, athletic, 32
National Prestige Classic points competition, 107
Neel, Mike
  on anti-Europe behavior, 184–185
  comments on team members, 118, 243
  on Dell'Oglio as sponsor, 177–178
  departure from team, 267–268
  early European career, 171–173
  as European insider for Team 7-Eleven, 173–174, *174*
  Gavia Pass (1988), 247–252, 257
  Giro d'Italia (1985), 182–183, 184–185, 189–190, 193
  life after Team 7-Eleven, 288
  with Ochowicz at 1976 Olympics, *172*
  Tour de France (1987), 228, 230
  U.S. Bicycling Hall of Fame inductee, 288
Newsweek magazine, 152
New York Times newspaper, 38, 48
nicknames of team members, 99–100
Nitz, Leonard "Harvey," team member, 92, 144, *145*, 150, 152, 157, 222, 224, 282
Northbrook, Illinois velodrome, 18, 33
Oakley sunglasses sponsorship, 246, *247*
obscurity of cycling as sport in U.S., 52–54, 56
Ochowicz, Alex, 34–35
Ochowicz, Elli, 34–35, 288
Ochowicz, Erv, 15–16, 24
Ochowicz, Jeanne, 23
Ochowicz, Jim
  on 1981 season, 108
  AMF Wheel Goods team, 11
  athlete-manager transition, 100–102
  athletic ability and perseverance, 18–19
  Borysewicz, friction with, 150
  chastised for team etiquette, 182
  comments on team members, 265, 268
  construction job, 19
  Coors Classic, 106–107, 259, 262
  and Dutch junior skating team, 20–21
  early athletic career, 14–15
  early cycling experience, 16–18
  on European team members, 218
  family with cycling trophies, *17*
  financial risk to save team, 279–280
  first La Primavera competition, 89
  Gavia Pass (1988), 246–252
  Ghent six-day track race, 14–15
  Giro d'Italia (1985), *166*, 193

on Gorski Olympic win and Southland, 154
as Heiden's advisor, 14
individual sponsorships, obtaining, 80–81
Inzell skating competition, 20
life after Team 7-Eleven, 288, *290, 291*
life levels, philosophy of, 282
long-range plans, 108–109
management style, 100–103
meeting with Winter and D. Thompson, 61
national championships (1966), 17–18
with Neel at Olympics (1976), *172*
nicknamed "Sergeant Rock," 18, 100
on Olympic boycott, 149
Olympics (1972) cycling team, *25,* 26
on overtraining, 105
Pan American Games, Cali, Colombia, 24–26
post-Olympic goals, 156
on "pot hunting," 222
pro-am cycling team concept, 41-42
race barking, 102
race strategies, 93, 165–166
as speed skating team manager, 29
team building, 64–65, *65, 82, 85,* 92–93
team recruitment, 66
on Team 7-Eleven's first European ride, 159
Tour de France (1986), 195, *201,* 203, *207,* 209–210, 212
Tour de France (1987), 230, 235, 239
Tour of Switzerland (1987), 227
U.S. Bicycling Hall of Fame inductee, 288
U.S. Speedskating team, 14–15
Varese track championships, 26
vision fulfilled, 282–285, *283*
work at Lake Placid for Olympics, 28
working with Taylor, 47–48
world championships (1973), 27
at World Sprint Championships, *22*
Ochowicz, Kate, 15, 28
Olympics, *25,* 26–29, 39, 52–53, 150, 154, 203
O'Reilly, Rory, team member, 150
pacelines, 96
pain
  Gavia Pass (1988), 255, 257–258
  Kiefel and Phinney, 6, 114
  and pleasure, 258
  as rider's lot, 4–5, 32, 45, 56–57, 124
Pan American Games, Cali, Colombia, 4, 24
Panasonic teams, 90, 107–108, 268–269, 274
Paris-Nice race, *195,* 245
Paris-Roubaix classic, 56, 264–265, 274
Parkinson's disease, 289
peloton, European, attitude toward Team 7-Eleven, 182–185
Perugia, Italy, Giro d'Italia (1985), 185–186
Petty, Sean, 54, 222, 288, *291*
Phinney, Damon, 118–119
Phinney, Davis
  AMF Wheel Goods team, 11
  aspiring to Team 7-Eleven, 88
  on Bradley, 79
  Coors Classic, 261–262
  crashing, 118, 209–210
  cycling ambition as teen, 2–3
  domination as cause of friction, 142
  early cycling career, 110–113
  on European racing, 212
  father as supporter, 118–119
  future after racing, thoughts on, 144
  Giro d'Italia (1985), *166,*
  Giro d'Italia (1988), *244*
  as goalsetter/daydreamer, 115, 119
  in interviews, *120*

and Kiefel, 124–129, *130*, 131–132, 142
Liège-Bastogne-Liège crash into car, 242–244, *243*,
life after Team 7-Eleven, 289, *290*, *291*
life goal, 112
nicknamed "Cash Register," 223
as Ochowicz's advisor, 141–142
Olympics (1984), 150, 203
original team member, *88*
Paris-Nice opener (1986), *194*
personality and demeanor, 119–121, 131–132
physical description, 117–118
post-Olympic goals, 156
on Puch women's team, 110
recruited by Ochowicz, 121
sprinting physique, *117*
Stieda, competition with, 143
Team 7-Eleven role (1987), 224
on Team 7-Eleven's purpose, 141
as team member, *186*
Tour de France (1986), 203, 206–210, 212
Tour de France (1987), 230–232, *231*, 235
Tour de Trump (1989), 268–269
Tour of Romandie (1988), 245
Tour of Texas (1985), 166
Tour of Texas (1987), *223*
U.S. Bicycling Hall of Fame inductee, 289
Phinney, Taylor, 289
Pierce, Jeff
  Life after Team 7-Eleven, *290*, *291*
  as pro cyclist, *31*
  on racing circuit, 33
  Team 7-Eleven role (1987), 224
  Tour de France (1986), 199, 205, 209, 212
  Tour de France (1987), 235–239, *238*, *239*
  on U.S. cycling, 30
  on Wolverine Sports Club, 36
Planckaert, Eddy, 274, *274*
politics and sporting events, 27
Post, Peter, 29, 252
post-Olympic goals, 154–156

pot hunting, 222
pro-am cycling team concept, 41–42
professional cycling requirements (ca. 1980), 1
promenade, 67
public relations for Southland, 97–98
quadriceps muscle development, 31–32
Race Across America, 286
race barking, 102
race caravan, described, 241
race earnings, (ca.1980), 1
racing terminology, 96
Raleigh bicycles, 190
Ranch Dog (car), 138–140
Reagan, Ronald, 195
recruitment of team, 66
Red Zinger Bicycle Classic, *See* Coors Classic
Redlands Classic, 195, 232
Renault/Gitane cycle team, 106
road racing circuit, early days, 33
Roche, Stephen, *239*
Rocky Mountain Championships, 116
Roll, Bob
  as domestique, 178
  Gavia Pass (1988), 255–257
  Liège-Bastogne-Liège accident, 241
  life after Team 7-Eleven, 289, *291*
  Merckx's bicycle for, 265
  Paris-Nice opener (1986), *194*
  Team 7-Eleven role (1987), *186*, *216*, 224–225, *225*
  as team clown, 184, 224–225, 285
  Tour de France (1986), 212
  Tour de France (1987), 229, 235
  Tour of Romandie (1988), 245
  Tour of Switzerland (1988), 227
Roto-Rooter team, 197
Russian team in Coors Classic, 106, 261
Rwandan cycling team, Boyer and, 287
Safir-Ludo team, Belgium, 75
San Diego, California training camp, 84–85, 159
Saronni, Giuseppe, 162, 180, 182
Schuler, Tom

Index

AMF Wheel Goods team, 11
  on animosity from other teams, 94
  in Charlottesville race (1981), 107
  future after racing, thoughts on, 144
  on Heiden and 7-Eleven team, 60
  at La Primavera, *90*
  life after Team 7-Eleven, 289, *290, 291*
  nicknamed "Ploughboy," 99–100
  original team member, 72–75, *74, 85, 88, 95*
  on race strategies, 93
  on racing in Europe, 181
  as rider-manager, *62*
  on speed skater training, 30–31
  on Stetina brothers as spoilers, 91
  Team 7-Eleven role, 186
  as team spokesman, 61–63, 96, 279
  U.S. Bicycling Hall of Fame inductee, 289
Schwinn sponsorship, 46–47, 80, 133
Scott, Bill, 108
service course, 82, 136
7-Eleven stores, 49–51, *See* Southland Corporation
Shapiro, Doug, team member, *194*, 195, 203–204, *204*, 210, 212, *290, 291*
silk tires, 1, 112–113
Simes III, Jackie, 4
skating versus cycling, preference, 36
skinsuits, 190, 198–199
Slurpees (derogatory nickname), 223
soigneurs, 82, 84, 113, 179, *179*, 184, 198, 248, 256, 267, 284, 288
Southland Corporation
  and 1981 season, 108
  Colorado Springs velodrome, 157
  Coors Classic, 259–260
  financial decline, 278–279
  Los Angeles Olympic Velodrome, 48, 54–55, *55*, 146
  Olympic boycott, 149
  sponsorship and support, 133–134, 158–159, 278–279, 282, 284
Soviet Union boycott of 1984 Olympics, 145
Spain, world championships (1973), 27
speed skaters, summer bike training, 30–31
sponsorship and support
  endemic/nonendemic sponsorships, 46, 47
  Giro d'Italia (1985), 164–165, 177–178
  Oakley sunglasses sponsorship, 246, *247*
  Ochowicz and individual sponsors, 80–81
  Schuler and Motorola, 279
  Schwinn bicycles, 46, 80, 133
  Southland Corporation, 133, 158–159, 278–279, 282, 284
  See Dell'Oglio, Erminio
sporting events and politics, 26–27
sports duos, 128–129
Sports Illustrated magazine, 9, 41, 48, 152
Sports Mondial marketing firm, 56
spring training camp (1987), 220–221
Stetina, Dale, 90
Stetina, Wayne, 10, 90–91, 100, 124, 262
Steve Bauer Bike Tours, 286
Stieda, Alex
  as first American to wear yellow jersey, 75, 200–201, 274–275
  future after racing, thoughts on, 144
  Ghent brothel as home base, 194–195
  on international travel for team, 222
  Liège-Bastogne-Liège accident, 241
  life after Team 7-Eleven, 289–290, *291*
  original team member, *88*, 133–134
  Paris-Nice opener (1986), *194*
  personality and demeanor, *134*, 197
  with Phinney after crash accident,

Index

241–242
Tour de France (1986), 75, 195, 197–202, *201*, *202*, 205, *206*, *207*, 212
taking a flyer, 96
Taylor, George, 43–48, 55–58, 103, 135, 157
team as family, concept of, 222
team aura/professionalism, 94
team directors, 267, *See* Neel, Mike
team doctors, 187
Team Saturn, 289
Team 7-Eleven
    defining role in U.S. professional cycling, *283*
    divided between Europe and U.S., 222
    in Europe, *183*
    first European win, 163
    inception, 57
    maturation of team (1987), 240
    reunions in Mexico, 286
    role in U.S. professional cycling, 284–285
    talents of team members, summary, 282
team-sponsor identification, 57–58
Team Sports management company, 289
Team Zed, 272–273, *272*, 277
Tesh, John, 210–212
Testa, Massimo "Max," 187–189, *189*, 250, 257, 287, *291*
Thomas Weisel Partners, 288
Thompson, Doug, 57, 61
Thompson, Inga, 262, *263*,
Thompson, Jere, 51, 53–54, 98, 278, 290
Thompson, John, 53–54
three-stack, 222
tifosi (Italian racing fans), 165
Time magazine, 9, 41, 52, 152
time trials, 190, 202–203, 234–235, 258
T.I.-Raleigh Story (Duker), 29, 155
The Tonight Show, Heiden on, 37, 46
Torriani, Vincenzo, 281
Tour de France
    1983, 174

1986, 194–209
1987, 228
1988, 258–259
1990, 274–277
1992, 287
Lauritzen as journalist for, 288
LeMond's performances in, 270
Tour de Trump (1989), 268, *269*
Tour of Lombardy (1990), 280–281
Tour of Romandie (1988), 245
Tour of Spain (Vuelta a España), 195
Tour of Switzerland (1987), 227
Tour of Texas, *34*, 136, 138, *151*, 166, 222, *223*
Tour of the Mediterranean, 160
Tour of Tuscany, 245
Trexlertown, Pennsylvania velodrome racing, 39
Trofeo Laigueglia race, 160, 163
Trump, Donald, 268
Twigg, Rebecca, 135, *136*, 145, 150–152, *151*
200-meter cone, 129
Ueberroth, Peter, 51–53
U.S. Bicycling Hall of Fame inductees, 286–289
U.S. Cycling Federation (amateur), 41
U.S. Postal cycling team, 287
U.S. Professional Racing Organization, 41
U.S. women's volleyball team, 86
Vails, Nelson, 148, 152
van der Velde, Johan, 252, 256
Van Haute, Danny,
    original team member, 71, *72*, 77, 85, 90–100, 90, 105, 126, 143, 291
Van Poppel, Jean-Paul, 230
Van Vliet, Teun, 230
Vande Velde, John, 24, 26–27, 279
Vanderaerden, Eric, 268–270
Varese, Italy, world track championships, 26
Vaseline as cold insulation, 248
vastus medialus muscle development, 31–32
Veggerby, Jens, team member, 217–218, *217*, *219*, 220, 222, 224, 254, 290, *291*

velodrome racing, 33, 36, 39, *55*
VeloNews, 46, 84, 103, 182, 232, 259, 289
Verses, Shelley, as soigneur, 179, *179*, 198
Versus television, 289
VO$_2$ max (maximal oxygen uptake), 32
Volvo-Cannondale mountain bike team, 289
Vuelta a España (Tour of Spain), 195
Walden, Mike, 35, 73
Walton, Bill, 39
Walton, Hugh, 90
Weaver, Andy, team member, 145, 152, 154–155, *291*
Weinmann/La Suisse team, 275
Wheat Ridge Cyclery, 123, 288
wheel sucking, 96
Wide World of Sports (ABC), 38, 46
Wilburn, April, 288
Wilcockson, John, 209
Winnen, Peter, 227
Winter, Roger, 57, 59, 61
Wolverine Sports Club, Detroit, Michigan, 28, 32, 35–36, 45, 72–73
women's 7-Eleven team, 133, 135, 145, 150, 157, 262, 284
World Champions I Have Known (Latour), 20
world championships (1973), 27
world pro road championships (1982), Boyer in, 174
World Sprint Championships, Inzell, Germany, 20–21
Worthy, Brian, team member, *88*
Yates, Sean, 281–282, *281*
yellow jersey, 75, 199–206, 237, 274–275, 282
Yellow Jersey bike shop, 11, 46
Young, Claire, 28
Young, Roger
    comments on team members, 13, 103, 128
    early racing in Europe, 69
    on familial relationships, 35
    and Ghent six-day track race, 14–15
    Mohawk placing (1981), 108
    move from rider to coach, 143
    and Ochowicz, 18, 28
    as original team member, 69–70, *70, 85, 90*
    public relations with Heiden, 98
    on race strategies, 93
    on racing for showers while training, 86–87
Young-Ochowicz, Sheila, 4, 15, 27–28, 31, 108, 154

ABOUT THE AUTHORS

Geoff Drake is the former editor of *Bicycling* magazine and *VeloNews* and has covered cycling events worldwide, including the Tour de France and the Olympic Games. He also writes regularly for national motorcycle magazines and is the author of *Smooth Riding*, a motorcycling book. He is an avid cyclist, a category II road racer, and an Ironman triathlete. He lives in Aptos, California.

Jim Ochowicz is a two-time Olympic cyclist and former speed skater who cofounded the 7-Eleven cycling team in 1981. He managed 7-Eleven through 1990 and its successor, the Motorola Cycling Team, through 1996. He served six years as president of the board of directors of USA Cycling and is currently the manager of the BMC Racing Team. He was inducted into the U.S. Bicycling Hall of Fame in 1997.

Made in the USA
Coppell, TX
24 April 2024